A Woman's Place Is in the House

A Woman's Place Is in the House

Campaigning for Congress in the Feminist Era

Barbara C. Burrell

Ann Arbor

THE UNIVERSITY OF MICHIGAN PRESS

1997   1996   1995   1994   4   3   2   1

A CIP catalogue record for this book is available from the British Library.

Library of Congress Cataloging-in-Publication Data

Burrell, Barbara C., 1947–
    A woman's place is in the House : campaigning for Congress in the
feminist era / Barbara C. Burrell.
        p.   cm.
    Includes bibliographical references and index.
    ISBN 0-472-10479-9 (acid-free paper)
    1. Women in politics—United States.   2. Women legislators—United
States.   3. Electioneering—United States.   4. United States.
Congress. House—Elections.   5. United States—Politics and
government—1945–1989.   6. United States—Politics and
government—1989–   I. Title.
HQ1236.5.U6B87   1994
320'.082—dc20   94-7641
                                                       CIP

320.082
B969w
1994

To the women who have taken the risk of running for national office because they believed in themselves and believed in women becoming part of elected political leadership. And to Caroline who I am sure will leave her mark on the world.

Contents

CHAPTER 1

Introduction

It took 66 years from the time the first woman was elected in 1916 before
the 100th made it in 1982 and before women became as much as 5 percent
of the membership of a single Congress.
                    —Irwin Gertzog, *Congressional Women*

In 1966, the National Organization for Women (NOW) was founded marking
the organizational beginning of the contemporary feminist movement. Margaret Chase Smith (R-Maine) and Maurine Neuberger (D-Oreg.) sat in the U.S.
Senate, and ten women served in the U.S. House of Representatives. Women
were 2 percent of the total congressional membership. Four years later, on the
fiftieth anniversary of women's suffrage, August 26, 1970, thousands of
women marched, picketed, and rallied in support of NOW's Women's Strike
for Equality Day, turning women's liberation into a mass movement (Freeman
1975).

Two decades later as the 102d Congress (1991–92) commenced, still
only two women sat in the U.S. Senate, Nancy Kassebaum (R-Kans.) and
Barbara Mikulski (D-Md.), and twenty-eight women were U.S. Representatives, plus one woman sat in the House as the nonvoting delegate from the
District of Columbia. Women had become 6.6 percent of the membership of
the U.S. Congress. Gains in the numerical representation of women in the
national legislature of the United States were incremental during the feminist
era. No real revolution had occurred. Indeed, columnist Ellen Goodman predicted in 1988 it would take 345 years for women to gain half the seats in
Congress![1] At the same time globally women were an average 11 percent of
democratically elected national parliamentary members. The U.S. Congress
had one of the lowest proportions of female members of any western democracy. (See fig. 1.1.)

Then the 1992 election occurred. It was a dramatic year for women in
politics in the United States. Women's candidacies received media attention as

---

1. Statistical analysis of projected trends in 1984 predicted at best only fifty-three congresswomen (12 percent of the House) by the year 2224, forty years later (Andersen and Thorson
1984).

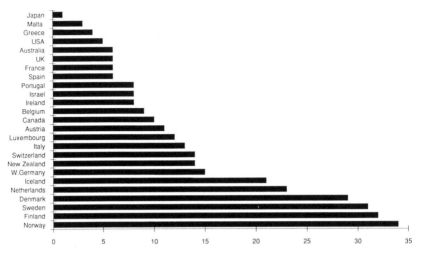

Fig. 1.1. Proportion of women in parliament in twenty-five democracies, 1985–87. (Adapted from Rule and Norris 1992. Reprinted with permission from Praeger Publishers.)

never before, and one women's group even raised six million dollars on behalf of women candidates! A favorable climate for women candidates and a pool of experienced female politicians positioned to undertake campaigns for national office allowed women to take advantage of the window of electoral opportunity 1992 afforded as a result of the redistricting of congressional seats after the 1990 census and the retirement of a larger than usual number of incumbents. The number of women in the U.S. Senate increased to six (6 percent of the body),[2] and twenty-four new women were elected to the House in the 103d Congress (1993–94). Previously no more than six women had been newly elected to that body in one election. Joining with the twenty-three female incumbents who were reelected, women now composed 11 percent of House membership, equaling the international average of female members of national parliaments. Comparing figure 1.2 with figure 1.1 shows that the United States moved up substantially, from fourth lowest in 1987 to eleventh lowest among twenty-five democratic nations. The United States was still in the bottom half, however, regarding female representation, and women's presence in Congress was still far from parity.

Over the course of the feminist era, women increasingly became involved in the political life of the nation's towns and states. The number of

2. In June, 1993, a seventh woman was elected to the U.S. Senate in the 103d Congress. Kay Bailey Hutchison (R-Tex.) was elected to fill the seat of Lloyd Bentsen, who had become Treasury Secretary.

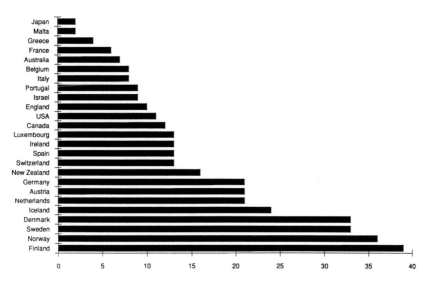

Fig. 1.2. Proportion of women in parliament in twenty-five democracies, 1992

women state legislators increased fivefold from 4 percent of all representatives in 1971 to over 20 percent in 1993. In 1990, sixteen of the one hundred largest, and four of the ten largest, cities in the United States had female mayors (CAWP Fact Sheet 1990). Women have become prominent at all levels of the party organizations, too. For example, they have been able to claim one-half of the state elected delegate seats at Democratic party national conventions since 1980. The parties have begun to feature women candidates, and new organizations have formed to promote women's candidacies. Some even claim it is now an advantage to be a woman when running for office (at least for a legislative position). (See, for example, Ehrenhalt 1982.) In 1992, women were the "in" candidates.

Within Congress, all of the women who served in 1966, when women began advocating nationally for greater political and economic equality, have left the House. A new cohort, more than triple in size, has replaced them. During the 101st Congress (1990–91), women won four of nine special elections to fill vacancies in House seats, giving them 44 percent of the victories. These wins were an impressive success rate given previous levels of victory. They were followed by even greater gains in the 1992 general election. Activists argue that "a new breed" of female candidate has emerged, more professional and more politically experienced. Although election outcomes more often than not had been unimpressive during the feminist era, women's quests for national office represented an important dynamic of this period, and a significant political feature of this time has been women organizing to gain greater influence through the acquisition of political leadership positions.

This study examines the experiences of the women who have run for a seat in the U.S. House of Representatives from 1968 through 1992, the feminist era, and compares their presence and performance with that of male candidates. Few women have been major party nominees for the U.S. Senate, although there were eleven such candidates in 1992 and ten in 1984. Thus, I have limited this research, mainly quantitative in nature, to elections for the U.S. House.

Women and Public Office Holding

In the past, women were socialized not to think of themselves as public citizens and were discouraged, if not prevented, from entering educational and occupational realms that would lead to political careers. It took fifty years of campaigning just to obtain suffrage for women and nearly another fifty years for women to vote in equal percentages as men.

The first women's movement in the United States, from 1848 to 1920, fought to gain women the right to vote. The second women's movement, which emerged in the 1960s, has campaigned not just for women to have a say in who the political leaders will be, but for women to be those leaders. Scholars have not explored the historical legacy for contemporary feminists of suffragist thinking on the idea of women as political leaders. Nor have we examined organized efforts to elect women to public office between 1920 and the reemergence of women's rights as a social movement in the 1960s, although historians have increasingly examined women's political activism during these years. (See, for example, Ware 1981; Rupp and Taylor 1987; Cott 1987.)

Did the organizational idea of encouraging women to run for office, promoting their campaigns, and arguing for the need for more women officeholders originate with contemporary women's rights activists or does the idea have a longer intellectual history? Ware argues that "Women viewed suffrage as the first step toward a wide range of social reforms: once they got the vote, women would purify the cities, abolish child labor, clean up politics, end all wars" (1981:5). But did the suffragists believe women would do this by voting for reform-minded men or by seeking elective office and becoming lawmakers themselves? Some have argued that the suffragists had no vision of women's political participation beyond exercising the franchise, and that their arguments, at least in the second half of their campaign precluded the idea that women should seek public office. "Women needed the ballot for reform so that women could better carry out their traditional responsibilities to their families" (Darcy, Welch, and Clark 1987:10). (See also Cott 1987.) This interpretation of suffrage history ignores calls for women to become active in party organizations, mentions of women as legislators in some suffragist public addresses, and organized efforts to elect women to office immediately after the vote was obtained, for example, in New York in 1916. The suffragists had strategic and tactical reasons to avoid mentioning wanting women in office. Convincing male office holders to extend the franchise to women would have been even more difficult had suffragists simultaneously promoted the idea of women competing for these politicians' seats.

The full meaning of women's citizenship for the suffragists awaits further research. We also must investigate the ideas and actions of the network of women who were engaged in political life in the years after the enactment of the Nineteenth Amendment in 1920 but before the revival of feminist activity in the 1960s. Did they promote the idea of more women in elective office and work toward such a goal? Efforts to have women appointed to public office were a prominent feature of women's rights activity during these decades (Ware 1981), but organized strategies to elect women to public office appear, at least on the surface, not to have been a focus of their attention. A closer examination may find a concern with this issue in those years. If not, we must ask why efforts to increase women's involvement in so many other facets of political life were not accompanied by campaigns to elect women to public office prior to the contemporary era.

Whatever its historical legacy, electing more women to public office has been a goal of the liberal women's rights movement, which emerged in the 1960s. The President's Commission on the Status of Women recommended in its 1963 report that "Women should be encouraged to seek elective and appointive posts at local, state, and national levels and in all three branches of government."[3]

The National Organization for Women's statement of purpose in 1966 called for action "to bring women into full participation in the mainstream of American society now, exercising all the privileges and responsibilities thereof in truly equal partnership with men." Women "must demand representation according to their numbers in the regularly constituted party committees . . . and in the informal power structure, participating fully in the selection of candidates and political decisionmaking, and *running for office themselves*" (emphasis added). The National Women's Political Caucus was founded in 1971 with the specific goal of increasing the number of women in public office, especially feminist women. Other organizations have developed since then, both to train women candidates and to provide them with financial and other assistance. Further, the 1977 National Women's Conference in

---

3. I wish to thank Janet Boles for pointing this recommendation of the commission out to me.

Houston, Texas, adopted the following as one of its National Plan of Action planks:

> The President, Governors, political parties, women's organizations and foundations should join in an effort to increase the number of women in office, including judgeships and policy-making positions, and women should seek elective and appointive office in larger numbers than at present on the Federal, State, and local level. (Bird 1979)

The plank urged chief executives to appoint more women to public positions and called for the political parties to encourage and recruit women to run for office and to create affirmative action offices for women.

The Theoretical Rationale for Electing More Women

Why organize to elect more women to public office? Theorist John Stuart Mill argued in 1869 that a more equitable involvement of women in government with men would benefit society because women could make informed and intelligent public policy contributions. If women have a capacity for political life, society will suffer without their involvement, he reasoned. Feminists endorse this basic argument, but they also believe that women officeholders can offer different and better solutions to policy problems because of their position in society.

The composition of governmental bodies contributes to the legitimacy of political regimes in democratic polities. The design of the U.S. political system has allowed its legislative assemblies to include representatives of various societal groups. Racial, ethnic, and religious groups have political identities based on their experience within the system. We accept the argument that ethnic minorities may be more passionately and fairly represented by someone of their own group, and that their members in elected office provide valuable role models. When citizens can identify with their representatives they become less alienated and more involved in the political system.

Women, too, have come to make a claim for representation based on their group identity. Women's rights activists believe women are excluded from political leadership positions because of their sex, not their lack of ability or achievements. Gender consciousness has increased in recent decades (Miller 1988). "Today, political decisions made by all-male or predominantly male governmental processes can no longer serve [a] legitimizing function" (Darcy, Welch, and Clark 1987). If half of the population has limited involvement in political decision making and believes its exclusion is not random or irrelevant, but rather the consequence of discrimination and larger societal processes, then the legitimacy of political decisions made by the governing structure, in this case a predominantly male one, is undermined. The scarcity of women in policy-making positions lessens the governors' ability to claim that their decisions are truly representative. The lack of substantial numbers of women in elective office in the United States also reduces the country's ability to serve as a democratic model for other nations.

Thus, who the governors are—the descriptive nature of representation—has great political importance. It does not, however, form a complete theory of democracy. The content, or substantive nature, of representation is also critical (Pitkin 1967). "What representatives do is as relevant to determining how representative they are as what they look like and where they come from" (Darcy, Welch, and Clark 1987:13). Women in elective office affect not only who makes political decisions, but how and with what results. Women bring distinct experiences to the legislative debate and particular concerns to the policy-making agenda. Their presence makes a difference in what are considered political questions, and how those questions are resolved. To borrow from Carol Gilligan (1982), women operate in "a different voice" from men.

Issues of special concern to women also are more likely to be addressed and to be given attention if women are present in the policy-making process to articulate them. As Carroll has shown, "predominantly male governing bodies frequently have not acted in response to the sentiments of their female constituents on policies dealing with women. Neither, it can be argued, have they apparently responded to an objective notion of the interests of women and pursued policies to further the welfare of their female constituents" (Carroll 1985:17). "Feminists assume that women officials more often than men will be conscious of and/or responsive to women's life experiences and their concerns and that women officials will work to insure that public policy adequately reflects women's interests" (Carroll and Taylor 1989). Indeed, studies have shown that female legislators give priority to issues of special relevance to women (Carroll and Taylor 1989; Dodson and Carroll 1991). Overall, the theoretical arguments for more women in public office are broad in scope, encompassing descriptive and substantive aspects of representation, societal needs, and concerns about governmental legitimacy.

Research on Women and the Pursuit of Public Office

Political scholars increasingly have asked why there are not more women in public office. They have sought to incorporate ideas about gender into theories of representation and democratic participation. They are also developing an empirical base for understanding the political status of women in our society. Both academics and activists have questioned why the number of female national lawmakers has not grown more quickly particularly since the number of female state legislators had slowly but steadily increased (table 1.1). We also want to place in context the phenomenon of 1992, in which women's candidacies were center stage, and historical gains were made in electoral success nationally.

Political scientists have adopted a variety of research strategies to explain the scarcity of women officeholders, especially at the national level. Some have focused on the beginning stages of the electoral process and asked why few women run for public office in general. They have explored socialization and situational background factors and have considered theories of male conspiracy. Observers have agreed that women were first socialized and then stereotyped into gender roles, particularly that their place is in the home, that offered few opportunities to exert political influence. Furthermore, women usually lacked resources such as law degrees that advance a political career. (See, e.g., Welch 1978; Githens 1983.)

Others have looked at electoral outcomes and sought to explain variations in the number of women recruited to serve in legislatures, especially state legislatures. Research has found women's presence in state legislatures to be related to political culture (Diamond 1977; Hill 1981; Darcy 1982; Nechemias 1987), socioeconomic environment (Jones and Nelson 1981; Nechemias 1987), and the population of states (Diamond 1977; Rule 1981). The percentage of women in state houses of representatives increases with the

TABLE 1.1.   Women in the U.S. House of
Representatives and State Legislatures

Year	U.S. House		State Legislatures	
	N	%	N	%
1967	11	2.5	—	—
1969	10	2.3	301	4.0
1971	12	2.8	344	4.5
1973	14	3.2	424	5.6
1975	18	4.1	604	5.6
1977	18	4.1	688	8.0
1979	16	3.7	770	9.1
1981	19	4.4	908	12.1
1983	21	4.8	991	13.3
1985	23	5.2	1,103	14.8
1987	23	5.2	1,170	15.7
1989	25	5.7	1,270	17.0
1991	28[a]	6.7	1,356	18.2
1993	47	10.8	1,516	20.4

Source: Figures for the state legislators come from CAWP Fact Sheet, 1991, Center for the American Woman and Politics.

[a]This number excludes Eleanor Holmes Norton, the nonvoting representative from the District of Columbia.

availability of relatively low-status political offices (Diamond 1977). Women have been more frequently recruited for Congress in more urbanized and populous states. But no relationship has been shown to exist between the percentages of women recruited to state legislatures and those serving in state congressional delegations (Rule 1981). Cross-national studies of recruitment show that the party-list/proportional representation systems provide the greatest political opportunity for women (Rule 1987). Thus, structural factors appear to be important elements in the presence of women in parliaments.

But what of those women who have run for national office? In the contemporary era who have they been, where have they run, and what have been their campaign experiences? Between the initial stage of the electoral process, considering a run for public office, and the final stage, actually being elected, are the campaigns themselves.

Campaigns matter. They affect outcomes. Mann (1978) has shown that incumbency advantage varies substantially across electoral districts. Some incumbents are much more successful than others. Swings in incumbents' margins of victory have also widened in recent elections (Jacobson 1987a). Campaign spending affects results. It is especially significant to challengers' success (Jacobson 1980). Goldenberg and Traugott (1984) have demonstrated the importance of media on electoral success in congressional campaigns. Periods of electoral upheaval enhance the ability of candidates without experience to get elected (Canon 1990). Ideally, too, campaigns are a major means for communication between representatives, would-be representatives, and the represented. Voters can indeed send a message as they did in 1990, when a backlash against incumbents occurred in the last days of the election (although only 15 of the 406 incumbents running for reelection were defeated, and they still received an average 63.5 percent of the vote). Campaigns also are an opportunity for citizens to become more involved in the political process by working on campaign committees.

What happens when women run for public office? No systematic longitudinal comparison of male and female campaign experiences and the role of gender in elections to the U.S. House of Representatives has been undertaken that examines both general and primary elections. Such an effort is essential if we are to go beyond the conventional wisdom about life on the campaign trail for women and its relationship to the scarcity of women in national office. We must develop an empirical base of knowledge about women's quests for a place in the national legislature. Yet little research has explored the role of sex in political campaigns. Anecdotes and case studies abound regarding the difficulties women candidates have faced. (See, e.g., Mandel 1981; Abzug 1984; Holtzman and Williams 1987.) These examples, however, do not allow for generalizations. Some studies have comprehensively surveyed women's experiences but have not made the crucial comparisons with men's campaigns. (See, e.g., Carroll 1985.) In such studies, conclusions are attributed to gender when in fact they may be the result of general trends and structural factors equally applicable to men's campaigns.

Previous research has made gender comparisons of certain aspects of campaign life focusing either on one election year (Uhlaner and Schlozman 1986; Burrell 1988) or one dimension (for example, women's presence in "hopeless races" [Gertzog and Simard 1981], voter behavior [Darcy and Schramm 1977; Clark et al. 1984], and general election fund-raising [Burrell 1985]). An exception is Darcy, Welch, and Clark's *Women, Elections, and Representation.* In their chapter "Women as Congressional Candidates," they test a number of the popular explanations for the paucity of U.S. congresswomen by systematically comparing men's and women's candidacies. They find gender not to be a discriminating factor in the campaign process.

A Woman's Place Is in the House goes beyond these studies through its dynamic and multidimensional focus. It traces women's campaign experiences and the role of gender in elections to the U.S. House of Representatives during the second women's rights movement from 1968 through 1992. It examines both women's distinct experiences as candidates for the U.S. House of Representatives (such as their presence in different types of races and organizational support for their candidacies) and differences in men's and women's election experiences over time (e.g., fund-raising and vote-getting ability) in both primary and general elections. It examines the background characteristics of the women who have taken the risk of running for high-level office. It traces organizational and financial support for their candidacies. Finally, it considers what the victorious women have done for women in the U.S. Congress.

An analysis of information on all of the major party nominees and open seat primary election contenders from 1968 to 1992 is the principal data base for this study. Quantitative variables include votes obtained, win ratios, age, political experience, occupation, and campaign receipts and expenditures and related financial data obtained from Federal Election Commission reports. Data on district characteristics are also included. The quantitative analysis is supplemented by anecdotal data obtained from interviews with female candidates, organizers within the women's rights community, and party officials.

Overview of Subsequent Chapters

Not long ago many people found the mere idea of a woman politician to be outrageous. But public acceptance of women in political life has increased in recent years, although the nature of that support varies by type of office. General public opinion conditions the opportunities for aspiring women politicians. Negative perceptions lessen the incentive for party leaders, consultants, and contributors to promote women's candidacies. Party activists can claim voter prejudice as a rationale for the lack of organizational support for women candidates. In such an atmosphere, women politicians lack credibility and are thus disinclined to run. As the idea of women in politics becomes more acceptable, reasons for nonsupport among the "movers and shakers" of the political world become less viable. The dynamics surrounding women's candidacies in general have changed as illustrated by the attention their campaigns received in 1992, and the themes they stressed in their campaigns that year. Chapter 2 reviews trends in public attitudes regarding female political activity and beliefs about the distinctive characteristics of female politicians, with special attention given to women as lawmakers. I compare the experimental literature on prejudice and stereotyping with the election outcomes literature and attempt to reconcile differences between the two approaches to explaining the small numbers of women in elective office.

Elections at the national level are a two-stage process beginning with campaigns to obtain a party's nomination. Chapter 3 examines the presence of women candidates in primary elections for the U.S. House and assesses their performance relative to male candidates. I pay special attention to open seat primary elections where the presence of an incumbent is not a factor.

If more women are to be elected, more women must run. Thus, chapter 3 (and chapter 7) explore trends in the number of female congressional candidates, the extent of their presence within each party, and regional variations in their candidacies from 1968 through 1992. Unfortunately, for groups underrepresented in the national legislature, unwinnable races for newcomers have dominated in recent years. Incumbents, whose ranks are populated by men, have enjoyed an increasing advantage and have been overwhelmingly reelected. In 1986 and 1988, for example, over 98 percent of incumbents seeking reelection won. Furthermore, the vast majority of incumbents have sought reelection during this period, leaving few realistic opportunities for new groups. This analysis of women's campaign presence takes into account the electoral situations that nonincumbent male and female candidates have faced and pays special attention to the numbers of women candidates in open seat primary and general election contests. Because of the absence of an incumbent, open seats are the most realistic opportunities for underrepresented groups to increase their legislative membership. The presence of so many more open seats in the U.S. House of Representatives in 1992 relative to other recent elections provided the opportunity for that election year to become "the year of the woman in American politics."

Women candidates may differ from their male counterparts in a number of ways that affect their electoral success. As Carroll has noted, "One popular explanation for the lack of women in public office focuses on previous experience and qualifications for officeholding" (1985:65). Backgrounds and credentials are important resources in establishing viability. They also provide connections to resource networks. Thus, chapter 4 compares the occupational status and prior office-holding experience of male and female candidates. I explore whether a gender gap has existed in these important assets, if it has closed over time, and whether women candidates have surpassed their male counterparts in electoral experience. At the same time, women candidates also may differ from male candidates in the experiences they bring to their campaigns, enhancing diversity in the electoral process.

Although congressional campaigns have increasingly become entrepreneurial affairs, organizational support continues to be critical. Chapter 5 assesses the impact of traditional power structures, namely party organizations, on women's campaigns. The current women and politics literature emphasizes the failure of parties to recruit women candidates. This perspective has largely ignored the dynamics of party life in recent years. It has not taken into account the impact of party decline on women's candidacies or the transformation of parties into more supportive agencies.

Traditionally, political parties operated as the major apparatus of support for candidates. In recent years, networks of interest groups and political action committees have challenged the parties' special relationship with candidates. Party organizations have become both less important to campaigns and evolved into new types of support structures. The parties were once viewed as barriers to women's candidacies. Democrats and Republicans traditionally supported women only in races they believed to be hopeless. Chapter 5 investigates whether this relationship has changed and whether and how other changes in the parties have affected women's candidacies. It may be that party organizational attitudes have evolved from one of "no women need apply" to one of "a woman could win this."

Chapters 6 and 7 investigate male and female campaign experiences. They focus on campaign contributions and voter response. As noted earlier, money is crucial to congressional campaigns. Popular myth suggests that women have lost national elections largely because they were unable to raise the same amount of money as male candidates. This study examines the empirical validity of that assumption and the relation of money to the electoral success of male and female candidates over time. I explore total receipts and expenditures, sources of funding, and the timing of contributions.

New organizations such as the Women's Campaign Fund, the National Women's Political Caucus, and EMILY's List have formed to promote women's candidacies. The Center for the American Woman and Politics's 1988 newsletter listed twenty-six women's political action committees. These groups have organized campaign schools for aspiring women politicians, established political action committees to aid such candidacies financially, and initiated public relations efforts to promote women's elections. Chapter 6 describes the efforts of some of these groups and evaluates their ability to counterbalance women's limited access to more traditional power networks.

It also may be a myth that women still face discrimination at the polls. Women candidates now may even draw more votes than similarly situated male candidates. It has previously been assumed that female candidates do less well than male candidates, although a few studies have shown voter indifference to the sex of candidates in congressional races (Darcy and Schramm 1977; Darcy, Welch, and Clark 1987; Burrell 1988). Chapter 7 addresses the question of voter reaction to women by gauging the relative performance of female and male candidates in general elections.

Chapter 8 considers the difference that elected women have made in public policy and the policy-making process. This chapter reflects on the ways that women in public office affect representation and lawmaking. It examines gender differences in voting behavior and explores the difference congresswomen have made for women through a discussion of the legislative priorities of the Congressional Caucus of Women's Issues.

Chapter 9 concludes the study with an assessment of women's status as congressional candidates based on the data analyzed in the earlier chapters. Proposals for accelerating women's entrance into the U.S. House are critiqued. The proposals are categorized as electoral system changes, legal reforms or changes within the present electoral structure, and informal efforts such as concentration on open seats and new seats. The chapter discusses how these proposed changes would theoretically affect women's candidacies for the national legislature and reflects upon the plausibility of their enactment. Being creative and assertive in pressuring the political elements to increase women's places in the House is essential to the building of a more democratic and representative political system.

CHAPTER 2

American Views of Women as Political Leaders: The Polls, Experiments, and Surveys

The stereotypes that used to work against us are now working for us.

—Ann Lewis

Politics has been a male domain and political leadership perceived as masculine endeavor. Feminist political theorists have considered the equating of politics with men and masculine behavior as a problematic to be understood. Feminist political theorists ask why it is that in virtually all known societies men appear to have power over women and how can this situation be changed (Bryson 1992). As Okin puts it, "The great tradition of political philosophy consists, generally speaking, of writings by men, for men, and about men" (1979). Elshtain has described the historical division of social life into public and private realms in which "women have, throughout much of Western history, been a silenced population in the arena of public speech" (1981:14–15). In 1972, less than a quarter century ago, half the U.S. electorate in a national survey felt "Women should take care of running their homes and leave running the country up to men," and 63 percent believed "Most men are better suited emotionally for politics than are most women" (Harris and Associates 1972). These polls reflected a general belief that women were not meant to be full participants in political life even in contemporary times.

Women candidates for public office have had to contemplate the risk of not only losing but challenging an environment that viewed political leadership as antithetical to a woman's role in society. To succeed as political candidates, women had to overcome stereotypes about their abilities, their personalities, and their traditional roles. They had to convince voters that they possessed the same leadership qualities as men and/or transform notions of leadership. They had to demonstrate strength and assertiveness without appearing masculine.

Leadership traits have often been equated with masculinity in the minds of the public, but traits usually ascribed to women, such as honesty, caring, and availability, have also become important for political leaders. Richard

15

Fenno has argued that U.S. House members generally strive to establish public images as trustworthy, hardworking persons deserving of support for their experience, service, and personal style rather than for their party identification or programmatic goals (1978). If Fenno's image is correct, we should expect women to make especially good U.S. representatives.

This review of a generation or more of studies of public attitudes toward and images of female candidates will show that support for the idea of women in public office has grown, but that gender-based stereotypes have not faded away. Gender politics has become more relevant than ever, and sometimes to the advantage of female candidates. This chapter explores our knowledge of sexism among the U.S. public in the contemporary era in order to assess the context within which women have sought elective office. It sets the stage for an analysis of the experiences of women who have run for national office. It reviews surveys and experiments which have examined sex discrimination among the public and stereotypes about male and female politicians.

To ascertain general sentiment toward women in politics, pollsters have asked people about their support for women in various types and levels of public positions and asked what difference a candidate's sex would make in their vote. Beyond a generalized sentiment toward or against women in public office, researchers have probed stereotypes about the performance of women officeholders. Stereotypes and prejudice have been examined through two research strategies. One has asked respondents to compare various traits and issue priorities men and women bring to office. The other approach has used experimental designs to assess discrimination, particularly nonconscious prejudice.

Attitudes toward Women in Public Office—the Polls

Public support for the idea of a woman as president interested pollsters long before women started to organize to promote women's election to public office in the second women's movement. In 1937, the Gallup organization asked a national sample "Would you vote for a woman for President, if she qualified in every other respect?" Thirty-four percent said yes, 66 percent said no. Forty-one percent of the women responded favorably, but only 27 percent of the men. While continuing to ask national samples about their support for a woman for president over the ensuing decades, Gallup changed the wording of the question to read "If your party nominated a woman for president, would you vote for her if she were qualified for the job?" By 1987, 82 percent expressed approval—83 percent of women and 81 percent of men. But notably, nearly 20 percent of the electorate still publicly refuses to consider voting for a female president.

Reviewing Gallup surveys taken between 1958 and 1969 and a General

Social Survey question asked in 1972, Feree (1974) found that the proportion of the American public willing to vote for a woman for president remained virtually constant from 1958 to 1969 (55 to 58 percent) but rose to 70 percent in 1972. This increase was more pronounced among women than men, who between 1958 and 1969 had been more supportive of a female president. In none of these surveys did education, age, religion, region, city size, or party affiliation prove to be powerful predictors of the willingness to vote for a woman presidential candidate, but these variables did explain a slightly greater proportion of the variance in 1972 than they had in earlier years.

Pollsters have also examined support for women in lower level offices. The idea of a woman serving in the national legislature was readily accepted by the 1980s. In 1984, 91 percent said they would vote for a woman for Congress. Men and women were equally supportive (Gallup 1984). A 1983 *New York Times* poll found 48 percent of a national sample believing Congress would do a better job if more women were elected (Raines 1983).

The degree of public support for the idea of a woman in a particular elected position is an abstract measure of prejudice among the electorate. It provides a baseline regarding the underlying sentiment about women's candidacies. One gains further insight into electoral approval when a woman's candidacy is posed against a man's. How well does a woman do when running against a man in a hypothetical situation? Are voters predisposed to pick one sex over the other?

In 1976, Hedlund and his associates found in a survey of primary election voters in Milwaukee, Wisconsin, that majorities reported that a candidate's sex made no difference to them in elections for school board and judicial office. Indeed, in recent national surveys, the modal response among the public has been that they are as likely to vote for a woman as for a man. For example, a Hickman-Maslin survey prepared for the National Women's Political Caucus (NWPC) in 1987, reported that majorities of both women and men, when asked to identify which of two candidates they were more likely to support, expressed an inability to choose between a candidate who was a man and one who was a woman when that was the only information given.

In addition, the study found that 57 percent of the electorate believed a woman would do as well as or better than a man as president. Thirty-one percent believed women would not do as well (20 percent of the women voters and 24 percent of the men voters). Some subgroups of the electorate—voters outside of urban areas, voters sixty and older, southern white women, voters with less than a college education, and voters in non-white-collar occupations—expressed a greater bias against a woman in the White House. The groups least resistant to a woman presidential candidate included Democrats, blacks, city residents, voters under sixty, and unmarried voters, and especially women in these subgroups (Hickman-Maslin 1987). Bias against women candidates also declined with the level of office. For example, only 13 percent of the electorate believed a woman would not do as well as a man as U.S. representative.

A 1992 survey by Greenberg-Lake for the NWPC, the Women's Campaign Fund, and EMILY's List concluded that "when all other factors are equal, both parties are more competitive when they nominate women for office" (Greenberg-Lake 1992). This conclusion was based on the finding that a generic Republican male candidate running for Congress beat a Democratic male candidate 48 percent to 40 percent. A generic Democratic woman candidate, however, nearly closed the gap, losing to the generic Republican male candidate by only two percentage points (45 percent to 47 percent). A generic Republican woman candidate won with the support of different voters than her male counterpart, but maintained the generic Republican advantage, beating a Democratic male candidate 48 percent to 40 percent. In 1992 also, a *Washington Post*/ABC News poll found "that all things being equal, voters give an edge to female candidates." Asked if they would be more inclined to vote for a male or female candidate if the two were "equally qualified," 37 percent picked the woman, 25 percent picked the man, and the rest said there was no difference, they could not make a choice (*Washington Post* 1992).

The Experiments

Poll data then have shown a declining hostility among the public toward female candidates and even growing bias in their favor. Research that has examined actual election outcomes also has tended in recent years to downplay voter prejudice toward women candidates. (See, for example, Darcy and Schramm 1977; Darcy, Welch, and Clark 1987; Burrell 1988.) Women seem to do as well as men at the polls. Leeper, however, has warned us that notwithstanding the findings of these empirical studies, stereotyping of male and female candidates may still exist. Stereotyping involves assigning characteristics to an individual because of his or her membership in a group, regardless of personal behavior. Voters have viewed men and women differently as political office seekers. Leeper (1991) argues first that lack of women in upper-level offices may draw attention to gender when women seek such offices. In addition, "voters may value and actually seek a candidate with traditional 'male' traits when casting a ballot for an executive or top-level leader." Third, in ambiguous electoral situations gender may be used as a "cue." A number of experimental studies have explored stereotyping in evaluation of male and female candidates. These studies explore the problem of nonconscious prejudice. As Sapiro has described the process:

Most of these studies ask for an evaluation of the performance of a person unknown to the respondent. All subjects in the study receive the same description of the performance. One treatment group receives the description with a male name attached, the other with a female name attached. Responses to questions about the performance and the performer are analyzed to determine whether there are systematic differences between the evaluation of the "male" and of the "female." (1981–82)

Stereotyping is complex, as Leeper points out, and as the scholars who have analyzed its presence through experimental methods have shown. First, sex may be used as a cue in evaluating candidates in ambiguous electoral contests. Second, gender roles may come into play through the perceived masculinity or femininity of the candidates. Third, candidates send out different messages about gender in their campaigns. Fourth, voters may also perceive political offices themselves as having masculine or feminine characteristics. (See Rosenwasser and Dean 1989.) Researchers employing experimental methodology have manipulated these situations to determine the extent to which prejudice exists in the minds of the electorate as it evaluates political candidates. Through simulations they have analyzed exposure to male and female candidates for different levels of office, presented in different settings, and projecting different images and different ideologies.

Sapiro began the experimental study of sexism in candidate evaluation with the ambiguous situation. In her widely cited study published in 1981–82, she presented students in two introductory political science classes with a short segment of a speech delivered by "a candidate for the U.S. House of Representatives." The ambiguous speech was actually part of a real speech previously delivered by Sen. Howard Baker. Half of the students were informed that the speech had been given by "John Leeds," and one half were told it had been delivered by "Joan Leeds."

The students evaluated the performance of these two candidates equally in terms of their understanding of the issues discussed in the speech, the clarity of their stands on the issues, and the effect their proposals would have if put into action. Stereotyping emerged according to Sapiro when the participants in the experiment were asked to evaluate the candidates' competence in thirteen issue areas not mentioned in the speech. But the sex of candidate had a significant effect on only three of these policies: improving our educational system, maintaining honesty and integrity in government, and dealing with health problems. On these issues, all areas in which women have traditionally been seen as especially interested, Joan received higher competency ratings than John. Significantly no difference was found in the measure of the compe-

To summarize their findings: (1) The male presidential candidate was rated higher on some items, mainly masculine duties, while the female candidate was rated higher on feminine duties, from which the researchers concluded that "overall relatively little evidence was found . . . to support the 'sexism' of voters hypothesis." (2) In a second study, however, participants rated masculine and neutral duties to be significantly more important for the presidency than feminine duties. Thus, women candidates who are viewed as better at feminine duties but less competent at masculine duties face a hurdle in running for the presidency. A female candidate may attempt to overcome that bias by adopting a more masculine image, if she is not already perceived that way. (3) "Masculine" candidates were rated more effective on masculine tasks (which here, too, were rated more important than feminine tasks) and "feminine" candidates were rated more effective on feminine tasks. Also, masculine male candidates were rated as being significantly more effective than feminine male candidates or masculine or feminine female candidates. No significant interaction effects were found on the feminine tasks, that is, feminine male and female candidates received essentially the same ratings on effectiveness.

These latter experiments highlight the problems women candidates face in attaining the highest political office in the United States. It is viewed in masculine terms and masculine duties are considered most important. So, although women appeared to be advantaged in the earlier simulations, women candidates would seem to face difficulties in seeking to be chief executive. For women to win the presidency, perceptions of the office must change,[4] or female candidates must become more masculine, an unattractive prospect for some feminist theorists.

The experimental studies described here are important because they have explored "nonconscious prejudice." Simulations as a research method minimize intentionally socially desirable responses, since participants are unaware of the role of sex in the experiment. These studies are limited, however, in their ability to generalize to the electorate. Surveys, on the other hand, allow us to explore explicitly the extent to which the electorate ascribe different characteristics to male and female candidates and to consider the implications of such stereotypes on voting behavior.

The Surveys

Male and female U.S. voters have long expressed differences on some major issues of the day and agreement on others. Women have consistently shown

---

4. An experimental study should be undertaken to determine whether indeed this has happened in the 1990s.

less support for military involvement in conflicts around the world. For example, 45 percent of men but only 33 percent of women supported U.S. military involvement in the Korean War. Fifty-five percent of men as opposed to 42 percent of women favored greater United States involvement in Vietnam. Women have also been less supportive of the death penalty. But on most domestic spending issues and other domestic concerns few differences existed between the sexes from the early surveys through the mid-1970s. Beginning in 1976, larger and more consistent differences between men's and women's attitudes on public issues emerged.

> On specific items, women were more likely than men to favor greater protection for the environment (51 to 35%), oppose the death penalty (77 to 67%), favor police permits for use of hand guns (80 to 65%), and support programs that would reduce the income gap between rich and poor (73% to 61%). On foreign policy, women were more isolationist than men (43 to 31%), more favorable toward having the United States stay out of world affairs (39 to 28%), less likely to support increased spending for the military (67 to 80%), less likely to support increased spending (39 to 52%). In addition to these specific issues, women expressed less confidence in their government and more concern that their country was in "deep and serious trouble" (27 to 39%, and 48 to 37%). (Simon and Danziger 1991:33)

These differences in male and female perspectives, what Sapiro has "called a woman's point of view" (1981–82), carry over into public perceptions of what men and women would bring to public office. National surveys conducted between 1972 and 1992 have shown that voters have distinct images of women and men candidates, and that those images have persisted over time.

The Virginia Slims American Women's Opinion Poll conducted by Louis Harris in 1972 asked participants whether they thought women in public office would do a better job, a worse job, or just as good a job as men on a number of issues. Cooper and Secrest Associates in a 1984 survey sponsored by the National Women's Political Caucus (NWPC) rated male and female candidates on a set of personal and professional characteristics. In 1987, the Caucus sponsored a second national survey in which Hickman-Maslin Research asked whether various descriptive phrases better described a male or female candidate, and who would deal better on a number of specific issues. The 1992 Greenberg-Lake survey asked voters about a set of issues male and female candidates would be better on and differences in traits male and female candidates possess. This latter study combined the gender issue with a partisan one by asking interviewers to compare a Republican woman candidate for

relatively simple extrapolations from women's private, domestic roles to public issues and problems" (1983:146).

Participants in the 1984 Cooper and Secrest Associates study rated
women candidates more positively on seven of ten measures of personal and
professional stereotypes. Women rated higher than men on being caring,
being effective in office, having strong opinions, having new ideas, fighting
for their beliefs, understanding voters' needs, and speaking to the point.
Women and men were rated equally on showing leadership and inspiring
confidence. However, men obtained higher ratings in ability to handle a crisis
(Cooper and Secrest Associates 1985).

The National Women's Political Caucus 1987 survey again revealed a
"clear pattern of stereotyping of candidates on the basis of sex" (Hickman-
Maslin Research 1987). Survey participants were asked whether they would
associate twenty-two qualities with a male or female candidate. Respondents
thought thirteen of the traits better described a female than a male candidate.
They felt eight of the traits better described male candidates, and only on one
trait—would take your position on most issues—did the respondents rate
male and female candidates equally.

Generally the phrases attributed by the survey participants as better describing women candidates parallel the findings of the earlier Virginia Slims
Poll. Puzzling, however, is the great advantage male candidates have in
"backing arms control." Thirty-four percent in the earlier poll felt women
would do a better job of working for world peace. Women have traditionally
been considered more peace oriented, and most public opinion polls have
found women more opposed to war than men. Perhaps the emphasis in the
latter poll on "arms" suggests a toughness usually attributed more to men than
women, even though the question is about *controlling* arms.

The poll also found that a majority of respondents gave women candidates an advantage on dealing with the issue of day-care for children, and
large minorities viewed women more favorably on issues concerning the poor
and needy, educational quality, cost of health care, government spending, and
civil rights. Interestingly, while women had the advantage in "holding down
government spending," male candidates had a slight advantage in dealing
with the federal budget. Male candidates also had the advantage in the military realm and foreign trade.

Women's image as weaker on foreign affairs and defense continued in
the 1992 Greenberg-Lake survey; however, the female disadvantage was quite
small. Women "lost" (the survey's term), on average, three points on foreign
affairs and seven points on defense. The authors of this study concluded that
stereotypes about character traits have proven more persistent than stereotypes about issues. They based this assertion on a comparison with previous
studies. But the advantages and disadvantages of women candidates were
much smaller in this study, as shown in table 2.1, than in the earlier na-

tional surveys, probably because of the confounding of gender and partisan cues.

As compared with the earlier studies, the Greenberg-Lake survey found voters still worried whether women candidates were tough enough to get the job done, even though they thought women would do fine on specific issues. They thought women of both parties were less likely than men to know the system, to be fighters, to be tough, and to be effective. At the same time, voters were more likely to think women would care about people, resist the influence of special interests and be honest—Democratic women gained an eleven point advantage over their male counterparts on this item. In addition, Republican women showed advantages over their male counterparts on sharing people's values, listening to people, and being part of the solution. Female Democratic candidates enhanced their party's strength on the domestic agenda; female Republican candidates often neutralized their party's disadvantage on domestic issues without losing traditional Republican advantages. The distinctive images voters have of the traits and issue concerns of male and female candidates drive the attention women candidates as a group have received in recent elections.

The Year of the Woman in American Politics

Nineteen hundred ninety-two was heralded as the Year of the Woman in American Politics when, early in the primary nomination season, Carol Moseley Braun defeated U.S. Senator Alan Dixon in the Illinois Democratic party primary. Several weeks later, Lynn Yeakel, a political newcomer, upset the establishment candidate in the Democratic party's U.S. Senate primary in Pennsylvania to face Republican incumbent Arlen Spector. Yeakel's main theme was anger at Senator Spector's treatment of law school professor Anita Hill in the infamous nomination proceedings regarding Clarence Thomas's appointment to the U.S. Supreme Court in the fall of 1991. Hill had accused Thomas of sexual harassment when they had earlier worked together. In June, Diane Feinstein and Barbara Boxer each won nomination to the U.S. Senate in California, further fueling the idea of 1992 as an opportune year for women. No state had ever had women in both senatorial seats at the same time.

But the ascribing of political significance to women's candidacies in terms of it being their "year" (or her year) was not initiated in 1992. Jules Witcover first used the phrase in the national media in 1974 to describe women's political opportunities.[5] In a column titled "Women Candidates Capitalizing on Clean Political Image," Witcover wrote:

---

5. Reference to this phrase can be traced even earlier. In 1972, *Life* magazine ran an article on women politicians in that year's election which began "It may not quite be the Year of the Woman" (June 9).

> While President Nixon laments the Year of Watergate, the great public disenchantment with elected officials that has mushroomed from it may be producing the Year of Women in American politics.
>
> Amid the clamor for fresh faces and clean images in politics, an explosion in candidacies of women at all levels of government is underway.

The headlines after that year's election read "Women Score Significant Gain at All Levels of Government" in the *New York Times* and "Notable Gains Scored by Blacks and Women" in the *Washington Post*. Six women were newly elected to the U.S. House of Representatives, a record number. Gallup concluded in 1976 that "Women are more likely than ever to win friendly reception from the electorate." He reported that "seven in 10 Americans say the nation would be governed as well, or better, if more women held political office." Just four years earlier 63 percent had expressed a belief that most men were better suited emotionally for politics than most women. Stereotypes and voter electoral concerns had begun to change to the advantage of women candidates. It was not that stereotypes vanished with gender becoming a neutral factor as suggested by the experiments. But rather, "feminine" political traits and issue agendas, once viewed as negative, became positive in the political arena for women politicians.

The theme of women's electoral advantage emerged again in 1982. Alan Ehrenhalt, in *Congressional Quarterly Weekly Report,* reported on "The Advantages of the Woman Candidate" (1982:551). Women candidates continued to be attractive because of their "outsider" status. Women had found, according to Ehrenhalt, that "not being 'one of the boys' is a political tool they can use against a male opponent. No woman has ever been involved in a congressional scandal. Women spend little time trumpeting their integrity; people believe in it."

Midway through the 1986 primary season, women activists were hailing that year as the year of the woman state house candidate. Women were seen as poised to make a political breakthrough at the statewide level when nine women won major party gubernatorial nominations. However, only two were successful in the general election. Feminists expressed disappointment at the outcome.

Nineteen hundred ninety, too, was not only trumpeted once again as the year of the woman as the campaign season got underway, but also as the beginning of the "decade of women in politics," a phrase coined by Mervin Field of the California Poll to describe the potential of female politicians in California (pers. com. 1992). More women were running than ever before for high-profile offices, the domestic issues dominating that campaign were right for them, and a public grown weary of scandals and seemingly out-of-touch politicians perceived women to have the right qualities for public office. (See Toner 1990a.)

As the 1990 campaign season neared its end, however, pundits were describing what was supposed to have been the year of the woman and how that was unlikely to materialize at the ballot box in November. *Newsweek* headlined its October 29th issue with "Sex Still Matters—Macho issues like war and recession make it tough for women candidates." It reported:

> A record number of female candidates are seeking elective office, and several high-profile contenders were thought to have the edge over their male opponents. But as Election Day approaches, the chances of winning are not good for many women candidates. The so-called caring issues of the environment and education that catapulted them to primary victories have all but vanished from the political agenda. In their place are fears of a Mideast war and of recession at home. (Clift 1990: 34–35)

Robin Toner (1990b) echoed the view, in the *New York Times* at the end of the campaign, that the issue agendas of the campaign appeared to have moved away from policies associated with women. However, more than one set of circumstances could account for the perception that women would not do as well at the polls as earlier expected. Without tracking polls one cannot determine whether support for women candidates diminished over time, or whether the reality of the structure of the electoral system accounted for women having a difficult time making major gains in their numbers in high-level office that year. Women may have simply been running uphill battles against advantaged incumbents, without gender being the issue. Only a handful of women had major party nominations in open seat contests (races without an incumbent running for reelection), and their opponents were certainly not conceding them victory without a fight. Only seven women were in open seat House races that year, and only two women had major party nominations in open seat Senate contests. The role of the electoral structure in analyses of the experiences of women who have run for national office is examined in the subsequent chapters of this book and is a major factor in their not making greater gains.

By 1992, women candidates were seen as agents of change, and change was what Americans appeared to want after years of scandals and inaction on domestic problems. Women still faced some resistance, and they still had to overcome structural barriers that limited their ability to make revolutionary strides in winning public office. But that year provided a window of opportunity regarding the electoral structure because of the open seats created by redistricting. Simultaneously the Clarence Thomas hearings provided a rallying cry for feminists, an opportunity to raise funds and gain new members by widely exposing the absence of women in the Senate.

More than ever, stereotypes played to women's advantage. Wendy Kaminer (1992) described the situation:

> That women candidates seem more accessible to voters is indeed part of the new conventional wisdom; it is evidenced by the tendency to call women in authority by their first names. . . . Political outsiders are in vogue. . . . Women are perceived as being more honest than men, so they benefit from general concern about corruption. Women are outsiders, so they benefit from the anti-incumbency mood (women embody change, everyone says). Women are perceived as being more compassionate than men and better at dealing with the quotidian domestic problems—day care, education, and potholes—that are displacing concern about communism and national defense (which men are considered better able to address). . . . Sometimes women's advantage on domestic issues is said to be offset by a lack of credibility in fiscal matters. But the presumption that women don't understand budgets is usually said to be balanced by the presumption that they're honest.

Women seized this advantage. In previous campaigns they had tried to neutralize stereotypes about women as politicians. Now they stressed their distinctiveness. Claire Sargeant, candidate for U.S. Senate in Arizona, for example, ran an ad with the tagline "You bet I'm different!" Perhaps the most famous theme of the campaign was Patty Murray's "just a mom in tennis shoes." Signs appeared along campaign trails proclaiming "Elect Women for a Change." Beryl Rothschild, Republican congressional candidate in Ohio's Eleventh District, began her campaign biography by emphasizing having been the first woman elected to the city council and the first woman elected mayor of University Heights. U.S. Senator Barbara Mikulski devoted a TV ad to breast cancer research. In her campaign for the U.S. House in Arkansas's First District, Blanche Lambert explained that "I would never ask you to vote for me simply because I am a woman, but it is time for a woman's perspective." Even politically conservative women candidates would stress the ability of women to balance budgets in their campaigns. "Difference" and "change" permeated women's campaign themes and literature in 1992 and were used to send messages to a receptive public in ways no male newcomer could.

On many dimensions, 1992 represented an evolutionary process in women's candidacies (which will be shown in subsequent chapters). Over the past several years, more and more women had been elected to lower offices, and had risen through the political ranks. What was clearly unique, perhaps revolutionary, in this campaign was the degree to which women ran "as women" rather than running away from their distinctive images. Republicans as well as Democrats took advantage of the stereotype, although not every woman candidate espoused it. (And some of the exceptions were dramatic: Donna Peterson, for example, Republican nominee for the House in Texas's Second District, castrated a bull, apparently to show how tough she was.) How women altered the political discourse on what leadership is all about may be the most profound legacy of the 1992 election.

Gender and Votes for Women

A subtext of this review of the environment in which women candidates have campaigned for public office is the issue of the voters' gender. Both surveys about attitudes toward women candidates in general and election exit polls of actual voter behavior have shown growing gender gaps in support for women candidates. Gender differences were present in the surveys reviewed above, which focused on stereotypes of male and female candidates. Further, in the *Washington Post*/ABC News 1992 Poll cited earlier, women chose the female candidate 48 percent to 25 percent; men chose the male candidate 27 percent to 24 percent for the female (*Washington Post* 1992).

Mervin Field's California Poll in 1990 asked Democratic primary voters "Suppose there were two candidates running for governor, one was a woman, and one was a man, both had equal experience, good personalities, and no major differences on issues, would you be more inclined to vote for the woman or the man?" Fifty-five percent of the women surveyed said the woman candidate, 14 percent said the male, and 31 percent said it depended on other factors. Twenty-nine percent of the male respondents picked the woman, 18 percent chose the man, and 53 percent said it depends, a twenty-six point gender gap. Field repeated the same question in 1992, with U.S. Senator substituted for governor. This time 65 percent of the female Democratic primary voters chose the woman, 9 percent chose the man, and 26 percent said it depends; 41 percent of the men chose the woman, 13 percent selected the man, and 46 percent said it depends, a 24 percent gender gap (DiCamillo 1993). Has a seemingly greater predisposition on the part of women voters to support women candidates been present in actual voting behavior? "Do women vote for women?"

In a review of exit polls from thirty-five senate or gubernatorial contests involving a woman running against a man between 1980 and 1990, *Public Perspective* (1992) concluded that "with few exceptions women have not voted for women in significantly greater numbers than men have." Significant difference was defined as "a 10 percentage point or more difference in the support of women for women." However, by the end of the 1992 election they had reached a different conclusion. In the 1992 primaries, significantly more women voted for the woman who was running. A nine point gender gap existed in Carol Moseley Braun's win over Alan Dixon in the Democratic Illinois Senate primary. Fifty-five percent of the women reported voting for Lynn Yeakel in the Pennsylvania primary compared with 40 percent of the men. Barbara Boxer in California got 47 percent of the votes of women compared with 39 percent of the men's votes. The gap was much narrower for Diane Feinstein, who received a majority of both men's and women's votes— 61 percent of the women and 58 percent of the men. In the general election, a gender gap emerged in every one of the eleven U.S. Senate races and in the three gubernatorial contests involving a woman. The gender gap in the Senate contests ranged from three points in Arizona to between 27 and 28 points in the two California races (*Public Perspective* 1993).

Reviewing the first *Public Perspective* article, Smith and Selfa (1992) showed that Democratic woman candidates almost always attracted women's votes, while Republican woman candidates rarely did so, and that the gender difference for Democrats appeared to be growing. They concluded that increasing numbers of women do vote for Democratic women candidates. This phenomenon has occurred, the authors contended, because Democratic women have usually included women's issues in their campaigns, while Republican women have often either ignored women's issues or been hostile to women's rights perspective (1992). *Public Perspective* concluded in 1993 that "Much of the margin of support that women candidates got among women voters in 1992 as compared to among men voters seemingly resulted from the general inclination of women voters to give more backing than men to Democratic candidates." Of course, ten of the eleven U.S. Senate races and two of the three gubernatorial races involved Democratic women candidates versus Republican male candidates, not a strong test of the Democratic advantage hypothesis.

Conclusion

Nineteen hundred ninety-two did not end in disappointment for women's rights activists as so many other election years had. More women than ever had run for national office; they had dominated the political debate, and they made substantial gains in their numbers elected to office. Feminists were celebratory. But the year also seemed to end in puzzlement about the progress women had made. The idea of the Year of the Woman was both cheered and jeered.[6] Women realized that their year had provided a unique opportunity for women candidates that likely would not be matched in the future. They also realized that the progress women had made in gaining a greater share of

---

6. Some feminists find the idea offensive.

political power was as much evolutionary as revolutionary, a result of the earlier advances and experiences women had gained in politics.

Further, stereotypes that played to women's advantage in 1992 could have a backlash in future elections. They place both an opportunity and a burden on the women who got elected. Women will have a disproportionate responsibility to achieve change in a system that does not easily produce change. Women in leadership positions will be looked to as agents of change. They may be evaluated on the extent to which change is achieved.

This review of voters' images of women as politicians has shown that the stereotypes that once haunted women who sought to be political leaders have not faded away, but rather that voters have come to value those qualities more in their politicians and that women can capitalize on their experiences and perspectives to gain greater representation in positions of power. Women will still have to deal with the masculine dimension of political leadership, and gender politics will continue as an important factor in the electoral process.

CHAPTER 3

The Presence and Performance of Women
Candidates in Primary Elections

Explanations centering on the concepts of supply factors and demand factors structure much of the comparative politics' research on women's marginal political role in national parliaments. (See Lapidus 1978; Randall 1987; Studlar and McAllister 1991; Norris and Lovenduski 1992.) The supply side examines the extent to which the small numbers of women holding public office are accounted for by few women seeking such positions. Questions concerning supply ask why so few women have run for public office and seek explanations in women's socialization and in adult life situations evolving around the personal lives and psychology of women themselves. Other explanations emphasize the demand side, seeing subtle and overt discrimination by political leaders and the public as the central factor in women's low level of political achievement. Women who on their own would achieve political influence are kept from doing so.

Activists and scholars now attribute women's small numbers in elective positions more to their scarcity as candidates than to the prejudices of voters and party leaders. In 1987, for example, former National Organization for Women (NOW) president Eleanor Smeal launched a "feminization of power" campaign with the goal of "flooding tickets" with women candidates. Smeal argued that "with all other factors in the candidacies of a man and woman being equal, a woman has a 3 to 15 percent better chance of winning" (Jacobs 1988). According to Smeal, the problem is the paucity of female candidates. She believes women, especially feminists, must be encouraged to run for public office. She urges audiences at her speeches and rallies to stand and take the pledge—the pledge to support only feminist candidates and to seek out women to run for public office. In summarizing data on female congressional candidacies, Darcy, Welch, and Clark concluded that "if more women run, more will be elected. . . . Why so few women run remains a problem" (1987:85).

In addition to increasing the sheer numbers of women who run, more women must enter races they can win. Female candidates may do as well at the polls as similarly situated male candidates, but if they are more likely to be slated against incumbents or in other nonwinnable races, the numbers of women legislators will remain small. What is critical is women's presence in that small subset of races where new candidates can win, principally open seat contests or races against particularly vulnerable incumbents. Women candidates must create a strategic presence.

These two factors—absolute numbers and strategic presence of women candidates—determine the likelihood of women increasing their membership in the U.S. House of Representatives. These factors are prior to campaign experiences in determining electoral outcomes. A third factor must also be taken into account in assessing the presence of women as candidates for national office in the contemporary era—opportunity. Efforts to increase women's candidacies have collided with limited political opportunities in recent elections.

The political opportunity structure conditions the viability of campaigns for public office. At the same time as the public became more supportive of the idea of women in political life, the competitiveness of seats for the House declined. Incumbents, predominantly men, insulated themselves from national trends in voter sentiment, making them extremely difficult to unseat. Further, few members retired in any election. Districts without incumbents seeking reelection—open seats—provide the greatest opportunities for new groups to increase their House membership. But these open seats were quite scarce in most recent election cycles. The 1992 election was an exception when 75 of the 435 districts did not have an incumbent running for reelection.

The structure of opportunity in contemporary congressional elections suggests that not running may often have been the rational choice for would-be candidates, regardless of gender. This factor of opportunity structure adds to structural and situational factors that have limited women's candidacies for the national legislature. The perceived hopelessness of so many races has meant that even if more women became candidates, their membership in the legislature would not have increased at more than a marginal rate. Any increase in the number of female nominees might simply have reflected a growth in the number of hopeless races forgone by potential male candidates.

Congressional elections' literature is replete with studies documenting the rise of incumbency advantage in the contemporary era and analyses of its implications. In 1974, David Mayhew reported that marginal districts had vanished. Since then, "competition in House elections has been looked at from practically every vantage point and with virtually all available measures. That competition had declined became the conventional wisdom" (Bauer and Hibbing 1989). From 1974 through 1990 the percentage of incumbents winning reelection never dropped below the 87.7 percent figure of 1974; in all subsequent elections their reelection rate topped 90 percent, and hit a record 98.3 percent in 1988 (Sorauf 1992).

Fowler and Maisel (1990) have gone so far as to characterize the 1980s as "the era of the vanishing candidates." They reported that in recent years, even in open seats, less than half of the contests involved two relatively well-matched competitors. The supply of House candidates has shrunk and the composition of competitors has altered to the detriment of the electoral process, they argue.

Jacobson (1987a) has challenged the idea of incumbent invincibility, arguing that incumbents were no safer in more contemporary elections, at least up through 1982, than they had been in the 1950s and that competition for House seats held by incumbents had in fact not declined. While the average percentage of the vote by which incumbents won reelection had increased, the chances of an incumbent winning by a large margin in one election and losing in the next had grown. Only in the 1980s, Jacobson later reported, did incumbents' reelection rates surpass those of the 1950s (1990).

Jacobson's analysis gives hope to potential challengers. For example, he argues that Republicans failed to increase their numbers in the House in the 1980s while dominating the White House, not so much because of the structural advantages of incumbency, but because they failed to field strong candidates (1990). Indeed, of those serving in the U.S. House in 1990, more than half (140) of the Democrats and nearly two-thirds (110) of the Republicans had been elected in 1980 or later, suggesting a good deal of turnover in membership viewed from a longer time perspective than one election.

House elections have become more candidate-centered than they use to be, and to the extent that these elections are candidate- rather than party-centered, competition depends not just on the presence of challengers but on the political talents and resources of those who run. Fowler and Maisel (1990) argue that "candidate recruitment is the key to understanding election outcomes in the House. Why some people run, while others remain on the sidelines thus becomes a critical question for congressional scholars."

The candidate centeredness of congressional elections and the significance of candidate quality are important to a consideration of the hopelessness of so many congressional races and to questions of women's presence and experience as congressional candidates. It suggests opportunities that might not be seen from a perspective that focuses only on the structure of incumbency advantage. Women, given the perception of their outsider status as discussed in chapter 2, might have been particularly appealing candidates in this era. It might have been a particular advantage to Republicans to have nominated women.

Table 3.1 describes the situation that aspiring candidates for the U.S. House have faced from 1968 through 1992. It shows the number of representatives not seeking reelection, the numbers defeated in primary and general elections, and the number of incumbents without a major party opponent in the general election. In nearly all of these election years, less than 10 percent

TABLE 3.1. Incumbent Retirements and Defeats, 1968–92

Year	Not Seeking Reelection	Defeats in Primary[a]	Defeats in General Election	No Opposition
1968	24	3	5	50
1970	28	6	10	59
1972	45	7	13	54
1974	44	7	40	59
1976	51	3	13	52
1978	53	5	19	69
1980	37	6	31	53
1982	42	4	29	53
1984	24	3	16	60
1986	42	3	6	71
1988	26	1	6	79
1990	28	1	15	82
1992	52	19	24	30

Source: Congressional Quarterly Weekly Report.
[a]Defeats do not include incumbent versus incumbent contests in redistricted districts.

of the House membership chose not to run for reelection—the percentage declined from an average of 9.4 percent in the first half of the period to 7.5 percent in the second half (not including 1992). The 1992 election marked a reversal of the trend when the retirement rate climbed to 12 percent. The figures also show 1992 to be distinctive in the number of members who were defeated in a primary election, and the small number of incumbents with no major party opponent in the general election compared with other recent elections. The number of representatives defeated in the general election was not so very different, however, from some of earlier elections.

In the analysis that follows I will often compare 1992 to trends in previous elections to provide a substantive basis of the ways in which it was (or was not) distinctive for women candidates. The 1992 election provided a greater opportunity structure for newcomers because redistricting, as a result of the 1990 census, displaced nineteen House seats, shifting them mainly from northeast and midwest states and moving them to western and southern states. California picked up seven seats; Florida gained four. In addition, the Voting Rights Act required increased minority-group representation.[1] *Congressional Quarterly Weekly Report* estimated that seventeen minority districts were drawn (Benenson 1992). Besides these objective measures of opportunity was the subjective sense that many incumbents would be more vulnerable than in recent elections as a result of the House bank scandal and a general atmosphere of displeasure with politicians. "Outsiders" had themes

---

1. In 1982, seventeen districts shifted from the northern to southern and western districts.

they could play on that had not been available to the same degree in earlier years.

Most studies of women's congressional candidacies have focused on women as major party *nominees* for the U.S. House. But this emphasis provides only half of the picture regarding women's presence as candidates for these offices. Election to the House is a two-stage process. Nominations must first be won. The supply of female nominees is contingent on how many women enter and win party primary elections. Only a few researchers have explored women's presence as primary election candidates for national office in the United States. (Bernstein 1986; Welch 1989; Burrell 1988).

This chapter first examines the scarcity hypothesis regarding women's candidacies for the House in the feminist era. It explores trends in the numbers of women who have entered primary elections and the types of primary situations in which they have run during this period. A more detailed analysis of women's presence in open seat primary elections follows. Open seats are where the primary action is because the potential of ultimate victory of newcomers is greatest in those races. If women are to increase their numerical representation in Congress, they must participate effectively in such primaries.

After analyzing their presence, this chapter examines female candidates' performance in open seat primary elections through a comparison of their voting power in these campaigns relative to that of male candidates. Research has found gender not to be a factor in general election outcomes for seats in the national legislature (i.e., female major party nominees average the same percentage of votes [Darcy and Schramm 1977; Darcy, Welch, and Clark 1987], raise the same amounts of money [Burrell 1985], and perform just as effectively [Darcy, Welch, and Clark 1987) as their male counterparts). Scholars have thus suggested that primary elections may be a "weak link" in increasing the numbers of women in elective positions, especially in national office (Darcy and Schramm 1977; Bernstein 1986). Based on an analysis of legislative elections in six states over time, Clark et al. (1984) concluded that while women were slightly disadvantaged in primaries without incumbents, primary elections were not serving to deny new women their party nomination for seats in state assemblies.

Prior Research

While research on the supply of women candidates for the U.S. House is rather limited, scholars have explored women's candidacies for public office in general. Studies of women's presence as legislative candidates at both the state and national level have shown that women tend to be a small minority of the nominees (even when only taking nonincumbents into account [Clark et al. 1984; Burrell 1988, 1990]) that changes in the nature of campaigning appear detrimental to women's candidacies in open seat primary races (Bernstein 1986), but that women no longer appear to be disproportionately slated as nominees in "hopeless" races (Darcy, Welch, and Clark 1987; Clark et al. 1984; Burrell 1988). Also, due to the increase in the number of women state legislators, contextual factors that once explained variations in women's legislative presence across the states no longer are such powerful predictors (Rule 1987; Nechemias 1987). Differences across states in the percentage of female legislators have diminished.

Structural factors such as women's absence from prestige educations and occupations have helped to explain the small numbers of women state legislators (Welch 1978; Williams 1990). Yet based on her review of the literature, Githens suggested that "the findings and conclusions drawn about structural constraints are contradictory" (1983:486). But women's roles as wives and mothers would seem to preclude their entrance into electoral politics or lead them to postpone their candidacies to later years, which especially constrains their ability to run viable campaigns for national offices.

The Data

For several elections now, women's groups and other organizations have tracked the number of female congressional nominees. Thus, we are familiar with trends in women's numerical presence as major party nominees. Scarcity characterizes women's presence among the pool of congressional candidates for the most part during this era. The number of nominations obtained by women doubled over the course of this period but remained relatively small prior to 1992. The number of women winning major party nominations soared in that election. One hundred and six women were nominated, a 50 percent increase over the previous high of sixty-nine in 1990. (Nomination patterns are examined in chapter 7.)

The task of tracking the numbers of female contestants in primary campaigns has not been undertaken, let alone an analysis of where and when women have entered these contests, and how well they have performed. Thus, we are unfamiliar with trends in the number of women who have sought a seat in the national legislature. We would suspect that the supply of female primary candidates has been small based on the general perceptions obtained from media coverage and the relatively small numbers of female nominees.

In order to assess trends in women's presence as congressional candidates one must be able to identify the players. Finding out who have been the contestants, even in races for such prominent positions as seats in the national legislature, is not a simple task. As one moves from the investigation of highly visible races to more obscure campaigns back in time, the candidate pool, and especially the sex of candidates, is not always easily determined.

Primary contests for the U.S. House in particular often receive little attention. *Congressional Quarterly Weekly Report* is the major source of information on congressional races and the main resource used in this research. It provides a complete list of general election candidates and offers some information about these individuals, usually age and occupation. Primary elections are also covered, although not as extensively.

Name identification is the principal means of classifying candidates by sex. The problem, however, is that some first names are androgynous, that is they are not distinctly male or female in reference (or as in one case, a Jerry turned out to be a woman candidate, and several Lynns were men). In the more highly visible races, press accounts usually refer to candidates in gender terms (i.e., as he or she, or him or her), which assists in identification if the name does not distinguish the sex of a candidate. For recent elections, Secretary of State's offices, state party headquarters, and winners' offices (for identification of opponents) have been good sources of information regarding candidates' sex when the name was not a clear indicator, and when news articles were not available.

Primary Entry Patterns

Two hypotheses drive the relationship between female candidates' primary election experiences and the numerical representation of women in the U.S. House of Representatives. A performance hypothesis suggests that the small numbers of female nominees result from losing primary efforts. A scarcity hypothesis states the problem in terms of few women mounting primary campaigns. These two hypotheses may work together—few women run in primaries, and those who do run perform less well at the polls than their male counterparts—resulting in few female nominees. To examine the scarcity hypothesis, data have been collected on the numbers of women in all primary contests from 1972 through 1992.[2] In the analysis that follows I focus primarily on nonincumbents. The performance hypothesis is tested by comparing the success of male and female candidates in open seat primary contests for both general and special elections from 1968 through 1992.

Primary contests consist of a number of situations: incumbency, challenges to incumbents, opposition party nominations to face an incumbent in the general election, and open seat contests. Women's presence in different types of primaries is examined here as a factor in the numbers of female U.S. representatives. Our expectations differ regarding trends in women's presence depending on the type of primary contest.

First, we expect that few women (and few men) would undertake pri-

---

2. Complete data are not available for the first two elections of this period, 1968 and 1970.

mary challenges to incumbents. Such campaigns traditionally have been overwhelmingly losing propositions, and in many districts little incentive exists to challenge the incumbent of one's party. Between 1968 and 1990 only one woman defeated an incumbent. In 1972, Elizabeth Holtzman (D-N.Y.) upset Rep. Emmanual Celler. This feat was not replicated until 1992, when Rep. Bill Alexander (D-Ark.) was defeated by a former aide Blanche Lambert. Rep. Stephen Solarz (D-N.Y.) also lost to Nydia Velazquez in a new district drawn to maximize the votes of minorities.

Secondly, women's candidacies in opposition party primaries to oppose an incumbent in the general election ought to have increased over this era, although we suspect that such an increase would have been conditioned, as for men, by the perceived difficulties of dislodging incumbents. A decline in the number of male candidates contesting such primaries may also have occurred during this period because the probability of victory against incumbents diminished.

Finally, we would expect that women's presence as open seat primary contestants would have increased during this time. Indeed, Bernstein notes the surge in female open seat candidacies in the 1974–80 period (1986). This last expectation follows from changes in women's lives, changes in public perceptions, and increased organized efforts to promote women's candidacies.

The numbers of female primary contenders during this era do not suggest an image of women "flooding party tickets," considering that 435 seats are up for election in each cycle, and that any number of candidates can enter a party's primary as figure 3.1 and table 3.2 indicate. Women's presence as primary election candidates did increase over the course of this era. In 1972, 67 women ran. Prior to 1992, 1986 was the high point with 134 female primary contestants. In 1992, 218 women ran.[3] If numbers of women running for national office are an indicator, it indeed was a year of the woman candidate compared with earlier elections.

Contrasting their numbers in primary elections to that of male candidates puts women's candidacies in a comparative context. Table 3.2 shows that women's presence as a proportion of all nonincumbent primary candidates is somewhat greater in more recent elections than in earlier elections of this period, but overall they have remained only a small minority of all nonincumbent candidates. Between 1972 and 1980, women were an average 7.4 percent of all nonincumbent primary contenders. That average increased to 10.3 percent between 1982 and 1990. Women's proportion achieved its highest rate in 1992 climbing to 13.2 percent, marginally exceeding their presence as a subset of nonincumbents in 1984 and 1986. The opportunities of the 1992 election attracted a surge in both male and female candidates. Overall, 1,825 individuals ran in primaries in 1992, compared with 1,195 in 1990.

---

3. Two other women were nominated after the primary.

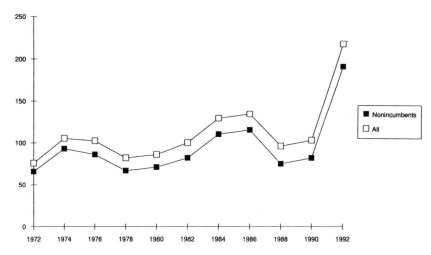

Fig. 3.1.   Number of women candidates in primary elections, 1972–92

Examining women's presence in different types of primary situations (the last three columns of table 3.2) addresses the strategic nature of their entrance into congressional races. The increase in the proportion over time of all nonincumbent primary candidates who were women results from women increasing the proportion of their candidacies in all types of primary election

TABLE 3.2.   Women's Presence in Primary Elections, 1968–92

Year	All Primary Candidates %	N	All Non-incumbents %	N	All Open Seat Candidates %	N	All Opposition Party Candidates %	N	All Incumbent Challengers %	N
1968	—		—		4.8	8	—		—	
1970	—		—		4.6	7	—		—	
1972	4.6	67	7.1	57	4.4	15	5.1	27	7.6	15
1974	5.7	87	8.2	93	6.4	20	8.7	55	9.4	18
1976	6.6	104	8.6	88	7.4	30	4.7	27	1.7	7
1978	6.1	83	6.4	68	6.5	21	6.1	32	12.3	13
1980	6.0	88	6.9	73	7.2	17	7.3	47	5.3	9
1982	8.2	81	8.1	81	10.7	36	7.3	39	3.2	7
1984	9.5	131	11.4	110	10.3	15	10.0	62	17.0	33
1986	10.2	134	12.4	115	11.3	27	11.7	61	16.0	26
1988	7.9	98	9.1	75	10.0	17	9.4	50	6.9	7
1990	9.0	105	10.3	81	12.0	20	10.5	52	7.7	10
1992	12.0	218	13.2	191	16.4	82	11.1	75	12.6	34

situations. Their presence as incumbent challengers is most variable, although on average higher, from the mid-1980s on than in earlier contests. Women's proportion of opposition party contenders shows a jump between 1982 and 1984 and then remains at a fairly steady state. Women's percentage as open seat candidates shows a fairly steady climb, so that by 1992, they had increased their presence in such races nearly fourfold from the beginning of the era. The largest contributor to the significant increase in the number of women running for primary nominations in 1992 was the relatively substantial number of women running in open seat primaries, an indicator of strategic presence.

Table 3.3 examines trends within the two major parties. I have combined the data into subsets of two election cycles for ease of presentation. The jump in the number of female primary entrants that occurred in 1984 and 1986 was fueled in part by the relatively large numbers of Democratic women challenging incumbents of their party in those two elections. None were successful. Few Republican women attempted to defeat an incumbent of their party during this era. In general, primary challenges to incumbents are Democratic party affairs for both sexes. Republicans tend not to mount challenges to their incumbents as indicated by these data and findings of other studies (Maisel 1981; Clark et al. 1984).

TABLE 3.3.   Partisan Distribution of Women Candidates in Primary Elections

	Incumbent Challengers	Opposition Party	Open Seat	Total
1972–74				
Democrats	31	59	28	118
Republicans	3	23	15	41
1976–78				
Democrats	20	46	36	102
Republicans	0	37	14	51
1978–82				
Democrats	14	39	27	80
Republicans	2	47	26	75
1984–86				
Democrats	55	61	21	137
Republicans	4	63	12	79
1988–90				
Democrats	17	49	27	93
Republicans	0	52	10	62
1992				
Democrats	23	40	58	121
Republicans	11	35	24	70

We should expect more Republican than Democratic women in opposition party primaries because the majority of incumbents are Democrats. Republican women would have more opportunities to gain opposition nominations. But as table 3.4 indicates, their presence has not been any greater than that of women in Democratic opposition primaries. Whether these figures reflect a lesser tendency on the part of Republican women in general to run for office, or a realization on the part of those positioned to run that campaigns against incumbents are not usually viable efforts is not known. The examination of women's presence in open seat primary elections allows us to explore partisan differences in more detail.

Women's Presence in Open Seat Primary Elections

Creating a presence in open seat primary elections is critical if women are to expand their numbers in Congress. In analyzing female candidates' presence in open seat primaries over time we must examine both the number of open seats in each election cycle and the distribution of female candidates across

TABLE 3.4.   Presence of Women Candidates in Open Seat Primaries, 1968–92

Year[a]	Number of Districts	Number of Women Candidates[b]			Proportion of Women Candidates per Race			Races with at Least One Woman Candidate[c]	
		Total	Dem.	Rep.	Total	Dem.	Rep.	Dem.	Rep.
1968	37	8	5	3	.11	.14	.08	11%	8%
1970	70	7	4	3	.05	.06	.04	6	4
1972	55	15	10	5	.14	.18	.09	16	9
1974	51	21	10	11	.21	.20	.22	18	22
1976	50	30	24	6	.30	.48	.10	34	10
1978	56	22	13	9	.20	.23	.16	18	16
1980	41	22	12	10	.27	.29	.24	29	20
1982	58	44	22	22	.38	.38	.38	19	24
1984	27	14	4	10	.26	.15	.37	15	26
1986	45	41	30	11	.46	.67	.24	40	20
1988	33	31	20	11	.47	.60	.33	54	30
1990	35	24	18	6	.35	.52	.17	43	17
1992	75	82	57	25	.55	.76	.33	55	27

Note: To obtain proportions in the total columns the number of districts was multiplied by two since there was a possibility of a primary in both parties in each district.

[a]Special elections in the year following a general election are included in that year's figures.

[b]The number of women candidates was obtained from the lists of primary candidates in *Congressional Quarterly Weekly Report.*

[c]These percentage figures differ from the proportion figures in column 4 because some races have more than one woman candidate.

races; that is, do female candidates tend to cluster in a few races or have they run in a range of contests? I measure presence by the number of female candidates per open seat race in each election, and by the percentage of each parties' contests with at least one female contender. This analysis includes primaries for special elections as well as primaries in the regular election cycle between 1968 and 1992. Table 3.4 describes the presence of women in open seat primaries by party from 1968 through 1992.[4]

Table 3.4 reveals a number of factors regarding women's presence as open seat candidates. The majority of open seat primary contests in each election cycle had no female entrants during this time period with the exception of 1992, when a bare majority of races had women candidates (55 percent). In a majority of the election cycles voters have had the opportunity to vote for a woman as their party's nominee (if they so desired) in less than one quarter of the races in any year (combining Democratic and Republican contests). At the same time, female candidates' presence did increase substantially in the second half of this era. Whereas a female candidate ran in an average of less than one in five contests (.16) between 1968 and 1978, she appeared in an average of one in three races between 1980 and 1990. Also, Democratic women tended to surpass their Republican counterparts in the number of their candidacies. This gap is especially notable in 1992. Looking at subgroups of elections, only in the 1980–84 election period did Republican women run as often as Democrat women did.

Context and the Presence of Women Candidates in Open Seat Primaries

Although women increased their presence in open seat contests as the feminist era progressed, they still tended to be infrequent candidates. Why had the supply of open seat female candidates tended to be quite small? The context in which they must seek office may hold a clue. Context provides the political opportunity for potential candidates.

The political context contributes to the differential participation rates of Democratic and Republican women. Perhaps more Democratic women have run because Democrats in general—as members of the majority party in the U.S. House throughout this era—were more likely to win. We would expect

---

4. Special elections are included in this analysis when they involve either a primary or an initial election with the possibility of a runoff if no candidate got 50 percent of the vote. Only the initial primary is included in these data, and such elections are not included in analyses of vote-getting power as they involve candidates of both parties. I have used these cases only in analyses measuring women candidates' presence and their characteristics. Some states have no provision for a primary when a seat becomes vacant outside of the regular retirement process. Party committees choose their nominees. Those cases, too, are excluded.

more candidates in the primaries of the party dominant in a district because the prospect of ultimate victory is greater for that party's primary winner. The larger number of female Democratic contenders in open seat primaries during this time may have been a function of more open seats in Democratic dominated districts attracting more ambitious women, just as they would have attracted a larger pool of ambitious male candidates. Between 1968 and 1992, 2,261 Democrats were open seat candidates compared to 1,682 Republicans. Democrats held the seat in 244 districts (i.e., the retiring incumbent was a member of that party) compared to 189 districts for the Republicans. Fifty-two races involved new districts.[5]

Partisan advantage contributes to the greater number of female Democratic candidates. Sixty-one percent of Democratic female contenders ran in districts where the "retiring" incumbent was a member of their party, compared to 40 percent of the Republican female candidates. (Seventeen percent of Democratic and 18 percent of Republican women ran in newly created districts.)

Partisan advantage, however, explains only part of the gap between the numbers of Democratic and Republican female primary entrants. If partisan advantage alone accounted for the larger number of female Democratic contenders, equal percentages of the "in party" districts for both parties would have had female candidates. But that was not the case. In the subset of districts currently held by one's party between 1968 and 1990, female Democrats held the advantage. Thirty-two percent of Democratic party open seat races in districts currently held by that party had a female candidate compared with only 19 percent of Republican districts with a "retiring" incumbent. The gap was significantly larger in 1992; 55 percent of the Democratic districts with either a retiring incumbent of that party or an overwhelmingly partisan advantage in a new district had a woman running in its primary. This was the case for only 18 percent of the Republican districts. Democratic women ran in 67 percent of the new districts in 1992, contrasted with Republican women, who ran in only 25 percent of these contests. One could call 1992 the "year of the Democratic woman," as some Republicans and conservatives have in disparagement, but in part that was the case because so many more Democratic women than Republican women took advantage of the window of opportunity provided by that election cycle.

This gap between the two parties in having had female contenders in open seat primaries in districts where they dominated suggests that partisan

---

5. Some of the "new" districts created in 1992, especially the new "minority" districts overwhelmingly favored one party. In those cases, even though technically they did not have a retiring incumbent of one party by which to classify them as "in" for a particular party, those districts were placed in either the "in" or "out" category for each party.

advantage alone does not explain the greater number of female Democratic party contenders. Another contributing factor is the larger pool of potential female Democratic candidates. As Nechemias has pointed out, "the recruitment pool of well-educated women professionals has expanded significantly and these women are more likely than their male colleagues to embrace liberal positions on politics, religious, economic and social issues" (1987:127). These women would have a more natural affiliation with the Democratic party. More Democratic than Republican women have also been positioned nationally to run for Congress. In 1992, for example, 59 percent of female members of the state assemblies were Democrats, as were 67 percent of the female state senators.[6] Further, the political culture of the Democratic party, where who you represent is important for influence, supports challenges to leadership. This culture more likely stimulates entrepreneurial campaigns by its female adherents than the Republican party culture, which stresses greater deference to leadership because influence flows from whom you know. (See Freeman 1986, 1987.)

Other elements of the political system may also affect the presence of women candidates. Welch studied the potential impact of variations in congressional election procedures on women's representation, particularly the significance of filing dates for candidates, the open or closed nature of primaries, and the use of party endorsements. In Democratic primaries, later filing dates seemed to produce more women candidates and increased the likelihood of a woman winning a primary. The party endorsement system did not affect the number of women candidates, but did improve their chances of winning. The open or closed nature of primaries had no impact on the presence or success of women candidates. None of these primary characteristics had an impact on women's candidacies in Republican primaries (1989).

In addition to partisan context and electoral rules, constituency factors reflected in the socioeconomic and political environment of the district may impact on women's candidacies. The social and economic environment of communities around the country varies in support for women in politics. Women have tended to be recruited to congressional office from urban areas (Rule 1981) and from districts outside the South. Mericle, Lenart, and Heilig have speculated on the basis of their experimental findings that women would do better as Democrats than as Republicans and would do better in liberal than in conservative districts (1989). These conclusions suggest that the types of

6. Overall, 60 percent of state assembly members were Democrats in 1992 as were 62 percent of state senators. Women are actually a slightly larger proportion of Republican assembly members—20 percent to 19 percent for the Democrats. Women are 16 percent of Democratic state senators and 13 percent of Republican state senators.

districts in which open seat primary contests have been held may have affected women's decisions to seek an open seat nomination (and their levels of success).

To explore the relationship between district characteristics and presence of women in open seat primaries, data were collected for all of the open seat districts on region (South, non-South), district urbanness, percent black, and median family income to represent the social and economic character of the districts. Data on the party's normal vote in the district,[7] and percent voting Democratic in presidential elections were also collected to represent the liberalism of the district. We would expect more female candidacies in districts outside the South, in urban districts, more affluent communities, communities with higher percentages of minorities, and districts more favorable to Democratic presidential candidates. Districts with and without female candidates are compared separately for each party on these features of district environment to test for contextual effects on the presence of female candidacies in open seat primaries between 1972 and 1990.[8]

Table 3.5 shows the simple bivariate relationships between the presence of women candidates and the socioeconomic and political characteristics of the districts for each of the parties. The correlations are presented first for the entire time period and then for two subgroups of elections—1972–80 and 1982–90—to look for suggestions of changes between the earlier and later years.

The percentage of blacks and the urbanness of the district had little effect, throughout the time period, on whether women ran in Democratic primaries (as opposed to the positive effect on the election of women to Congress). The effects were slightly stronger for Republicans (especially in more recent elections): their female partisans were more likely to run in more urban districts, and they were less likely to run in districts more highly populated with minorities. Income was the major indicator of whether women ran in both parties' open seat primaries. Women in both parties tended to run in wealthier districts (as measured by median family income). The relationship was especially strong for Republican women in the 1980s. These districts are more likely to have a higher pool of professionally employed women with advanced degrees eligible to run for high-level office.

Region had the expected effect on the presence of women candidates. Women in both parties were more likely to run outside of the South. However,

---

7. I wish to thank David Canon for providing me with his normal vote data. The normal vote is based upon the average percentage of the district vote the party's candidates received for U.S. Senator, governor, and president in the previous six years. See Canon 1990.

8. Because of redistricting, district level data are not yet available for 1992.

TABLE 3.5. Bivariate Analysis of Impact of Constituency Factors on the Presence of Women Candidates in Open Seat Primaries, 1972–90

Constituency Factor	Democrats	Republicans
1972–90		
Percentage of population in urban areas	.03	.06
Percentage of population that is black	.03	−.08
Income	.12*	.19**
Region	−.10	−.10
Normal vote	.06	.00
Presidential vote	.09	.01
1972–80		
Percentage urban	−.01	−.02
Percentage black	−.02	−.08
Income	.12	.12
Region	−.06	−.16*
Normal vote	.01	.04
Presidential vote	.01	.15
1982–90		
Percentage urban	.04	.18*
Percentage black	.08	−.10
Income	.08	.26**
Region	−.16	−.05
Normal vote	.12	−.07
Presidential vote	.17	−.09

Source: Congressional Districts in the 1970s; Congressional Districts in the 1980s; Barone and Ujifusa 1990.
  *Significant at the .01 level.
  **Significant at the .001 level.

this relationship reverses in the 1992 election among the Democrats. At least one woman ran in 63 percent of the southern Democratic open seat primaries compared with 50 percent of the nonsouthern races. Florida sent five women to the House—three Democrats and two Republicans; Georgia and North Carolina each sent a black woman to the House, and Arkansas also elected its first woman in this era. Republican women were still less likely to run in the South. Nineteen percent of their southern races had a woman candidate compared with 31 percent of the nonsouthern contests.

Democratic women were slightly more likely to run in districts friendly to their party, based on the correlations between the normal vote for their party and the votes their party's presidential candidates obtained. The friendliness of the district toward Republicans made little difference overall in whether a Republican woman ran in her party's open seat primaries, but this correlation masks a slight reversal in the relationship between the early years, when they tended to run in unfavorable districts, and the later years, when they had a greater presence in friendlier districts.

Table 3.6 presents the results of a multivariate probit analysis examining the joint impact of these variables on the presence of Democratic and Republican women between 1972 and 1990. Only two constituency factors are significant in the Democratic analysis. Open seat primaries in the South were negatively related to the presence of female Democratic candidates, while the median family income of the district was positively related. Neither the Democratic party's normal vote nor the urbanness or percent of the black population in the district had an impact on Democratic women running for an open seat nomination. In a parallel regression analysis only 4 percent of the variance was explained by these factors. Only 4 percent of the variance was also explained in the Republican model, and here only one factor was significant: the median family income of the district, which was positively related to the presence of female candidates. Separate analyses of the early and late time periods produced very similar results. (Region was only significant for the Democrats in the 1982–90 period.) Clearly greater idiosyncrasy is present in the decision to enter a race as opposed to actually getting elected (extrapolating from other studies that have found significant relations between some of these factors and the recruitment of women to Congress).

Sex and the Vote in Open Seat Primaries

If primary election experiences impede women's candidacies for the House, we would expect women to do less well than male candidates in these races. They would win less often and obtain a smaller average percentage of the

TABLE 3.6. **Probit Analysis of the Impact of Constituency Factors on the Presence of Women Candidates in Open Seat Primaries, 1972–90**

	Democrats		Republicans	
Constituency Factor	Probit Coefficient	Standard Error	Probit Coefficient	Standard Error
% of population in urban areas	.003	.003	.000	.003
% of poulation that is black	−.009	.006	.004	.007
Income	.030	.010**	−.040	.010
Region	−.430	.180*	−.240	.200
Normal vote[a]	−.010	.007	.004	.007

[a]The normal vote and the presidential vote are highly correlated as only one was entered in the equations. Which one was included did not affect the results.

*Significant at the .01 level.

**Significant at the .001 level.

vote. Also, they would raise smaller amounts of money to finance their campaigns during this stage of the electoral process. If this is indeed so and not just a perception, we need to ask why women do not perform better at this stage.

The traditional argument has been that primary elections hurt female candidates' opportunities to gain national elective office because male party leaders oppose their nomination except in situations considered hopeless for the party. If a woman seeks a party's nomination in a contested primary, she is unlikely to receive the necessary support from party leaders and other influential forces (Buchanan 1978; Kendrigan 1984). When party nominations are won, many institutionalized benefits automatically become available, even to women candidates, making gender less of a factor in general than in primary elections.

The theory that male leadership opposition accounts for few women winning major party nominations for national office loses force in the contemporary era as party organizations have declined in their ability to control nominations (Crotty 1980). Female activists have also increased their leverage within the parties (Glenney 1982). Many local party organizations are now run by women, and women have advanced into leadership positions at the national level (discussed in more detail in chapter 5). Therefore, competitive primaries in recent elections should have become less of a hurdle for female candidates.

The supposed declining influence of party organizations in the electoral process, however, does not necessarily benefit women's opportunities for recruitment to public office. Several scholars have argued that strong parties and party systems increase political opportunities for women. (See, for example, Matthews 1984; Deber 1982; and Bledsoe and Herring 1990.)

Indeed, Robert Bernstein has shown that a decline occurred in the percentage of women winning open seat races (i.e., races without an incumbent) for the U.S. House of Representatives in the 1970s compared with the 1960s. He argued that a breakdown in party control, which made it increasingly possible for ambitious candidates to compete for congressional nominations, contributed to this decline. "Contests for open seat nominations have increasingly pitted 'young men in a hurry' . . . against women without that drive. Consequently women have become less competitive in open seat primaries" (1986:158). Darcy, Welch, and Clark (1987) have shown that little difference existed in the types of general election situations in which nonincumbent men and women candidates ran between 1970 and 1984, suggesting that, contrary to Bernstein, women were not disadvantaged in the nomination process. Their analysis, however, does not tell us about the role of sex in primary elections among nonincumbents, especially in those races where the potential for victory in November is greatest for one's party, namely open seat races.

Bernstein concluded that "when women have tried for open seat nominations . . . their success rate has been lower than that for men" (1986:157). Yet he did not reach this conclusion through a comparison of male and female candidates' success rates. Rather, his analysis is based upon a comparison of women's success rates in opposition party primaries with their success in open seat primaries, and a longitudinal analysis of women's open seat primary success rates. Indeed, his data show that female open seat primary candidates' success rate was only marginally lower than that for male candidates (15 percent to 19 percent).

A very different interpretation can be put on women's performance as open seat primary contenders in the 1970s if we account for context. Bernstein may have captured a transforming period in women's quest for congressional office. He shows that women performed poorly as open seat candidates in the 1970s compared with their experience in an earlier period. But at the same time, the 1970s was a decade of surge in the number of female open seat candidacies, as he has noted (ninety-one female candidates between 1974 and 1980 compared with nineteen from 1964 to 1970). Bernstein suggested that weakened parties operated to the detriment of female candidates as those who had run in the previous decade had greater success rates.

But we need to consider that prior to the emergence of an active feminist movement in the 1970s, the nomination process was either literally or subjectively closed to most would-be female candidates. Those who ran for open seats in the earlier period may have done very well relative to male candidates, but they were only a select few. Winners may have been principally "widows." (And those nominated may have been selected disproportionately by minority parties as sacrificial lambs since the number of female U.S. representatives declined during the 1960s.) Anecdotal data hardly present this earlier period as a golden era in party organizational attitudes toward women candidates. (See, for example, Tolchin and Tolchin 1973.) With party organizations in control of the nomination process fewer women were likely to try for a nomination, and most female party activists probably did not even contemplate a run. The more open system that developed in the 1970s allowed a broader range of candidates and new groups to compete. At first many may have failed, as voters had to become accustomed to the idea of such individuals as political leaders, and newcomers had to learn how to acquire the resources to run adequate campaigns. But at least the voters had more opportunities to select such individuals. Thus, the political environment and the pool of candidates, as well as their performance, must be assessed before concluding that the earlier period was better for women candidates.

Have female candidates performed poorly in open seat primary elections in the contemporary era? Table 3.7 presents data on the relative performance of male and female open seat primary candidates in races from 1968 through

TABLE 3.7. Percent of Winners and Average Percentage of the Vote Obtained in Open Seat Primaries, by Sex, 1968–92

Year	Winners		Votes Obtained in Contested Open Seat Primaries		Uncontested Open Seat Primaries	
	Men (%)	Women (%)	Men (%)	Women (%)	Men (N)	Women (N)
1968–72	33	33	27.1	24.8	68	3
	(668)	(30)	(581)	(27)		
	$X^2 = .000,$		$F = 0.27$, n.s.,			
	$p = .99$, n.s.		eta = .02			
1974–78	26	19	22.8	18.7	54	3
	(1052)	(73)	(983)	(68)		
	$X^2 = 1.50,$		$F = 2.89$, n.s.,			
	$p = .22$, n.s.		eta = .05			
1980–84	28	34	24.9	22.9	40	9
	(764)	(85)	(679)	(69)		
	$X^2 = 1.23,$		$F = 0.61$, n.s.,			
	$p = .27$, n.s.		eta = .02			
1986–90	29	26	24.0	29.3	47	3
	(686)	(96)	(551)	(76)		
	$X^2 = .26,$		$F = 4.58, p = .03,$			
	$p = .61$, n.s.		eta = .005			
1992	26	43	23.1	30.6	22	6
	(418)	(82)	(391)	(76)		
	$X^2 = 8.427,$		$F = 9.84,$			
	$p = .004$		$p = .002$, eta = .14			

Source: Data compiled from *Congressional Quarterly Weekly Report.*
*Note: N*s for columns 1–4 are given in parentheses.

1992 to answer this question. Because of the small numbers of female candidates in any one election cycle, the period has been divided into four subgroups of elections, plus 1992, for longitudinal analysis, rather than presenting data separately for each election year. Measures of election performance are the percent of a group's candidates who won their party's nomination and the average percent of the vote received by male and female candidates.

The data show that the electoral performance of female candidates has not been appreciably worse than that of male candidates. Statistically significant differences did not emerge between the success rates of the sexes, except in 1992 when women did substantially better than men. Women did least well relative to male candidates in the 1974–78 subgroup of elections, a large portion of the time frame of Bernstein's analysis. Female candidates' success rate equalled that of male candidates between 1968 and 1972, and then surpassed them in the 1980–84 period. Women also outpolled men in the 1986–90 elections and in 1992. Women have not been less competitive in open seat primary elections in the contemporary era. Their performance hardly suggests that primary elections are a weak link in the recruitment of women to the U.S. House. It is their lack of presence (i.e., the scarcity of female candidates), not their performance that has made primaries a weak link in increasing the number of women in the U.S. Congress. Women's increased presence in open seat primaries in 1992, taking advantage of the window of opportunity in that election, and their strong performance in that year's open seat primaries make primary performance as a negative factor in women's representation in the U.S. House an even more outmoded (if ever descriptive) feature of women's candidacies for public office.

Conclusion

This chapter has explored the primary election experiences of women candidates. I have tested both a scarcity hypothesis and a performance hypothesis in primary elections to explain why so few women have served in the U.S. House of Representatives. It has been the scarcity (not the performance) of female candidates in the primaries and their seeming lack of opportunity to mount successful campaigns in the general election that have contributed to their small numbers in the House. While women did increase the number of their candidacies over this era, they remained a very minor proportion of all nonincumbents. In part that was caused by the lack of incentive to run a campaign against overwhelmingly advantaged incumbents. The political opportunity structure has not been kind to newcomers in general. But neither did women greatly expand their presence in open seat races where incumbency was not a factor. With expanded opportunities in 1992, women made substantial gains, and they did it strategically through the targeting of open seats. But it was primarily a Democratic party affair.

The window of opportunity, with so many open seats and vulnerable incumbents, that 1992 presented will not be repeated at least until 2002, after the next census mandates redistricting. Women's candidacies received the media attention in 1992, but men still dominated the campaign process as candidates. Who the women candidates have been may give us clues as to the potential of even more women running for national office.

CHAPTER 4

The Backgrounds of Female Candidates for the U.S. House of Representatives, 1968–92

Women have the advantage of being the outsider.
                    —Ellen Malcolm, founder of EMILY's List

Mr. Bilirakis, This is Cheryl Davis Knapp, the nurse from Safety Harbor
who is running for your congressional seat . . .
                                        —Radio ad, 1990

Who become the governors is a most important political question, particularly
in democratic societies. Traditionally, seeking to become one of the governors
was an activity in which only men engaged. Yet it is a process in which
women increasingly have become involved. Who have been the women who
have stepped outside of traditional female roles to seek high-level office in the
United States? We can imagine they must be extraordinary individuals, or at
least exceptionally well connected politically to break the mold and take the
risk of seeking such positions. But a popular thesis has been that women
candidates have lacked the credentials and the experience necessary for public
office holding (Carroll 1985:65–66), and this deficiency relative to male candidates was a major factor in there being so few women in elective office. This
chapter examines the backgrounds and experiences of female congressional
candidates, with a special focus on open seat primary contenders, and traces
changes in the demographics of female candidates in the feminist era to
determine whether women's routes to candidacy differ from men's routes and
whether winners differ from losers. I also assess trends in the characteristics
of newly elected female representatives and their male colleagues.

The media have focused attention on a new type of female politician in
recent elections. The *New York Times* reported that 1980 was "a time to
recognize that a new breed of woman has entered politics. In the last decade,
nearly every woman elected to public office was the first woman in her field,
but today she is simply joining the ranks. She comes from a background
similar to her male colleagues—business and law—instead of the traditional
route of community organizations or the accidents of marriage or birth. . . .

Women are developing a farm system from which congresswomen, women mayors and women governors will be drawn in the 1980s" (Shreve and Clemans 1980).

By 1986, many of the women running for major offices were reported to be "seasoned by numerous campaigns and years of elective office." According to Ruth Mandel, director of the Center for the American Woman and Politics, "There are women with experience, they are building political careers. . . . The ones you now see have the credibility and the constituency to mount races for high level office" (Toner 1986). Many viewed 1992 as the culmination of an evolutionary process in which substantial numbers of women had developed political careers similar to men's so that they were in a position to run viable campaigns for national office when the political opportunity emerged. As Mandel puts it, "Women achieved unprecedented success in 1992 because of a generation of work and preparation which resulted in a state of readiness. They were able to take advantage of these special conditions and opportunities because of 20 years of sowing seeds and moving women in lower elective offices and because of changing social aspirations and more public acceptance" (Schiegel 1992).

Celinda Lake, former campaign director for the Women's Campaign Fund, has described the evolution of female politicians' career paths as a "three wave" pattern. "We're seeing the fruits of the third wave of recruitment. The first wave—which accounted for almost all the victories up to the 1970s—were the women who won as wives, widows, or, in a few cases, daughters of male politicians. The second wave, dominant in the past decade, were the women who shifted their energies from volunteer work in civic groups to politics, and used their private-sector credentials as an entry pass to public office. In this third wave, women who have made their marks in lower political offices are setting their sights higher—just as men have done all along" (Broder 1986). (Her description remains to be empirically tested as to its historical accuracy concerning U.S. House candidates.) These statements attest to the importance placed on qualifications in the American campaign process. Who leads and how they get there are among the most significant political questions we ask. The backgrounds of political candidates are theoretically important because they appear to be related to success in the political sphere, illustrate the degree of openness in the political system, and may affect interests and behaviors in public office, although these latter empirical relationships are complex.

Establishing one's credentials and promoting one's experience are crucial to earning support, particularly for women, in our electoral campaigns in which who the candidates are is often more important than what their ideology or party affiliation is. Successful candidates have convinced the voters they are qualified to hold public office. Because political leadership has traditionally been a male preserve, possession of certain credentials and experience is even more critical for aspiring female politicians. Would-be female officeholders have had to overcome stereotypes about their lack of leadership ability. Consultants advise women candidates to "establish early on your experience. It is critical that women establish their competence and their managerial ability" (Broder 1986). We would expect to see fewer female amateurs who lack prior political experience successfully pursuing high-level elective office.

Competence, especially, is a word that appears throughout discussions of women and political leadership. (See, for example, Cantor and Bernay 1992.) Competence reflects judgments about the candidates' political experience and qualifications for office (Miller 1990) and appears important generally in voters' assessment of congressional candidates. When asked in the National Election Studies what they liked and disliked about the congressional candidates in their district, voters emphasized candidates' personal characteristics (Jacobson 1987b). Within the domain of personal characteristics, cues concerning candidate competence have been the criteria most frequently used for judging candidates (Miller 1990). Prior political experience, advanced education, and a high-status occupation are normally viewed as measures of competence for holding national office.

Besides the traditional view of acquiring political credentials another lens should also guide our analysis of female politicians' backgrounds. Most political activists and observers assume that women candidates should acquire professional credentials and connections and rise through the ranks much as men have. According to this wisdom, women must develop these career structures to create viable candidacies. A convergence in the career paths of male and female congressional candidates becomes a measure of female politicians' coming of age. Most scholars have structured their research in terms of female deficiencies vis-à-vis male politicians (Carroll 1985; Mandel 1981). Yet the stress on the male model limits our political vision. In 1992, women candidates, for example, capitalized on themes of change and difference with an implicit, and sometimes explicit, message that stressed the significance of women's experiences as well as gender distinctions.

Who the female candidates have been has implications for the democratic creed—which states that every citizen has a chance of winning office—beyond expansion of political opportunity to half of the population previously excluded. Does the presence of female candidates expand the categories of potential governors to include a wider range of groups based on experience, age, and occupations as well as gender? By emphasizing the male model we risk ignoring other assets female candidates (and newcomers in general) may bring to political life. Diversity of backgrounds provides a variety of experiences relevant to political discussion. Activists have long argued that women's different experiences make their presence in public life important. The criteria by which one is considered qualified should also be reassessed.

Voter preferences, too, for experienced candidates may be overstated (Canon 1989). Voters may be responsive to different backgrounds and experiential concerns, especially for legislative office. For example, Celinda Lake argued in a 1991 speech that "the public very, very much wants outsiders, they want politicians that they think have not been tied to special interests, they want politicians to embody change, they want honest politicians . . . and women seem in a very very fundamental way to them to embody those notions. Women represent by their very essence change. They think they're honest and been outsiders, not enmeshed in special interests."

Indeed, "not being one of the boys" has become a political asset both observers and female candidates believe can be used positively in electoral campaigns. This idea usually refers to not having been involved in traditional politics and seeming less susceptible to political corruption. But it may also provide the opportunity to expand our notions of "career" structures. Why, for example, did Cheryl Davis Knapp, quoted in the epigraph to this chapter, make her occupation as nurse part of her challenge to the incumbent?

In this examination of the backgrounds of female candidates for the U.S. House of Representatives between 1968 and 1992 we want both to consider the emergence of career structures typical of male candidates and to be sensitive to alternative achievements and experiences that women may have successfully brought to political campaigns. The presence of female candidates and elected officials may expand the experiential base of representation, bringing with it important policy implications.

Scholars have investigated the backgrounds and precongressional careers of women who have been elected to the House in the past. (See Werner 1966; Bullock and Heys 1972; Gehlen 1977; Gertzog 1984; Thompson 1985b.) Prior to World War II, a majority of congresswomen were widows of former legislators. Thompson reports that even in the period from 1968 to 1975, approximately one of every four new women in the House was the widow of a congressman or congressional candidate (1985b). In the 103d Congress (1993–94), however, only two of the forty-seven female House members had followed the "widow's route" to Congress—Cardiss Collins, who replaced her congressman husband in 1973, and Marilyn Lloyd, who stepped in for her husband as a congressional candidate when he was killed during the 1974 campaign.

Using grouped data, Gehlen (1977) reported that the median and modal age of women newly elected to the U.S. House between 1916 and 1969 was 45 to 50 years of age. Two of the 63 women were under 35 and 6 were over 60 years old. First-term congresswomen as a group tended to be older than first-term House members generally, but Gertzog (1984) reported that the median age of beginning congresswomen was declining in both relative and absolute terms through the Ninety-eighth Congress (1981–82). The median age of newly elected female members between 1965 and 1982 was 43.

Although the majority of women elected between 1916 and 1969 were well educated, 20 percent had not gone beyond high school (Werner 1966; Gehlen 1977). Thompson reported that it was among congresswomen that postgraduate education in fields other than law was first common (1985b:75).

Legal training has been pervasive among American politicians. "The law degree has clearly been the most common professional credential acquired by public office holders, particularly those who rise to the highest levels" (Gertzog 1984:39). Yet, congresswomen in the years after the suffrage were distinctive in their lack of legal training. Only 17 percent of the regularly elected congresswomen (as opposed to those who entered via the "widow's route") serving between 1917 and 1970 had law degrees (Bullock and Heys 1972). The most frequent college major for these women had been education, and teaching the most frequent precongressional occupation (Werner 1966). A major finding of Thompson's research has been the convergence over time in the proportion of male and female representatives who had law backgrounds. Between 1920 and 1975 the proportion of attorneys among congressmen had declined somewhat from 6 to 5 in 10 and that among the congresswomen had risen from 0 to nearly 4 in 10.

Prior elected office experience is common among members of Congress, but this was less true for female members in the past. The presence of experienced officeholders among female representatives has increased over time. Before World War II, less than one in five (19 percent) of all congresswomen, but 42 percent of the nonwidows, had been elected to public office before they entered the House. The percentage grew between 1965 and 1982—over 50 percent of all congresswomen and 67 percent of the nonwidows had held elective office before running for a seat in the House (Gertzog 1984:40–41).

The Congressional Candidates

The political process is, among other things, about competition for public office. Knowing who the competitors are, how they have come to compete, and with what effect are central to the study of the political process. The study of the recruitment to candidacy for high-level positions has not received as much scholarly attention as election to those offices has. While the campaign process has become the focus of scholarly interest in recent years (see, for example, Goldenberg and Trauggott 1984), the candidates themselves have not received as much attention. Major exceptions have been Fishel's *Party and*

Opposition (1973); Carroll's *Women as Candidates in American Politics* (1985); and Jacobson and Kernell's *Strategy and Choice* (1983).

As cited earlier in this chapter, the characteristics and credentials candidates bring to elections are important features of campaigns. What brings women in particular to announce their candidacies for high-level office, what they do with the opportunity, how their presence affects outcome, and who wins are significant political questions. Here I focus on the initial question of which women have been major party nominees for the U.S. House of Representatives during the feminist era. Even that is a difficult question to examine in a historical time frame. Much is known about winners, but losers often fade quickly into obscurity. Of course, even gaining attention during the campaign has been a problem for challengers. Thus, addressing this basic "who" question has required a major sleuthing effort, especially as we go back ten to twenty years. I have focused on prominent demographic factors that contribute to a candidate's public profile including age, education, occupation, previous elective office holding, marital status, and number of children. I have used *Congressional Quarterly Weekly Report,* personal interviews, newspapers, *Who's Who in American Politics,* party organizations, and informal sources to collect these biographical data. The Women's Campaign Fund in Washington has been especially helpful. Their files contain the biographies and résumés of many female House candidates during this period. The National Women's Political Caucus supplied important information on the 1992 nominees.

The "new breed" idea and the "three wave" thesis suggest increasing numbers of female congressional candidates would be experienced public officeholders and would have had extensive party involvement. These theories also suggest an expansion of the pool of female congressional candidates because more women would have the necessary credentials of an advanced education and a high-status occupation to be considered viable contenders and thus, presumably to have the ambition to run. More women work outside the home. Women now comprise half of the college graduates and are an increasing percentage of lawyers and business executives. Most importantly they have expanded their presence as state legislators in each election over the past twenty years. Paths to public office holding are an empirical element of the "new breed" idea.[1]

Age, too, is a factor in the development of a political career, although it

---

1. A second dimension of the "new breed" idea involves style, which is not explored here. The new breed is seen as being less ideological and more pragmatic. According to Harrison Hickman, "They've come up the traditional route, they're not ideologues" (Peterson 1986). They are considered to be more sophisticated (Mann 1986). The contemporary female politician approaches politics in the same way as men do. "They are more like their male counterparts in qualifications and in agenda than they are different" (Hornblower 1992).

has not been as clearly articulated as an element in discussions of the career paths of female politicians. Age has been related to political ambition more generally. As Schlesinger has observed, "The younger a man is when he enters politics, the greater the range of his ambition and the likelihood of his developing a career commitment to politics" (1965:176). We would assume that female politicians would run at younger ages over the course of the contemporary era as political ambition becomes more characteristic of women. We may be incorrect.

A problem for female congressional candidates in the 1970s noted by Bernstein (1986) was that in open seat primaries for the U.S. House of Representatives they faced younger, seemingly more ambitious, male candidates and were defeated by them. Yet pollster Peter Hart has noted that "the interesting thing about women running in 1986 is you don't have women aged 30 and 40. They're women aged 50 and 60. They're serious and professional candidates. They have their names at the top of the ticket because the party is looking for proven vote-getters" (Dionne 1986). Hart was referring more to women running for executive positions than to legislative seats, but he suggests that younger is not always better for women candidates. Voters may perceive young male and female candidates differently—perhaps to the detriment of female politicians. Further, political ambition in women can not be separated from the realities of their lives, which often involve motherhood, leading to later political careers.

Sex, Age, and Political Experience in Open Seat Primaries

I begin this analysis of background characteristics and candidacies with a focus on open seat primary contenders. We saw in chapter 3 that female open seat primary candidates performed as well as their male counterparts, contrary to Bernstein's idea (1986). According to Bernstein, women's weak performance in open seat primaries, which he believed characterized the 1970s election period, resulted from older, seemingly less ambitious, female candidates facing younger, more ambitious men.

Table 4.1 examines the relationship between sex and age in open seat primaries between 1968 and 1992, and between sex and political experience, measured as having held public office. The average female open seat primary candidate between 1968 and 1992 was 47; the average male candidate was 44. Five percent of male and 4 percent of female candidates were under 30 years of age. Male candidates were more likely to run while in their thirties (31 percent to 18 percent), while female candidates were more likely to run when fifty or older (38 percent to 29 percent), lending some initial credence to Bernstein's thesis. However, as table 4.1 shows, examined in a longitudinal time frame, age differences are small and statistically insignificant for the most part within subgroups of elections, and the age gap diminishes even further among the more recent cohorts. The average age of both male and female candidates rose over the course of this era. The correlation between age at time of candidacy and election year was .11 for the female candidates and .15 for the male candidates.

Open seat primary election winners in general tended to be only slightly older than losers. (The average age of winners and losers was respectively 43 and 41, $p = .001$, eta $= .05$.) This relationship between winning and age obtained for both male and female candidates as separate groups. Female open seat primary winners, with an average age of 46, were somewhat older than male winners, whose average age was 43 ($p = .003$, eta $= .09$). A statistically significant difference existed in the first half of the period with female winners being older than male victors, but disappeared in the 1980s when the average age of male winners increased from 41 to 44 while female winners' average age remained constant.

"Good" congressional candidates according to Jacobson (1980) are those persons who have held elective office prior to running for a House seat. On

TABLE 4.1. **Average Age and Experience of Open Seat Primary Candidates, by Sex, 1968–92**

Year	Average Age		Percentage Having Held Public Office		Number of Candidates	
	Men	Women	Men	Women	Men	Women
1968–72	43	45	34	46	668	30
	eta = .04, p = .41, m = 222		X^2 = 1.22, n.s.			
1974–78	42	45	33	26	1052	73
	eta = .07, p = .02, m = 93		X^2 = 1.07, n.s.			
1980–84	44	47	36	38	764	85
	eta = .08, p = .04, m = 104		X^2 = .005, n.s.			
1986–90	46	47	42	47	686	96
	eta = .03, p = .49, m = 56		X^2 = .66, n.s.			
1992	47	48	38	43	418	82
	eta = .05, p = .24, m = 2		X^2 = .44, n.s.			

Source: Data compiled from *Congressional Quarterly Weekly Report.*
m = number of candidates whose age is not known.

this criterion, female open seat primary candidates have equalled males. Forty percent of female and 36 percent of male candidates had held public office. In the earliest and most recent subsets of elections larger percentages of women than men held public office prior to running for Congress.

Since politics has traditionally been considered a masculine pursuit, credentials should be more important for female candidates. Thus, we would expect more prior elective office-holding experience among female open seat primary winners than among male winners. Female winners would less likely be amateurs than male winners, although we would expect the majority of winners of both sexes to have held public office.

Sixty percent of the female and 58 percent of the male open seat primary winners had held public office—a difference that was neither substantively nor statistically significant. Also, equal percentages of male and female candidates in open seat general elections had been state legislators (34 percent of each group). The similarities in age and experience refute Bernstein's thesis that young, ambitious males have pushed out older, less ambitious women for open seat nominations.

Background Characteristics of Female Major Party Nominees

There have been 471 female nonincumbent general election nominees for the House between 1968 and 1992. The number of women who have been general election candidates for U.S. representative is somewhat lower because some women have been nominated more than once.

Age

Female nominees have ranged in age from 25 to 75. Their median age was 47. Table 4.2 presents the age distribution of the women candidates by decades and their average age by subgroups of elections. As with the open seat contenders, female nominees in general tended to be older as the contemporary period progressed. The correlation between age and election year is .12. No statistically significant difference existed between the ages of general election winners and the losers. (Data not shown.) Losers were neither more likely to be younger individuals, perhaps out for the challenge of running, or older persons contesting hopeless races, perhaps given the "honor" of running for their service to their party.

Data are available on the ages of the male nominees in the most recent elections (1986–92). A comparison of the average ages of the male and female nominees in this period shows that the relationship between age and sex has continued with women candidates tending to be older than their male counterparts. This is true for all nonincumbent major party nominees and for

TABLE 4.2.   Background Characteristics of Female Major Party Nominees, 1968–92

Age Distribution	
Age	Percentage
Under 30	3
30–39	21
40–49	37
50–59	29
60 and over	10
$N =$	443

Average Age by Election Years	
Election Years	Average Age
1968–72	44.0
1974–78	45.7
1980–84	47.4
1986–90	47.5
1992	48.2
Total = 46.8, F = 1.66, n.s. eta = .12	

Education		
Education Level	%	N
High school or less	1	3
Some college	14	44
College graduate	25	79
Some post college	6	41
Master's degree	24	74
Professional degree	4	14
Law degree	19	59

challengers and open seat candidates considered separately. Women tended on the average to be three years older than the men. The mean age of male nonincumbent nominees was 45; the mean age of female nominees was 48.

Education

Data have been collected on the educational backgrounds of two-thirds of the female candidates.[2] Advanced education has been considered one of the key

---

2. Missing information on education spread throughout the years, so the results should not be distorted.

TABLE 4.2—*Continued*

Occupation				
	1968–90		1992	
Occupation	%	N	%	N
Professionals	30	127	35	28
Lawyer	9	33	11	9
Educator	12	42	8	6
College professor	5	17	6	5
Nurse	3	10	3	2
Other			8	6
Journalist, newscaster	3	12	5	4
Administrator, manager, director	10	36	8	6
Nonprofit agency	3	11	1	1
Government appointee	3	12	5	4
College	1	5	1	1
Public administration-general	2	6	—	—
Social worker	4	13	4	3
Technical	2	6	—	0
Business owner	6	23	21	17
Businesswoman	8	29	8	6
Elected official	8	27	8	6
Legislative or administrative aide	4	13	4	3
Artist, writer, designer	3	12	—	—
Farmer, rancher	3	11	—	—
Sales	5	5	4	3
Real estate	2	8		
Administrative assistant/clerical	3	9	—	—
Supervisor	1	2	—	—
Laborer	.3	1	—	—
Homemaker	8	28	1	1
Political or civic activist	4	13	3	2
Retired	1	11	1	1
Unemployed	.3	1	—	—

credentials in proving oneself as qualified for high public office. On this measure, female congressional nominees have been qualified. Only three of the female nominees between 1968 and 1992 for whom we have information had not attended college; over 50 percent had more than a bachelor's degree, and 47 percent had an advanced degree (see table 4.2). Twenty-three percent had either a professional or a law degree. Interestingly, the losers had somewhat greater educational credentials than the winners (Tau-$_c$ = .05), mainly because they were more likely to have Ph.D's or M.D.'s. No winners had these credentials, compared with fourteen of the losers. Overall, 25 percent of the losers had professional degrees, compared to 20 percent of the winners.

Occupations

In her study of female candidates for statewide and congressional office in 1976, Carroll reported that, as has been found in previous studies of predominantly male officeholders and candidates, the vast majority of female candidates had professional or managerial occupations, but that contrary to the precongressional careers of male candidates few of the women were lawyers, and the largest percentage were teachers (1985:67).

Women who were congressional nominees between 1968 and 1990 had been, among other things, homemakers, civic activists, political appointees, nurses, ministers, social workers, teachers, stockbrokers, newscasters, businessowners, lawyers, and farmers. Their occupational backgrounds were many and varied. But the general picture is similar to Carroll's. The most frequent occupation has been elementary or secondary education, closely followed by administration in nonprivate sectors. Fourteen percent were either business owners or businesswomen employed in the private sector, and 9 percent were lawyers, although another 11 percent had law degrees,[3] but still they were only a small proportion of all candidates. Together, lawyers and businesspeople—the predominant occupational categories of male members of Congress—made up less than half of the pool of female congressional candidates.

The vast majority of the female nominees had some type of a professional or business background, 18 percent had been in traditionally female occupations (elementary and secondary school teachers, nurses, or social workers), and a number administered social welfare organizations. Another 12 percent ran as homemakers or political and community activists outside the workforce. These data suggest that a wider variety of precongressional experiences have been represented in the backgrounds of the female nominees than we would expect to find in that of the male nominees.

In 1992, business, the legal profession, and education were the dominant occupations of female nominees. Twenty-six of the eighty nonincumbent nominees were in private business, ten were lawyers, thirteen were in education (seven at the elementary or secondary level and six at the college level). The social work area was poorly represented: only three women could be classified as working in that sector, and only one woman said she was a housewife. The most outstanding feature of the occupational backgrounds of the 1992 nominees compared with the backgrounds of previous nominees was the increase in those employed in the business world. It may suggest a trend toward convergence in the backgrounds of male and female politicians.

---

3. Some of the candidates with law degrees have occupations categorized here as public officials or administrators where that seemed the more appropriate classification, as opposed to lawyer.

Elective Office Experience

Nonincumbent female major party nominees were just as likely as male candidates to have had prior elective office experience between 1968 and 1990.[4] Twenty-nine percent of each sex had held public office. The female candidates were somewhat less likely to have been state legislators (12 percent compared to 17 percent). Since few female candidates had held statewide office, we can assume there is a slightly greater tendency for female congressional candidates to have run from local office experience.[5]

Prior public office experience was not more prevalent among the more recent female congressional nominees than those nominated in the earlier part of this era. Thirty percent of the women nominated between 1968 and 1972 had held elective office compared with 29 percent of the women nominated between 1986 and 1990. A 10 percent increase in female officeholders among the nominees broke this pattern in 1992. In that election, 40 percent of the female nominees had held public office. We might have expected the presence of experienced candidates to have increased over time prior to 1992 as women increasingly gained lower-level offices. But the lack of greater office-holding experience among the female nominees during this period up to 1992 may have been part of a larger phenomenon of congressional elections increasingly pitting weak challengers against overwhelmingly advantaged incumbents rather than being a gender-specific feature of these elections. Few women in state legislatures or other good lower-level elective positions would have had incentive to give up these offices to run in a seemingly unwinnable race. The increase in elected office experience among female nominees in 1992, when the chance for victory was greater than in earlier years, confirms the importance of opportunity as a major factor in so few women having run prior to that year.

Significant differences existed between the political experience of open seat nominees and incumbent challengers, but not between men and women in each of these categories. Whereas a majority of open seat nominees had held public office, less than 25 percent of male and female incumbent challengers had elective office experience (22 percent of the women and 23 percent of the men).

Female winners were much more likely to have had elected office experience than female losers (66 percent compared to 28 percent, $Tau_b = .27$).[6]

---

4. I would like to thank Gary Jacobson for providing me with the data on prior office-holding experience. The data for male candidates in 1992 is not yet available.

5. This cannot be empirically confirmed with the present data, as we do not have information on the types of offices male nominees have had other than state legislative positions.

6. The 1992 nominees were included in this calculation. They enhance the relationship. Seventy-five percent of the winners in that year's election had elected office experience compared with 25 percent of the losers.

TABLE 4.3. Occupations and Elective Office Experience of First Term Congresswomen, 103d Congress (1993–94)

Name	Occupation	Elected Office
Karan English	Public official	state senate
Blanche Lambert	Lobbyist, former congressional aide	none
Lynn Woolsey	Personnel service owner	city council
Anna Eshoo	Public official	county supervisor
Lucille Roybal-Allard	Public relations, fundraiser	state assembly
Jane Harman	Lawyer—deputy secretary in Carter cabinet	none
Lynn Schenk	Lawyer—state cabinet official	port commissioner
Corrine Brown	College guidance counselor	state assembly
Tillie Fowler	Lawyer	city council
Karen Thurman	Teacher	state senate
Carrie Meek	Educational administrator	state senate
Cynthia McKinney	Professor	state assembly
Pat Danner	State senator, small business owner	state senate
Nydia Velaquez	Professor	city council
Carolyn Maloney	Teacher	city council
Eva Clayton	County commissioner, assistant state cabinet official, college minority recruiter	county commission
Deborah Price	County judge	judge
Elizabeth Furse	Political activist, vineyard owner	none
Marjorie Margolis-Mezvensky	Television journalist	none
Eddie Bernice Johnson	Airport shop owner, consultant, nurse	state senate
Karen Shepherd	University official, English teacher and social services director	state senate
Leslie Byrne	President—business consulting firm	state assembly
Maria Cantwell	Public relations consultant, owner, public relations firm	state assembly
Jennifer Dunn	Chair, Washington State Republican party	none

Source: Congressional Quarterly Weekly Report.

Experienced female candidates were more likely to win because they were more likely to run in open seat elections.

The Winners

In 1972, five women were newly elected to the U.S. House. Their median age was thirty-eight years. They all had law degrees and three had prior public office-holding experience. Two had served in their state legislatures and one had been county clerk. In 1992, twenty-four women won their first election to the House. They were older than the earlier cohort, having an median age of forty-nine. Only four of the twenty-four, or 17 percent, had law degrees, but 75 percent had held elected office.

Seventy-six women won election to the U.S. House of Representatives between 1968 and 1992.[7] Table 4.3 presents background characteristics of these women and those of a sample of men elected to the House during the same era. A random sample of 120 newly elected male members stratified by year of election between 1968 and 1990 was drawn, and data were collected on their backgrounds to examine similarities and differences between newly elected male and female officials. Similar information has been collected on all of the eighty-six men first elected to the 103rd Congress in 1992.

Age

The median age of the women elected to the House between 1968 and 1990 was forty-eight years while that of their male colleagues was forty-three (table 4.3).[8] The age gap was slightly wider in 1992: the twenty-four newly elected women had a median age of forty-nine, and the men had a median age of forty-three. That women enter the House at an older age than male members is not particularly surprising, given that women still tend to wait until their children are older before undertaking a political career. Women may also feel the need to acquire more qualifications and maturity than men do before they feel comfortable running for office.

But contrary to expectations, the women's movement has not spawned successful younger female candidates for national office. (See also Johnson and Stanwick 1976). As table 4.4 shows, while the average age at entrance for male members was quite stable over the course of this era, the average age of newly elected female House members increased over time. The product moment correlation between year elected and age for the female members was .26.[9] This trend is contrary to that found by Gertzog who examined the backgrounds of female members between 1917 and 1982 and reported a downward trend in the median ages of congresswomen over time.

This trend may reflect changes in the type of women running in the 1970s and the 1980s. Candidates in the 1970s reflected concerns raised by the

7. This figure includes those women elected to finish their husbands' terms but who did not run for reelection, such as Jean Ashbrook in 1982.

8. The presence of congressional widows contributes slightly to the higher average age of women representatives. The median age of the eight congressional widows elected to replace their husbands during this time frame was 49.5 years. The median age of the noncongressional widows was 47. But even excluding widows, women enter Congress later in life than men.

9. Over a longer period, the trend in age at entrance for women members may be curvilinear. Emmy Werner (1966) reports that "the modal age at which congresswomen first obtained their seats on Capitol Hill [between 1916 and 1964] was 52." (This figure, however, includes women elected or appointed to the U.S. Senate.) But Gehlen's (1977) figures also confirm this curvilinear trend.

TABLE 4.4. Background Characteristics of Newly Elected U.S. Representatives, by Sex, 1968–90

Characteristic	1968–90 Women (%)	1968–90 Men (%)	1992 Women (%)	1992 Men (%)
Age				
Under 30	—	2	0	0
30–34	8	12	8	9
35–39	10	21	8	21
40–44	19	29	13	26
45–49	19	12	25	16
50–54	17	15	25	20
55–59	15	8	17	5
60 and over	12	3	4	4
Median Age	48	43	49	43
	$\chi^2 = 14.7, p > .04$			
Education				
High school or less	0	2	—	2
Some college	23	8	8	4
College degree	29	24	38	17
Postgraduate work	10	5	13	1
Master's degree	19	12	25	14
Professional degree	2	8	—	8
Law degree	17	43	17	54
N	52	120	24	86
	$\text{Tau}_c = .27$		$\text{Tau}_c = .29$	
Elected Positions Held				
None	42 (34)[a]	24	25	26
School board	4 (5)	1	—	1
City council	10 (11)	8	17	7
Mayor	2 (2)	3	—	6
County legislator	2 (2)	3	8	2
Other county office	2 (2)	1	—	2
State representative	14 (16)	23	21	22
State Senator	17 (21)	19	25	27
Statewide	4 (5)	4	—	3
Judicial	— —	4	4	2
Former U.S. representative	2 (2)	7		
Party and Civic/Community Activity				
Party	65	35		
Civic/community	73	49		
Occupation[b]				
Lawyer	16	40	13	49
Business (owner, executive, banker)	10	20	20	17
Educator	20	3	8	2

TABLE 4.4—*Continued*

Characteristic	1968–90		1992	
	Women (%)	Men (%)	Women (%)	Men (%)
College professor	2	3	4	4
Professional	4	9	4	5
Administrator	10	2	20	17
Journalist, newscaster	4	2	4	2
Public official	12	5	17	12
Social worker	2	—	—	—
Farmer	4	4	—	4
Sales	—	9	—	4
Real Estate	—	3	—	1
Legislative/administrative aide	4	—	4	—
Administrative assistant/clerical	2	—	—	—
Homemaker	4	—	—	—
Civic leader, political activist	6	—	4	—
N	50	118	24	86
Marital Status				
Never married	12	8	8	7
Married	58	87	67	83
Divorced	8	3	25	11
Widowed	8	3	—	—
Congressional widow	15	—	—	—
Number of children[c]				
None	20	8	9	19
One	4	9	14	8
Two	33	30	46	34
Three	28	21	5	23
Four or more	15	32	27	18

[a]Numbers in parentheses exclude "widows" from analysis.

[b]This classification relies on the occupation listed in the short biographies in *Congressional Quarterly* for the most part. It tends to underestimate the diversity of occupational backgrounds.

[c]Figures are based on representatives who have been married only.

activism of the 1960s. Shirley Chisholm, Pat Schroeder, Elizabeth Holtzman, and Martha Keyes, for example, addressed the challenges of the younger generation in an unprecedented way. The backgrounds of women elected in more recent years may reflect the time-consuming process of developing traditional (i.e., male) political careers characteristic of the "new breed" idea, such as climbing the political ladder and acquiring credentials. (This may also have been the case for the nonwidows in earlier periods.) It is important to note that with the exception of Pat Schroeder (and the widows Cardiss Collins

TABLE 4.5. Trends in the Average Age and Elective Office Experience of Newly Elected Members of the U.S. House of Representatives, by Sex

Election Years	Women Age	N	Men Age	N
1968–72	44	11	44	26
1974–78	47	12	42	39
1980–84	48	15	45	34
1986–90	51	14	44	21
1992	49	24	43	86

	Percentage with Prior Elective Office Experience		
1968–72	55	(67)[a]	73
1974–78	42	(56)	69
1980–84	53	(67)	76
1986–90	71	(71)	81

[a]"Widows" excluded from the analysis.

and Marilyn Lloyd), none of the women elected in the early part of this period (prior to 1978) today serve in the House. Representation and seniority on Capitol Hill would look very different if more congresswomen had sustained their congressional careers. Does the age trend reflect changes in backgrounds?

Education

Earlier studies showed that only 8 percent of congresswomen had obtained advanced degrees. But 38 percent of those elected between 1968 and 1990 had done so, and 42 percent of the class of 1992 had either a master's or a law degree. Nonetheless, contemporary female representatives are less highly educated than their male colleagues, 62 percent of whom possessed post-graduate degrees.[10] Seventy-six percent of the newly elected male members of the House in 1992 had advanced degrees. The major difference between the sexes lies in the significantly greater proportion of male members elected between 1968 and 1990 who have had law degrees (43 percent to 17 percent). Fifty-four percent of the male members of the class of 1992 had law degrees compared with 17 percent of the female members.

10. The education gap between the sexes is lessened somewhat if we exclude the widows for the analysis. The Tau-$_c$ measure of association declines from .27 to .19. Five of the eight congressional widows had some college education, and the other three had bachelor's degrees.

The proportion of first term congressmen in the 103rd Congress with law degrees represents a reversal of a downward trend in law as the major occupation among members of the House. The large gender gap in legal training, which has been sustained and even enhanced in recent elections, suggests a movement away from the convergence in career paths between male and female representatives that Thompson had earlier noted.

The absence of female lawyers in Congress is intriguing. Bullock and Heys (1972) reported that 17 percent of the regularly elected congresswomen serving between 1917 and 1970 had law degrees. Thus, no trend exists toward an increasing presence of female members with law degrees. Only two women elected to the House after 1972, Geraldine Ferraro and the returning Patsy Mink, had law degrees prior to 1992, when they were joined by four more women with legal training. From a dynamic perspective it is important to consider the extent to which female lawyers have been positioned to mount congressional campaigns. The number of female law degree recipients in the country has increased dramatically in recent years (Williams 1990). Where have they gone? Women in the statehouses are in good positions to run for Congress. To what extent do they and prominent female local officials have law backgrounds? It may be that female lawyers are pursuing interests other than public office holding. Why that may be so should be pursued. (See Briscoe 1989.)

Prior Elective Office Holding

Bullock and Heys (1972) reported that 57 percent of the nonwidows elected to the House between 1916 and 1964 had previously held public office. Two factors stand out from the figures on contemporary congresswomen's prior elective office holding. First, surprisingly, the women elected to the House between 1968 and 1990 were significantly less likely to have held elective office than their male counterparts (42 percent to 24 percent had not held office). The gap decreases somewhat, however, if the "widows" are excluded. Thirty-four percent of the newly elected female representatives who did not succeed their spouses had never held elective office. Secondly, over time the presence of previously elected officials among female representatives increased. Consequently, the gap between the sexes has narrowed. A 10 percent gap existed in the public office-holding experience of male and female newly elected representatives between 1986 and 1990. The gap vanished in 1992 when three-fourths of both the new congresswomen and the new congressmen had held elected office prior to running for a seat in the House. Forty-six percent of the new congresswomen and 49 percent of the new congressmen in 1993 had been state legislators. The "new breed" thesis would have led us to expect such a convergence.

Partisan and Community Activism

We should expect to find that high levels of involvement in party and community activities are characteristic of House members' backgrounds in general, and that such activism is especially prevalent among congresswomen. Female candidates would need more personal resources to compete successfully in this traditional male arena. Scholars have previously commented on the importance of partisan and community involvement to female politicians either as compensatory modes of gaining recognition when private achievement credentials have not been available, or as alternative means of gaining credibility in the political arena (Mandel 1981; Carroll 1985).

I measure partisan activity and civic and community involvement only roughly in this study. Individuals have been credited with being active in their party or in civic associations if their résumés included any partisan activity, such as having been a convention delegate or a party committee member, or listed membership in any civic or community groups such as the League of Women Voters or the Rotary. For example, *Women in Congress, 1917–1990* describes Nancy Johnson as having used "her experience in community and civic affairs as an effective foundation for her later career in elective politics. Before her election to the Connecticut Senate in 1976, she worked as a volunteer in local school programs, community children's services, and fund raising campaigns for libraries and charities" (1991:115).

The data on political and community activism were collected from information in *Who's Who in American Politics, Congressional Quarterly Weekly Report*, and *Women in Congress*. Participation may be underestimated using this method, as one could be active in various organizations without having that activity, especially party work, recorded in the these publications. Candidate surveys would have been more accurate sources of information, but were beyond the resources of this study. We talk, then, in terms of the percent of the representatives who have this involvement featured in their backgrounds rather than who has and who has not been active. Also, no attempt is made to place activism on a continuum; one is simply credited with participation if any membership is listed or any party involvement is recorded. Thus, a convention delegate gets the same credit at this point as a state party chair or a member of her party's national committee, and the number of community associations one belongs to is not given, only whether any membership in a civic organization appears in one's biography.

As the data on party and community activity indicate (table 4.4), such involvement is much more prevalent in the biographies of female members of the House, although without more definitive data we cannot make concrete conclusions about an activity gap. But the greater prominence of party and community activity in the biographies of congresswomen suggests the large importance women attach to these activities in their routes to office.

Occupations

Lake's second wave of recruitment centered on volunteerism in civic activities leading to political office. Conceptualizing this route as an "ideal type," does it describe any of the contemporary female members of the House?

None of the contemporary congresswomen had gone from civic volunteerism directly into a successful run for a House seat. Nonetheless, community involvement has often led to a career in local or state level politics for women, which in turn served as a base for a congressional career. It was the path for several of the women elected to the House during this period. A good example is Gladys Spellman. A biography describes her as coming

> to politics with a strong interest in educational issues and a background as a school teacher and strong supporter of the PTA. On the surface her credentials appear to be in the traditional mold of suburban wife and mother during the 1940s and 1950s. As a young mother, for example, she raised quite a ruckus with the County Board of Commissioners when she came before them, four-year-old in tow, to demand kindergartens for local children. . . . Although her own career pattern centered around the birth and rearing of three children, as a member of Prince Georges County Council in Maryland during the 1970s, Spellman initiated much progressive, women-related legislation directed to the needs of working women with children, single women, and sexually assaulted and battered women. (Stineman 1980)

A variant of the volunteer path, stemming from a commitment to issue politics, is present in the backgrounds of some contemporary female representatives. An example is Bobbi Fiedler. As a young adult, her goal was to

> "be a good mother, homemaker and a good citizen." Although she switched to the Republican Party in the early 1970s, Fiedler played no active role in politics until 1976. That year, as a parent volunteer in an elementary school, she learned of a proposed mandatory busing plan for the Los Angeles area. With a few other parents, Fiedler began an impromptu anti-busing organization called BUSTOP. . . . In 1977, Fiedler defeated an incumbent school board member in a city wide election. She was the first anti-busing candidate in Los Angeles to win using that issue. Three years later the one-time drugstore owner and interior decorator took on the chairman of the Democratic Congressional Campaign Committee and beat him by 776 votes. (*Congressional Quarterly Weekly Report,* January 3, 1981, 6)

Civil rights and antiwar activism propelled several of the women elected early in this era into successful House bids without first holding any lower-level office. Examples are Bella Abzug, Pat Schroeder, Elizabeth Holtzman, and Martha Keyes. (All except Martha Keyes were lawyers, too.)

Examples of the "third wave" of recruitment of rising through the political ranks are abundantly present throughout this time period. The careers of Barbara Jordan, Barbara Kennelly, Connie Morella, and Elizabeth Patterson come to mind. Elizabeth Patterson, for example, "worked as a recruiting officer for the Peace Corps and Vista, as Head Start Coordinator for the South Carolina Office of Economic Opportunity, and as a staff member for South Carolina U.S. Representative James R. Mann. She first held political office when she served on the Spartanburg County Council in 1975 and 1976. Patterson was a member of the South Carolina Senate from 1979 to 1987" (*Women in Congress*, 193–94). Eddie Bernice Johnson, elected in 1992, is another prominent example of this contemporary path to high level office. A nurse with a master's degree in public administration, she served in the Texas House from 1972 to 1977. She resigned her seat to accept an appointment in the Carter administration as regional director for the Department of Health, Education, and Welfare. Afterward she turned to private business—setting up Eddie Bernice Johnson and Associates, which helped businesses expand or relocate in the Dallas-Fort Worth area—and was elected to the state senate in 1986. As chair of the Texas Senate Redistricting Committee she "drew herself the open seat" she won in 1992 (*Congressional Quarterly* 1993).

Contemporary congresswomen have differed from their male colleagues in their occupational histories. Data on occupations are taken from the official listing of professions in *Congressional Quarterly Almanac* and *Weekly Report*. Lawyering and business backgrounds have predominated among the male members, while education fields distinguished the backgrounds of the female members. Further, 10 percent of the female members listed their profession as either homemaker or civic leader (not a paid position). While over time the female members of the House are becoming more like their male counterparts in their prior office-holding experience, their distinctive occupational backgrounds and apparently greater community involvement bring experiential diversity to the legislative arena.

In 1992, the first term congressmen and women continued to be primarily distinguished by the dominance of the legal profession among the male members. Forty-nine percent listed lawyer as their occupation compared with only 13 percent of the women. The female members were more likely to have had administrative positions, particularly in the public sector, and to have listed their former elected position as their occupation. Business careers of the new male and female members, however, are much more similar than in earlier elections.

Marital Status and Families

Writing on the characteristics of women in Congress from 1917 to 1964, Emmy Werner noted that "Contrary to the popular stereotype of the suffragette spinster, 90 percent of the congresswomen have been married" (1966:20). Eighty-eight percent of the female members of the House elected between 1968 and 1990 had been married. Ninety-two percent of the male members had been married. Eight female representatives were congressional widows. Eight and 3 percent respectively of the female and male members were divorced at the time they entered Congress. We do not know from biographies how many representatives have been divorced and remarried (and whether that is of consequence). Thus, vast majorities of both the men and women have been married, but the women were slightly more likely to be single or divorced. The divorce rate was higher among the new congresswomen in 1992 (26 percent), while 11 percent of the new congressmen were divorced. Two of the women elected that year were single, as were six of the men.

Among those representatives who have been married, women had fewer children than their male counterparts. Twenty percent of the women had no children compared with only 9 percent of the men. At the same time, nearly 33 percent of the men had four or more children, whereas only 16 percent of the women had this large a family. (Of the first-term congressmen in 1993, 41 percent had three or more children compared with 32 percent of their female counterparts.) The older ages of the female representatives, their smaller family sizes, and the slightly greater likelihood of their being single illustrate the incompatibility of wifehood and motherhood with political lives for women.

We don't know how many women have run and been elected with children still at home, since most biographies only list the number, not the ages, of children. We can make an estimate that women under the age of forty-five are more likely to have children at home than those over forty-five. Twenty-one women were elected to the House under the age of forty-five (37 percent of the female members) between 1968 and 1992. Sixty-four percent of them had no children ($N=14$), and only one had four or more children. Thus, only eight women have made a successful run for the House in this era while potentially having children at home. We can assume then that very few congresswomen follow the model of Pat Schroeder, described as a prototype of the new woman politician, "2 babies, a husband, and briefcase. She's going to be the scene tomorrow" (Witcover 1974).

Conclusion

This chapter has described the characteristics of female congressional candidates during the feminist era. Credentials and experiences are important to the campaign process and to representation within the political arena in the United States. Beyond description, we have sought to determine whether women climb the "political" ladder in the same way men do. The general perception has been that women's political résumés have increasingly resembled men's, that a "new breed" has emerged. We have found that while elements of this perspective are true, women have continued to bring different experiences to their quests for public office.

Age is an important characteristic because of its seeming relation to ambition in political science literature, and because young officeholders have a greater opportunity to develop seniority and influence in the political system. Women are viewed as disadvantaged in this realm because they tend to start their political careers later in life than do men. Bernstein (1986) has also suggested that in contemporary politics women are increasingly disadvantaged because as candidates for public office they are challenged by younger, seemingly more ambitious men who beat them.

In the contemporary era, the average age of women elected to the U.S. House of Representatives was forty-eight. The average age of female nominees was forty-seven. Female open seat primary contenders had an average age of forty-six years. Female representatives are older than their male counterparts, and, contrary to expectations, their average age at entrance has increased during the feminist era. But there is little evidence that younger men are besting older women in the crucial open seat primary elections and thus contributing to the small number of women in Congress.

Women who run for the House are a highly educated group. Fewer women winners than men are lawyers or businesswomen, but an equal number have held office. The trend is toward convergence in previous office holding. There are few amateurs among the women members of the House, but women bring a wider variety of occupational experiences to the campaign process.

Is there a "new breed" of women politicians running for and winning national office? Yes and no. Winners are increasingly likely to have prior elective office experience. But the presence of officeholders among nominees remained static until 1992. A substantial minority of the female nominees listed their occupation as homemaker or political or civic activist, traditional routes for women. Education continued to be the most frequent occupation of women nominees. Thus, regarding the symbolic nature of representation, women's candidacies have enlarged the composition of political leadership and not just in terms of gender. The substantive impact of this change remains problematic. Chapter 8 explores the consequences of having more women in public office.

CHAPTER 5

Political Parties and Women's Candidacies

Political parties are key actors in the electoral process. They even have been deemed essential to democracy (Schattschneider 1942). Parties can fill many roles, including identifying with citizens, mobilizing supporters in the electorate, developing platforms for elected officials, and perhaps most importantly, selecting or nominating candidates for office. Most party scholars agree with E. E. Schattschneider's evaluation that "whatever else they may or may not do, *the parties must make nominations*" (1942:101; emphasis in the original).

American political parties are weaker institutions than party organizations in most other western democracies, in part because our system of primary elections has taken the selection of nominees for public office away from the parties. American parties nominate candidates only in the weakest sense. They have no mechanism for formally controlling whom they nominate for public office. Voters, rather than involved party members, select the nominees. In our primary election system, candidate selection is a governmental function, that is, the state determines who can participate in the selection process and how it will be conducted. State laws, not party rules, govern the process. Primaries allow outsider or insurgent candidates to run under the party label and perhaps to be selected by individuals with no loyalty or concern for the party organization. Candidates often recruit themselves or are encouraged to run by groups other than the parties.

A major theme of contemporary U.S. parties' literature has been the declining status of parties in American political life. American political parties as campaign organizations have become weaker and less meaningful and have diminished as symbols of identification for the general public. Voters have become more independent in their political attitudes, making split tickets (where voters choose candidates from different parties for different offices) more common. As patronage politics has declined and the media's influence has grown, local organizations have atrophied according to many scholars. (For example, see Sorauf 1984; Crotty and Jacobson 1984; Wattenberg 1986; Polsby 1983; Ladd and Hadley 1975.)

Other scholars argue that the case for party organizational atrophy, even at the local level, has been overstated. Eldersveld claims that local party organizations are active, combative, adaptive, and linked to electoral success

(1982:17–18). The work of Cotter and associates (1984) has shown increasingly organizationally secure state party committees, and Joseph Schlesinger (1991) believes that greater independence on the part of the electorate has resulted in party organizational growth and competition nationally. Herrnson has described party organizations as being in a period of transition rather than a period of decline:

> Proponents of this perspective contend that party organizations have taken on new functions to suit the current political environment and, to some extent, to compensate for areas in which party influence has diminished. . . . national party organizations, especially those of the Republican party, have taken an active role in encouraging candidates to run for Congress, as well as for state and local offices. Moreover, these organizations are supplying more campaign services to candidates, including training sessions, survey data, and media assistance. These findings challenge the claim that parties are in decline. They suggest instead that parties are finally beginning to make the transition to the modern, cash-base campaign economy. (1988:4)

Party decline has implications for our understanding of women's experience as candidates. Women's rights activists have viewed party organizations as obstacles to electing more women. Party organizations have been considered bastions of male domination closed to women. For example, at the end of the 1986 election, a Women's Campaign Fund spokesperson complained that parties discriminate against women in statewide races, and that "the old boys couldn't stand these women getting so close to the nominations for governorships." Instances of local party opposition to women's candidacies for top positions exist in recent elections. Both Harriett Woods, who ran for the U.S. Senate in Missouri in 1982, and Betty Tamposi, who sought the Republican nomination for U.S. Congress in New Hampshire's Second District in 1988 felt this bias. Woods remarked that when she entered the Missouri Democratic primary, the state Democratic leaders rejected her because she "was too liberal, too urban, and even worse, a woman" (Abzug 1984). Tamposi was publicly scolded by her state's U.S. Senator Gordon Humphrey, who said she should stay home with her children. According to Senator Humphrey, "there is no way a mother of a two-year old child can serve her constituents" (Kiernan 1988). Although Senator Humphrey was forced to apologize, Betty Tamposi lost that primary.

The negative influence of party leaders on women's candidacies has been a theme in much of the women and politics literature, too. (See, for example, Tolchin and Tolchin 1973). Some argue that the parties were a greater obstacle to women's achieving elective office than voter prejudice was. In 1977, Darcy and Schramm examined voter response to women candidates in U.S. House races for 1970 through 1974. They found the electorate indifferent to the sex of congressional candidates at the general election stage, that is, female candidates did as well as male candidates in similar situations. They concluded that the recruitment and nomination process was the true impediment to women's elections. They wrote that "the districts in which the nomination process manages to draw women are still the few, atypical, largely Democratic urban districts." This conclusion was, however, only an assertion on the authors' part, not the result of an empirical analysis of the nomination process.

It has long been argued that women receive a party's nomination primarily in situations where the party has little hope of winning the contest. Former Connecticut state party and Democratic National Committee Chair John Bailey is noted for his comment that "the only time to run a woman is when things look so bad that your only chance is to do something dramatic" (Lamson 1968). Gertzog and Simard (1981) tested the idea that women candidates received party backing disproportionately for congressional seats in districts dominated by the opposition party. Analyzing nominations for the U.S. House of Representatives between 1916 and 1978, they concluded that "women have been nominated for hopeless contests more often than men." But they also speculated that with increasing numbers of women running for public office the percentage in the hopeless category should decline. However, a trend toward more female candidates has run up against a shrinking opportunity structure for newcomers in general, as described in chapter 3. Incumbents have become more entrenched while challengers, both male and female, have become more hopeless. Nineteen hundred ninety-two was somewhat of an exception.

If parties have declined, then they should be less of a barrier to women's candidacies. They would have become irrelevant. Male and female candidates would organize their own campaigns and depend upon their own resources to win elections. Thus, it would be less meaningful to talk about party organizations as negative gatekeepers blocking women's rise to power in the contemporary era. If party organizations traditionally tended to pose an obstacle to women's recruitment, their lessened influence should have had favorable consequences for women candidates.

But a number of authors have suggested that the decline of parties has adversely affected women's political opportunities. From a cross-national perspective, Matthews (1984) has found that weak political parties, the entrepreneurial style of primary nominations, and candidate-oriented election campaigns seem "to discriminate against women politicians. . . . In countries with stronger parties, nominations controlled by established party leaders and proportional representation elections, women have a somewhat easier time of it." Some U.S. scholars have called for stronger parties in the belief that they would benefit women candidates. Bernstein (1986) believed that the declining success rate for female open seat primary contenders was a result of weakened parties and the rise of entrepreneurial campaigns. Deber, reflecting on the poor record of women being nominated for the U.S. Congress in Pennsylvania, suggested that "those women who won office were those who did receive organizational backing from a major party organization or from another strong faction. To the extent that party loyalty can elect candidates who are 'different,' 'reform' can act to remove the one force that has elevated outsiders" (1982:478). Finding women politicians more ambivalent about taking risks to achieve higher political office than men, Bledsoe and Herring have suggested that "strengthened political parties . . . would increase political opportunities for women" (1990). Thus, even though instances of sexism within the organizations still exist, it is important to consider the importance of a strong party system on women's recruitment to office, especially in an age of party transformation.

Party Transformation and Women's Candidacies

Party organizations, however, have not become totally irrelevant in American elections. As noted at the beginning of this chapter, the national organizations (the Democratic and Republican national committees and their senatorial and congressional campaign committees) especially have become institutionalized, with more resources than ever to assist their candidates. They have adapted to new technologies and to the candidate-centered nature of contemporary campaigns. Party transformation has also involved development of a more favorable organizational climate for women candidates.

A number of factors account for this transformation in attitude: changes in party leadership personnel, the "gender gap" in voting behavior, and women organizing on behalf of women within the parties.

Women as Party Activists

Party organization personnel include formal party committee members, national convention delegates, and staffers. When passage of the suffrage amendment seemed imminent, and some men feared that women would use this new tool of citizenship too independently, party leaders took steps to co-opt women into their organizations. In 1919, the Democratic party's national committee (DNC) agreed to have the national committeeman from each state appoint a woman to join him on the committee, doubling the size of that body. At their 1920 national convention, the Democrats went further and voted that each state would elect a national committeeman and a national committeewoman.

The Republican National Committee (RNC) in 1918 created a "Republican National Women's Executive Committee" as a permanent auxiliary to the RNC, and in 1919 it formed the "Republican Women's Advisory Council of One Hundred." At their national convention in 1920, the Republicans voted to increase the membership of their National Executive Committee from ten to fifteen, and promised to appoint seven women to the fifteen vacancies created. At their 1924 national convention the Republicans joined the Democrats in voting to elect a national committeeman and a national committeewoman from each state. Women attempted to duplicate this system of equal numbers of men and women on committees at the state level, and by 1928 eighteen states had adopted this arrangement. (See Lemons 1973; Andersen 1990.)

In 1932, women were included for the first time on all Democratic party convention standing committees. In 1940, the platform committee was required to be half female, and in 1944 women chaired convention committees and held convention offices. In the Republican party, eight women served on convention committees in 1928. They were represented equally on the platform committee in 1944 and served as officers and chairs in 1948 (Freeman 1987; Cotter and Bibby 1980).

A few women had been national convention delegates prior to women's suffrage. In the quarter century after suffrage, women were never more than about 10 to 12 percent of the Republican party's national convention delegates. Their highest number during this period was 120 in 1924. Their numbers declined after that but began to increase marginally in 1940, although not reaching the 1924 high. The Democratic party, on the other hand, showed a pattern of steady increase after women obtained the vote that continued through 1936, when 252 women (14 percent of the convention), were seated as delegates (Fisher and Whitehead 1944). After that their numbers declined. Between 1948 and 1968 women were on the average 13 percent of the Democratic party's and 15 percent of the Republican party's national convention delegates (Jennings 1990).

National committeewomen apparently were not considered to be influential in the parties during these years. Based on a survey of political observers and participants in the states, Cotter and Hennessy (1964) reported that Republican women were judged to be somewhat more influential in the GOP than were Democratic women in their party; however, very little power was attributed to either group in their state. The authors inferred that since these women were credited with so little influence, no other women had much influence in state political parties.

The period between the 1968 and 1972 elections was crucial to increasing women's status in the U.S. party system. The importance of that period lies primarily in the Democratic party's adoption of presidential nomination reforms recommended by the McGovern-Fraser Commission. The commission's guidelines A-1 and A-2 required each state's delegation to include representation of minority groups, women, and young people "in reasonable relationship to their presence in the population of the state" (Ranney 1976). The guidelines' significance for women's role in party politics cannot be overstated. As Jennings has shown, "beginning in 1972 and continuing for the next four conventions, women far exceeded their earlier presence" as national convention delegates (1990:224). Women were 40 percent of the Democratic and 30 percent of the Republican delegates in 1972. In 1978, the Democratic party wrote equal representation of women and men as national convention delegates into its rules.

The Republican party was concerned with appearance too, although it was not as reform oriented as the Democratic party. After its 1968 convention, it established a Committee on Delegates and Organizations (DO Committee) to review its rules. Its July 1971 report declared that each state should "endeavor to have equal representation of men and women in its delegation to the Republican National Convention," and to take action to achieve the broadest possible participation of everyone in party affairs. These recommendations were adopted as formal rules by the party's rules committee in 1972 (Freeman 1987). The Republicans encouraged change; the Democrats mandated equality.

The Democratic party rules were not adopted without a great deal of acrimony, however, and they have been blamed for the party's inability to mount successful presidential campaigns in subsequent elections. Also, significant numbers of the women who entered the ranks of party elites continued to view men within their party as negative gatekeepers. The University of Michigan's Center for Political Studies, in a series of surveys of delegates to the Republican and Democratic national conventions from 1972 through 1984, found women were far more likely than men to agree that men try to exclude women.[1] Moreover, the gap was fully as large among Democrats in 1984 as it was in 1972 and was still substantial even among the 1984 Republicans. But over time, the trends were in the direction of more positive perceptions (Jennings 1990:240).

At the time suffrage was obtained, both parties had established women's divisions within their national and some of their state organizations to encourage women to engage in party work. As recently as 1984, Mary Lou Kendrigan described the most common role of women in the political party organizations as "that of the volunteer who pours coffee, rings door bells, licks envelopes, 'mans' booths, and takes care of many of the other petty details that need to be done. . . . As within the traditional family, women are

---

1. They were asked their agreement with the statement "most men in the party organization try to keep women out of leadership roles."

quite visible and very unequal" (1984:27). This description, however, ignored the fact that women won the convention delegate selection battle in the Democratic party (Crotty 1983; Shafer 1983), and it did not consider the effect of party transformation on women's roles inside the parties. It accepted the traditional stereotype of women as playing only supportive roles.

The status of women has changed within party organizations beyond their greater presence as national convention delegates. Women have become both "insiders" and leaders. Some theorists would discount the significance of this change, arguing that women have become leaders of organizations with little life or influence in the electoral process, while others argue that the parties have revived and that women have been major players in that revival. The role of gender has not been extensively analyzed in the transformational process of the party organizations. It may be that the "good old boys" in the organizations are being replaced by women who often consider themselves feminists. Baer has recently suggested that "an entire area of political science *central* to the political influence of women—political parties—has been both ignored and misunderstood" (1990). She also argues that the growth in women's presence and influence has "coincided with an increase in power of the national parties."

Observers have described a "backstage revolution" within the parties and campaigns in which "a new breed of women political professionals" have developed an expertise in the practical day-to-day details of politics (Glenney 1982; Romney and Harrison 1988). Republican women and Democratic women have taken different routes to power. Men at the Republican National Committee have been credited with cultivating women as campaign professionals. Within the Democratic party, Romney and Harrison describe a process in which women have taken advantage of the interest group or constituency based nature of the Democratic party. Women who gained expertise through involvement in women's and feminist organizations later moved into campaign positions within the party (1988:206). The diverse paths women have taken to leadership within the parties reflect a process congruent with Jo Freeman's conception of the parties' distinctive cultures described in chapter 3.

Feminists have obtained positions of leadership in the national party organizations at the same time that national party organizations have expanded their resources and role in federal and state level campaigning. Ann Lewis, a columnist for *Ms.* magazine and former political director of the Democratic National Committee in the early 1980s, is a major example. Mary Louise Smith, who served as chair of the Republican National Committee during the Ford administration, had been a founding member of the Iowa Women's Political Caucus. These leaders have been positioned to use party resources to recruit and assist women candidates. Indeed, Lynn Cutler, vice-chair of the Democratic National Committee was a founder of EMILY's List, described in chapter 6 as one of the major women's political action committees.

By 1982, according to *Campaigns & Elections,* a woman was directing the Republican National Committee's field division with three female political directors and two female regional finance directors working under her. The Democrats had two women in top executive slots (Lynn Cutler and Polly Baca Barragan), while Ann Lewis, noted above, headed the political staff. Women were the directors of campaign services, polling, and finance, and a woman served as counsel to the DNC. Women were also in top positions in the congressional campaign committees. Especially notable was Nancy Sinnott, the youngest and first female executive director of the National Republican Congressional Committee. In 1986, women were campaign managers in sixteen U.S. Senate campaigns. In 1988, Susan Estrich became the first woman to manage a presidential campaign. The positions women have attained in the parties in recent elections contradict the image of women as the lickers, the stickers, and the pourers of coffee.

Women have emerged as leaders at the state level also. In 1991, five of the Democratic and seven of the Republican state party chairs were women;[2] The Democratic party had women as executive directors in seventeen states, and the Republicans had eight female executive directors.[3] Massachusetts provides an example of the difference female presence can make at the state party leadership level. The Massachusetts Democratic party's female executive director played an instrumental role in establishing the Women's Impact Network (WIN) in 1988. Realizing that the party organization could not favor female candidates, especially in primary contests, she developed a network outside the formal party structure dedicated to raising money for progressive Democratic women candidates.

Betsy Toole, New York State's Democratic party vice-chairwoman offers another example. When Barber Conable announced his retirement in 1984 as U.S. representative from the Thirtieth Congressional District, Toole said, "Women—that's what went through my mind when I first heard Conable's seat was vacant. The right woman could win in this district, you know" (Fowler and McClure 1989). Indeed, a woman won the seat in 1986.

Whereas no woman has won a top leadership position in the U.S. Congress, been a member of the inner Cabinet in the White House, or won the presidency, at least an occasional woman has cracked the "glass ceiling" within the party organizations. Women have served as spokespersons for their

2. The Democratic national list of state chairs in 1988 listed ten women in those positions.

3. In 1992, Jennifer Dunn, chair of the Republican state committee in Washington State was elected to the House. Earlier Nancy Pelosi, former state party chair was elected to the House from California.

party. They have directed congressional campaign committees, managed a presidential campaign, and chaired the national committees of both parties, albeit only for short periods in the 1970s.[4] But when strategy is made at the top levels of the parties and within presidential campaigns, does the presence of women continue to be the exception rather than the rule? Although it has been cracked, does the "glass ceiling" still primarily describe women's status within the parties as well as in other political and economic structures?

In 1987, Ann Lewis described presidential campaigns as still "the last locker room in American politics" (Alters 1987). The *Boston Globe* characterized women's role in the upcoming 1988 presidential campaign as being "so thin, and their influence so spotty, that they will have almost no power to shape issues or call the shots in campaigns" (Alters 1987). Yet one year later, Ellen Goodman described women at the 1988 Democratic convention as "'the new insiders.' . . . Women are no longer a special interest group in Atlanta. Nor are they outsiders agitating for a place at the table. They are simply players . . . in the inner circles of campaigns and conventions" (1988).

Thus, the issue of the influence and presence of women at the top remains unsettled. The presidential candidates were quizzed about the presence of women among their top advisors in the third presidential debate of the 1992 election. Susan Rook asked the candidates, "I acknowledge that all of you have women and ethnic minorities working for you and working with you, but when we look at the circle of the key people closest to you—your inner circle of advisors—we see white men only. Why and when will that change?"[5] President Bush, in response, cited Margaret Tutwiler as a key person and then listed his cabinet appointees and noted his appointment record in general. Mr. Perot emphasized his history of hiring women in his business and the presence of his wife and "four beautiful daughters." Governor Clinton responded that he disagreed "that there are no women and minorities in important positions in my campaign. There are many." He went on to talk about his appointment record in Arkansas.

Women held prominent positions in the Clinton campaign including his former chief of staff Betsy Wright, his political director, Stephanie Solien, and his press secretary, Dee Dee Myers. The most visible female advisor in the Republican campaign was President Bush's deputy campaign manager Mary Matalin, often described as a Bush strategist, a term usually reserved for members of the inner circle. Torie Clarke also served as spokesperson for the

---

4. In addition to Mary Louise Smith, who chaired the RNC during Gerald Ford's administration, the Democrats appointed Jean Westwood chair during the McGovern campaign in 1972.

5. Anna Quindlen in a *New York Times* editorial earlier in the election year raised the same point suggesting women were nonexistent in the inner circle of the Bush reelection effort and that jokes had circulated among the press about it. She described Clinton's closest advisers as the "standard issue white guys" (April 26, 1992).

campaign. When James Baker temporarily resigned as secretary of state to become White House chief-of-staff in order to oversee the president's reelection effort, he brought with him Margaret Tutwiler and Janet Mullins as two of his four aides. The Center for the American Woman and Politics has concluded that "both the Bush-Quayle and the Clinton-Gore tickets boast a large number of women in high-level positions, as well as at mid-level and entry-level positions" (Neuman and Walker 1992). Thus, this last most important bastion of male dominance in the parties has been stormed by women.

The Gender Gap

If women's increased prominence within the parties has forced change from inside, the gender gap in voting behavior has forced change from the outside. The gender gap, which emerged as a political phenomenon in the aftermath of the 1980 election, describes differences in men's and women's voting behavior, political party identification, and political attitudes. By the 1988 election, the media were crediting women with commanding the balance of power (Matlack 1987) and having "power at the ballot box" (Alters 1987) because of their numbers and distinctive voting behavior.

An 8 percent gender gap emerged in the 1980 election. Women split their vote evenly between Ronald Reagan and Jimmy Carter, while men gave 55 percent of their votes to Reagan and only 38 percent to Carter (Frankovic 1982). In 1984, 64 percent of men cast Reagan ballots, but only 55 percent of women, a 9 percent gender gap (Kenski 1988). The gender gap was seven percentage points in 1988. The Republicans obtained a majority of men's

TABLE 5.1. Presidential Politics—Male and Female Differences, 1968–88

Year	National Convention Delegates (% Women)		Turnout (%)		Presidential Preference Republican (% Vote)	
	Dem.	Rep.	Male	Female	Male	Female
1968	13	17	69.8	66.0	43	43
1972	40	30	64.1	62.0	62	63
1976	34	31	59.6	58.8	45	51
1980	50	36	59.1	59.4	55	47
1984	50	44	59.0	60.8	64	55
1988	49	37	56.4	58.3	57	50
1992	50	42	60.2	62.3	38[a]	37

[a]A gender gap existed in the votes for Bill Clinton and Ross Perot. Forty-six percent of women voted for Bill Clinton, 41 percent of men; 17 percent of women voted for Ross Perot, 21 percent of men.

votes (57 to 41 percent), while women divided their vote evenly between George Bush and Michael Dukakis (Farah and Klein 1989). (See table 5.1.)

The 1980 election also marked the first time that women voted at higher rates than men and this voting gap has been growing with each election since then (table 5.1). As stated by Mueller (1988), "Given the numeric superiority of women in the population, the change in voting rates made a dramatic difference in the composition of the electorate. By 1984, women made up 53.5 percent of voters—7 percent more than did men, a plurality of 3 million."

Sex differences in voting in the 1980s were not restricted to presidential elections. Heiderpriem and Lake report that "in 1982, [the] presidential phenomenon spread to congressional races. In apparent reaction to the Reagan recession, the pro-Democratic [gender] gap was particularly pronounced in open and in incumbent Republican seats" (1987). In 1984 and 1986, exit poll data showed women voting differently from men in 28 top statewide races and providing the margin of victory in 14 states (Women's Agenda Conference 1988:5).

Party identification has also taken on a gender dimension. The *National Journal* characterized the trend in a party identification gap between the sexes as "the feminization of the Democratic party." Up to the late 1970s, poll data showed no significant differences in men's and women's patterns of party support. But by 1982, a 26 point gap emerged between Democratic and Republican party affiliation of women, but only a 13 point male differential (Kirschten 1983). The gap between young men and young women in party affiliation was especially notable in the 1984 campaign, with many more young men identifying themselves as Republican (Keeter 1985:104).

The party identification gap continued into the 1990s. In polls taken between October, 1991 and May, 1992, the Gallup organization found Republican identifiers outnumbering Democrats by twenty percentage points among 18- to 21-year-old men, but Democrats predominating by 8 points among this group of voting-age women (Ladd 1992). Further, asked in November of 1991 which party would be best able to handle the problem they considered to be most important facing the nation, 38 percent of the men but only 25 percent of the women cited the Republican party.

The significance of the gender gap in voting behavior and party identification for this study lies in its effect on party activities. Just as they responded in 1920 to the threat of a women's voting bloc and the creation of a women's party after passage of the suffrage amendment, the parties reacted to the gender gap between 1980 and 1984. The response was especially noticeable in the Republican party which felt it was being hurt by the gender gap. The Senate Republican Policy Committee in 1982 even produced an internal report "The Gender Gap: Do Republicans have a Woman Problem?" and the

White House commissioned its own internal study paper on the subject (Bone-fede 1982; Mueller 1988).

The parties believed it to their advantage to develop positive action strategies on behalf of women. In 1983, both parties held leadership confer-ences for women. The leaders of both parties said the gender gap stimulated these meetings (Klemesrud 1983). In anticipation of the 1984 election, the Reagan-Bush campaign committee acted vigorously to involve women in party affairs. Margaret Tutwiler was named the liaison between the White House and the various Republican political arms and campaign committees. "In that capacity, Tutwiler . . . crashed the top-level strategy meetings of the Reagan White House" (Kirschten 1984:1084). Sonia Landau was made chair of "Women for Reagan-Bush." Women became respectively national cochair, campaign treasurer, director of voter registration, and a regional director. Jo Freeman describes the attention paid to women by the Republican party convention apparatus in 1984:

> Republican women were cajoled into running for delegate spots and men discouraged by top party leaders, including the President. . . . party leaders had to exert steady pressure to persuade men originally selected as delegates to step aside for the "envelope stuffers and precinct walkers." One-third of the major speakers were women, and for the first time the Republican convention had a large booth in the press area solely to provide information on women. The Republican Women Information Services also set up interviews and sponsored or advertised receptions, luncheons, and breakfasts aimed at women. (1987:232).

And, as we will see in the next section, the Republican party found it advan-tageous to promote women's candidacies. They began in 1983 to search for female Senate candidates in part to counter Democratic stress on the "gender gap" (Muscatine 1984). Feminists within the Republican party, however, were not impressed with the public relations activities regarding women's political involvement surrounding the 1984 Republican National Convention. For ex-ample, Mary Purcell, president of the American Association of University Women, called the GOP's showcasing of women at the 1984 convention, "a blatant display of window dressing" (Jordan 1984).

Freeman (1987) has described the near total exclusion of feminists from the Republican party after 1976. The 1976 national convention reversed the party's historic support for women's rights issues. The GOP narrowly main-tained its endorsement of the Equal Rights Amendment (ERA) but adopted an antiabortion plank. The Republican Women's Task Force of the National Women's Political Caucus complained that women held fewer important posts at the 1976 convention and that the GOP was alienating the mainstream

Republican women. In 1980, the party's forty year commitment to the ERA was reversed and its platform included a plank endorsing a constitutional ban on abortion (Baer and Bositis 1987). "On July 14, the day the convention opened, ten thousand women marched through downtown Detroit to the GOP meeting place in a demonstration of support for the ERA; leading Republican women and the nine pro-ERA Platform Committee members were visibly up front" (Abzug 1984:82).

Freeman (1989) reports that a feminist presence reemerged at the 1988 Republican National Convention. The feminists were unable, however, to reverse the party's all encompassing and rigid antiabortion plank, but did see the adoption of planks encouraging more women candidates and recognizing the importance of child care. The 1992 convention, however, was dominated by those opposed to changing the status of women. The result was a public relations disaster for the party, especially as the Democratic party showcased its female Senate nominees on the first night of its convention.

Party Activities on Behalf of Women Candidates

As early as 1974, the Democratic party had sponsored a Campaign Conference for Democratic Women aimed at electing more women to political office (Scott 1974). Twelve hundred women attended this workshop where they passed resolutions urging the party to do more for potential women candidates. Similar conferences did not occur within the Republican party until nearly a decade later, when it became politically expedient to do so to offset the gender gap.

This later start does not mean that the Republican party has been less receptive to female candidacies. Indeed, Eleanor Smeal, former chair of the National Organization for Women, has argued just the opposite (Freeman 1989). Women in the Republican arty have tended to credit men for bringing them into the organization (Romney and Harrison 1988). But the Democratic party has been the site of early action, primarily because of its different culture (Freeman 1987). Feminists, as an accepted organized group within the Democratic party, were able early on to impose themselves on leadership, in addition to having a sympathetic ear within the liberal wing of the party. Nearly all of the female members of the U.S. House of Representatives in the 1970s were Democrats.[6] A number of these women won their seats not because they were championed within their local party organizations, but because they challenged the local party structure and beat it.

In the 1980s it became politically expedient to promote women candidates. The Republicans even publicly acknowledged this fact. Republican

---

6. This was a trend away from more equal representation between the parties.

Senatorial Campaign Committee (RSCC) chair Sen. Richard Lugar issued a press statement in 1982 declaring that "a concerted drive by the Republican party to stamp itself as the party of the woman elected official would serve our nation as well as it served our own political interests. . . . The full political participation of women is a moral imperative for our society, and intelligent political goal for the Republican party." Thus, he pledged to "commit the RSCC to the maximum legal funding and support for any Republican woman who is nominated next year, regardless of how Democratic the state or apparently formidable the Democratic candidate. I am prepared to consider direct assistance to women candidates even prior to their nomination, a sharp departure from our usual policy" (Lugar 1983).

This pledge, however, did not result in even the close election of any new Republican women to the U.S. Senate in 1984, although the party did break precedent by giving female senatorial candidates $15,000 each to use in their *primaries* against other GOP contenders (Muscatine 1984). It is relatively easy for a party with a flush treasury, as the Republican party had in 1983, to make a big public relations splash by advocating women's candidacies in seemingly hopeless situations. The real test comes when the office is perceived as being winnable. Women need early support in open seat primaries, but neither party is likely to contribute to such campaigns because of the potential backlash from other candidates. Nonetheless, in 1990 the Republicans made a major effort on behalf of three women senatorial candidates with much greater chance of victory. All three were U.S. representatives. However, two lost to incumbents and the third, Pat Saiki, lost in a close race in Hawaii, which traditionally has overwhelmingly favored the Democratic party.

The Democrats have also adopted special strategies for women candidates for federal office. For example, U.S. Representative Tony Coelho, as chair of the Democratic Congressional Campaign Committee, established the Women's Congressional Council (WCC) to raise money for female House candidates. According to Mr. Coelho, as reported in the "Washington Talk" section of the *New York Times,* "Not only have we not done enough, but what the women candidates legitimately have said is that we don't give them enough help up front. . . . it is important to 'invest' in women running for the House by aiding them early in their electoral efforts" (May 28, 1986). The WCC raised $100,000 in 1984 and had a goal of $200,000 for women running for the House of Representatives in 1986. The council solicited memberships with dues of $500. Members received invitations to luncheons with members of Congress and to the annual Geraldine Ferraro Women Making History Award Reception, and received legislative updates on issues of concern to women. This project was in existence during Coelho's tenure as chair of the Democratic Congressional Campaign Committee.[7]

---

7. This effort, however, has recently been described as a flop. (See Donovan 1992.)

Senator Lugar's and Representative Coehlo's activities are representative of the nature of efforts by the parties on behalf of women during the 1980s. These efforts have been dependent on the interest and creativity of powerful party officials. They were not institutionalized as part of the party structures.

In 1983, both parties sponsored national conferences for female party activists to inform them of party policies, urge them to run for office, and provide training workshops in campaigning (Williams 1984). In 1985, Republican National Committee chair Frank Fahrenkopf, cochair Betty Heitman, and Edward Rollins, then a White House political aide, established the Alliance for Opportunity, a program "to help women turn the challenges of their personal and professional lives into opportunities" ("Washington Talk," *New York Times,* September 19, 1985).[8]

The national parties have also established units to aid women candidates. In 1982, the Democratic party created the Eleanor Roosevelt Fund, which provided support to women running for state and local office. This fund was active through 1986, and contributed more than $300,000 nationwide. In 1986, six candidates for statewide office received financial support from the fund. The fund also provided in-kind services, such as direct mailings, training sessions, and networking with political action committees. In keeping with the 1984 Democratic party platform, it assisted progressive women candidates who were pro-choice on abortion. In addition, the fund developed a recruitment project in four states to encourage women's involvement in party politics. Through 1990, the Democratic party also held special sessions for women as part of its regional training workshops for new candidates.

In May, 1992, building on the splash women candidates had made in the primaries, the Democratic Senatorial Campaign Committee initiated the Women's Council. The DSCC's Women's Council was touted as the "only official party organization dedicated to recruiting and supporting women candidates" in its fact sheet. However, at least in 1992, it did not help female candidates until they had been officially nominated by the party. It did not get involved in primaries, and was created too late to be active in recruiting efforts. The Women's Council raised and allocated $1.5 million to the ten Democratic women Senate nominees. It received an average contribution of $125 from over ten thousand individual donors. It hosted three events in Washington, Philadelphia, and San Francisco as well as undertaking a direct mail donor program. It also raised money through the sale of contemporary art donated to the Women's Council by a group of prominent artists. Founders, of whom there were 150, contributed $1,500 each. While this was certainly a positive effort on the part of the national party, it could be characterized as an

---

8. Evans Witt in *Public Opinion* described these workshops, which were "aimed at the working women of America," as sessions on "managing money, managing time, managing the family, Jazzercize, and—almost incidentally—on politics" (1985; emphasis in original).

opportunity for the party to capitalize on the excitement the women candidates had generated to raise money for the Democratic Senatorial Campaign Committee rather than an effort to support underfunded and disadvantaged candidates. Potential donors perhaps would be more inclined to give to an effort directly in behalf of the women candidates or attend an event in their honor than to donate to the committee on a more generic basis. It remains to be seen how the recruitment effort works in the future.

For female GOP candidates, the National Federation of Republican Women (NFRW) is an autonomous, financially independent affiliate of the Republican National Committee. This grass-roots organization, which lists 160,000 dues-paying members, runs regional candidate seminars and campaign-management schools for women activists. The NFRW has expanded its focus from women as volunteers within the Republican party to recruiting and training women candidates and campaign managers. In 1989, the NFRW sponsored five regional weekend campaign-management schools for members, a program begun in 1979 (Baer 1990). In 1990, the federation established Project '90, a candidate recruitment program to find and train Republican women club members to run for state and local office. As part of Project '90, the federation conducted a women's candidates' seminar in Washington. As Baer states, the NFRW "advances[s] the cause of women in the party" (1990).

In 1988, for the first time, both national party platforms included statements endorsing "full and equal access of women and minorities to elective office and party endorsement" (Democrats) and "strong support for the efforts of women in seeking an equal role in government and [commitment] to the vigorous recruitment, training and campaign support for women candidates at all levels" (Republicans). These planks were indeed only symbolic statements, not substantive mandates to implement specific action. Their significance lies in the recognition of the problems of women candidates, and in the ability of influential party women to make that recognition explicit and public.

Since parties do not control the nomination of their candidates, the major support they can provide their nominees is financial assistance. The Federal Elections Campaign Act, however, limits the financial backing that party organizations can give to congressional candidates. National, congressional, and state party organizations are each allowed to contribute no more than $5,000 to House candidates during the general election. They can also give $5,000 in the primary election. National party organizations and state party committees also can make coordinated expenditures on behalf of their candidates. Originally set at $10,000 each for a state and national committee, the limits for coordinated expenditures on behalf of House candidates are adjusted for inflation and reached $23,140 in 1990. (See Herrnson 1992.) Table 5.2 shows the average amount the Democratic and Republican parties have given

TABLE 5.2.   Average Party Contributions and Coordinated Expenditures, by Sex, 1980–90

Year	Contributions			Coordinated $		
	Men	Women	Difference	Men	Women	Difference
Democrats						
1980	$ 2,429	$ 1,922	$ 507	$ 581	$ 872	$ −291
1982	2,423	2,512	−89	1,592	1,543	49
1984	3,449	3,474	−26	4,756	4,295	461
1986	2,660	1,953	709	4,873	5,363	−490
1988	2,560	4,735	−2,175	6,098	9,396	−3,286
1990	1,751	2,361	−610	8,388	10,247	−1,859
Republicans						
1980	$ 8,626	$10,317	$−1,691	$ 5,434	$ 6,853	$−1,419
1982	11,787	13,684	−1,897	13,199	15,780	−2,501
1984	10,657	11,651	−994	16,597	18,415	−1,818
1986	6,685	7,804	−1,119	11,510	9,243	2,267
1988	6,561	6,684	−123	10,558	9,661	897
1990	4,227	4,471	−244	7,109	7,304	−195

to their male and female nominees in the elections between 1980 and 1990 (the years for which data are available).

In each election, Republicans contributed a larger average amount to their female candidates than to their male nominees. In four of the six elections, they were also more generous to their female nominees in their coordinated expenditures. Democratic female nominees also did better in acquiring direct contributions and coordinated expenditures from their party in four of the six elections.

Because women were more likely to be challengers, we might have expected them to have received less support from their party, aside from any question of sexism. The parties' goal is to maintain their incumbents in office and pick up as many of the other competitive seats as possible. Therefore, rationally, they should target their funds to competitive situations rather than supplying all nominees with equal support. Table 5.3 presents the regression coefficients from a multivariate model showing the effect of sex on campaign contributions, controlling for incumbency and open seat contests. In no election in either party were women candidates significantly advantaged or disadvantaged statistically once these other factors were taken into account. More often than not, however, as indicated in the bivariate case, women candidates came out ahead in both the Democratic and Republican parties. Thus, the parties have tended to match their rhetoric with their dollars.

TABLE 5.3. Effect of Sex on Party Contributions and Coordinated Expenditures, 1980–90

Year	Constant	Sex	Open	Incumbent	R^2
		Unstandardized Regression Coefficients			
			Democrats—Contributions		
1980	$ 1,623	$ −537	$ 3,739**	$ 762	.09
1982	3,014	−130	81	−1,169*	.02
1984	2,768	141	5,734**	484	.06
1986	1,436	806	1,746	−1,565	.06
1988	3,104	1,452	5,902**	−1,475*	.14
1990	1,659	168	3,333**	−256	.06
			Democrats—Coordinated Expenditures		
1980	$ 596	$ 252	$ 367	$ −82	.01
1982	1,995	−196	38	−792	.01
1984	3,724	−293	8,308**	842	.05
1986	6,141	−210	3,782*	−3,216**	.07
1988	6,237	2,526	8,379**	−1,055*	.05
1990	9,900	366	6,670*	−3,385	.05
			Republicans—Contributions		
1980	$ 7,402	$ 2,066	$ 7,973**	$ 1,056	.08
1982	8,711	1,993	8,021**	4,419**	.11
1984	9,966	1,131	9,185**	115	.07
1986	8,063	−1,761	9,899**	2,079	.16
1988	5,404	1,190	14,762**	212	.17
1990	3,212	901	13,566**	−358	.20
			Republicans—Coordinated Expenditures		
1980	$ 5,809	$ 1,039	$ 8,647**	$−3,436**	.14
1982	10,616	1,892	13,161**	1,583	.07
1984	16,136	1,120	17,204**	−7,094	.10
1986	5,081	1,257	24,701**	1,697	.18
1988	9,321	1,044	27,284**	−1,663	.13
1990	4,504	1,557	26,547**	1,056	.17

*Significant at the .01 level.
**Significant at the .001 level.

Conclusion

Women seeking public office in the United States operate in what Pippa Norris has called "a free market system." Those individuals who wish to seek public office are free to compete for the support of the general public. The party organizations contain no monopoly over recruitment of candidates nor over selection of nominees. The major parties are used by the candidates. However, the parties do attempt to recruit candidates, offer training programs for potential candidates, and provide a substantial support base for their nominees for national office.

Traditionally the operative message from party leaders was "no woman need apply" for a party nomination. In the 1980s, while female candidacies were still rare, women's campaigns were highlighted by the parties, and "a woman could win this" became an occasional theme. In the 1990s, women candidates have become mainstreamed in the parties, and are treated like any other candidates. The Democrats, for example, have developed a "coordinated campaign" in which national party staff work with candidates at all levels. There are no special programs for women. In 1992, however, the Democratic women members of Congress pledged to adopt campaigns of female nonincumbent nominees. Women candidates in the 1990s have the advantage of being perceived as "outsiders" of a scandal-ridden era, although they have access to the resources of the party establishment.

This transformation in the relation between political parties in the United States and women's candidacies has been accomplished by the changing status of women within party organizations and the importance of women as voters in the 1980s. Party organizations are no longer negative "gatekeepers" for women candidates. Rather they have become positive forces.

American parties will never be really strong until they once again control the nomination of their candidates. Stronger parties are not something women have to fear given the changes they have brought about in these organizations and the importance of women voters to the electoral success of the parties. Strengthened parties should enhance women's candidacies. Stronger parties should help the United States advance its position among democracies in the percentage of national legislators who are women. The lack of substantial numbers of women in elective office in the United States reduces the country's ability to serve as a democratic model for other nations.

CHAPTER 6

Sex and Money: The Financing of Women's and Men's Campaigns for the U.S. House of Representatives, 1972–92

Congressional campaigns have become increasingly expensive undertakings. Spending in U.S. House and Senate races rose from $99 million in 1976 to $678 million in 1992. The rise was particularly striking between 1976 and 1982. The rate of growth in spending then leveled off and actually declined in 1990,[1] but rose dramatically in the 1992 election cycle increasing 52 percent over 1990 (FEC press release, March 3, 1993). General election House candidates spent $407 million in 1992, a 53 percent increase over the previous election cycle. Fifty candidates spent over $1 million each (forty-four men and six women).[2] The average cost of a U.S. House race in 1974 was $52,000. It was nearly $389,000 in 1992. A newly elected House member spent an average $517,000 in 1992 to obtain that seat.

Money matters in congressional campaigns, too (Jacobson 1980). Contributions impact on outcomes. How well candidates do on election day is a direct function of how much money they raise and spend (Jacobson 1987a). In campaigns against incumbents the more challengers spend, the more votes they receive, and the more likely they are to win (Jacobson 1990). For challengers, however, it has become increasingly difficult to raise the money needed to be competitive. They have difficulty raising funds because they are not viewed as being competitive. Incumbents are seen as being overwhelmingly advantaged. The gap in spending between incumbents and challengers has grown over time (Makinson 1989).

The relationship between spending and votes is negative for incumbents. The more they spend, the lower their vote and the greater the chances of their losing. This is the case because incumbents spend more money the stronger the challenge they face. They also tend to keep a large treasury to scare off potential challengers. Thus the more money they have at the beginning of the

---

1. It rose 3 percent in House campaigns but declined in Senate races.

2. This figure compares with twenty House campaigns topping a million dollars in 1988 and fifteen candidates in 1990.

campaign season, the weaker will be their challenger. Strong challengers usually opt not to take the risk when faced with an incumbent with a substantial treasury to bankroll his or her reelection. At the same time, open seat races are the most expensive contests of all.

Money plays a particularly distinctive role in the consideration of women's campaigns. Romney and Harrison have called it "the special relationship of political women and money" (1988:74). The popular belief has been that women cannot raise the same kinds of money as men. This disadvantage has been accorded prominence in explaining the dearth of women in the national legislature. Commentary in the 1990 elections illustrates this perception. Dan Rather on the *CBS Evening News* stated, "On this closing day of Campaign '90, it turns out the money gap also exists for women candidates seeking campaign cash" (November 5, 1990). According to the *Christian Science Monitor* "women receive smaller contributions from a larger number of donors; men receive larger donations from fewer sources" (Brown 1991). *Newsweek* also proclaimed money to be a problem for women candidates in that election year. "It's been a very eye-opening year for the problems women candidates face," it quotes one major political figure, "The chief problem: fundraising" (Clift 1990). These observations represent longstanding conventional wisdom regarding the relationship between sex, money, and election campaigns. A major story of the 1992 election was the amount of money flowing to women candidates, and the role of the women's PACs in obtaining these funds.

The basis of this assumption is that women have more difficulty raising campaign contributions than male candidates. That assumption has been little challenged and has received only modest scholarly attention. (See Burrell 1985; Uhlaner and Schlozman 1986; Theilman and Wilhite 1991.) Three theories drive this assumption. First, it is assumed that women are psychologically unsuited to asking for money for themselves (Carroll 1985). According to Ruth Mandel,

> Women must usually surmount inner obstacles before asking for other people's support to further their own personal ambitions. But that challenge pales when compared with conflicts experienced by women in soliciting money on their own behalf. . . . Women have developed valuable expertise in organizing fund-raising events and donation drives for community projects, hospitals, ballet societies, museums, parks, and certainly many a political candidate. But when it comes to raising money for herself, a woman recoils. (1981:181)

Whether women have been handicapped in their ability to ask for money is an empirical question. So far the handicap has existed mainly in the realm of perception and in the eyes of consultants. Why should we make such an

assumption, especially concerning candidates for higher office? In fact, we might make the opposite assumption. Given that it is quite unusual for women to seek these positions, those who do step out of traditional female roles would be extraordinary individuals—more capable, more experienced, and more assertive than their typical male counterparts, at least as a group. Consequently, they should not be particularly timid about fund-raising. Women may not like asking for money, but men may not be any more comfortable. Even the most outgoing of politicians, former vice-president and presidential nominee Hubert Humphrey, expressed his dismay at the humiliation of seeking financial backing for his quest for the White House.

Secondly, women are believed to have been handicapped in acquiring substantial campaign treasuries because they have not been involved in established formal and informal financial and political circles. To the extent that their candidacies have emerged more from community volunteerism and less from political and professional careers, women would not have access to the large contributors who finance major political campaigns. These people are not likely to know the aspiring female politician, and thus, are less likely to contribute to her campaign. As Carroll has put it, "most women are not well integrated into occupational and social networks that often serve as a major source of campaign funds. As a result they may have difficulty obtaining money from sources commonly available to male candidates" (1985:50). However, as female politicians have increasingly gained political experience similar to that of male politicians (as discussed in chapter 4), they should have become more integrated into these networks.

Perhaps women have requested campaign contributions from the same donors and to the same degree as men, but have been less likely to obtain it. Sexism and/or a belief that women cannot win and are, therefore, a poor investment may have limited contributions to women's campaigns. Many women candidates believe discrimination still exists, but whether it continues is unproven.

Given the prominence of the idea that financial disadvantages have handicapped women's efforts to gain elective office, one would expect a substantial body of research in this area, but only a few analyses have compared the monetary aspects of male and female congressional campaigns. In 1984, the Women's Campaign Fund published the first systematic comparison of the financing of men's and women's campaigns for national office. The study, based on an analysis of the financial reports of Democratic and Republican nominees for the U.S. House of Representatives from 1976 to 1982, reported that "in similar campaign situations, female candidates on the average raise as much money as do male candidates" (Newman et al. 1984:5). Similar campaign situations meant comparing male and female incumbents, challengers, and open seat candidates of the same party separately. They concluded that "the perception that women candidates cannot raise money is no longer true.

By 1982, female candidates did as well on average as male candidates in similar campaign situations. In almost every category and difficulty of race in 1982, women raised as much money as men did" (1984:7). I reached a similar conclusion in my analysis of the relationship between gender and campaign finances for the 1972 through 1982 congressional elections:

> The data suggest that the gender gap in congressional representation does not result primarily from a gender gap in campaign financing. Fund raising is not a structural constraint once women obtain a major party nomination, and this has been true for a number of years. Although women average fewer receipts than men, this disparity is accounted for more by their candidate status than by their gender and has been decreasing in most recent elections. (1985:267)

This chapter updates these earlier works by examining the impact of sex on the raising and spending of money in congressional campaigns through 1992. I focus not only on the fund-raising capabilities of male and female House candidates but also on the structure of giving to their campaigns—who contributes and how much they contribute. Further, I extend this analysis to include the role of money in primary races in the most recent elections to assess the relationship between gender and *early* money. I conclude with a description of the women's PACs that have funded female congressional campaigns in this era.

The basic hypothesis that I test is that women have been less successful fund-raisers than men. I question whether women have raised smaller amounts of money and thus have had less to spend, have not had the same access to interest group money as men, and have had to depend on smaller size donations. The attention given to women candidates in 1992 suggests that these relationships may have been reversed in the 1992 election cycle.

This research uses information on all major party nominees from 1972 through 1992 for the U.S. House of Representatives. The data are taken from the financial reports of the candidates filed with the Federal Elections Commission (FEC). Financial data prior to 1972 is not available. In 1971, Congress passed the Federal Elections Campaign Act, which required that all money raised and spent in future elections be accounted for and recorded with the FEC. Candidates for federal office must report their financial activity four times during the course of an election year.

Receipts and Expenditures

If women have had greater difficulty asking for money for their campaigns and have had less access to financial support, an analysis of receipts and expendi-

Incumbents

In the past, male incumbents, more often than not, raised and spent more than their female counterparts, but in the 1988 and 1990 election cycles, female Democratic incumbents acquired significantly greater amounts than male Democratic incumbents. In 1992, they raised slightly less while female Republican incumbents surpassed their male counterparts (figures 6.4 and 6.5). Smaller campaign treasuries in earlier elections, however, did not lead to weaker performances at the polls. The average percent of the vote female incumbents have obtained has equaled that of male incumbents throughout this period (Darcy, Welch, and Clark 1987). The lack of imposing challengers as much as any inability to accumulate vast sums may have accounted for female incumbents' previous failure to acquire campaign treasuries as formidable as male incumbents'. In the past, male incumbents also had greater seniority in Congress, gaining them most of the committee and subcommittee chairs. These positions attract campaign contributors. Female members are now moving into positions of seniority. Whatever the source of this previous male incumbency financial advantage, it has disappeared in recent elections.

Challengers

Running as a challenger to a House incumbent is a daunting task. Incumbents running for reelection in contemporary times have tended to win over 90 percent of their races. In 1988, for example, only 6 out of 408 incumbents were defeated in the general election. Critics of the current campaign finance system have argued that these elections are essentially not campaigns between the Democratic and Republican parties but between an "incumbent" party and a "challenger" party. As cited above, challengers have operated at a great disadvantage in acquiring a campaign treasury.

Women have disproportionately been challengers and therefore have had difficulty in attracting contributors. But they have not been particularly disadvantaged vis-à-vis male challengers. They have raised amounts similar to those of male challengers of their party. In six of the eleven elections, female Democratic challengers surpassed their male counterparts in accumulating campaign dollars (figure 6.6), and Republican female challengers were financially advantaged in five of the eleven campaigns (figure 6.7). These figures suggest that women nominated as major party challengers have not been more likely "tokens" or "sacrificial lambs" than men nominated in such situations in contemporary elections. If we consider that most challenges to incumbents are viewed as hopeless affairs from the beginning of the campaign season, female challengers would not appear to have been nominated in the most hopeless of

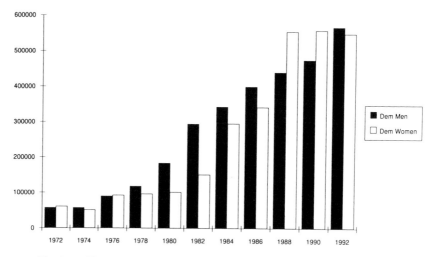

Fig. 6.4. Mean receipts of male and female Democratic incumbents, 1972–92

these discouraging situations, at least as reflected in the amounts of money they have been able to raise for their campaigns.

Open Seat Candidates

Open seat races, where incumbency is not a factor, are the crucial arenas for increasing the number of women in the national legislature. If female candidates are disadvantaged in campaign financing in these races, then little progress will be made in achieving numerical equality in the U.S. House no matter how well they do as incumbents. But female open seat nominees have not been disadvantaged in fund-raising (figures 6.8 and 6.9). In recent elections especially, they have been formidable fund-raisers compared to their male counterparts. In each of the election cycles beginning with 1984, female Democratic open seat nominees raised more than male contenders in these races. For example, in 1990, the seven female Democratic open seat nominees raised 27 percent more than their male counterparts; in 1992, the twenty-five open seat female Democratic nominees also raised 27 percent more. The one Republican female open seat nominee in 1990 raised 21 percent more than her male counterparts, but the thirteen female Republican open seat nominees in 1992 did not do quite as well as the male contenders. However, in that year Michael Huffington spent over $5,000,000 of his own money to defeat GOP Representative Robert Lagomarsino in the primary and win the general election. If we remove this outlier case from the Republican open seat

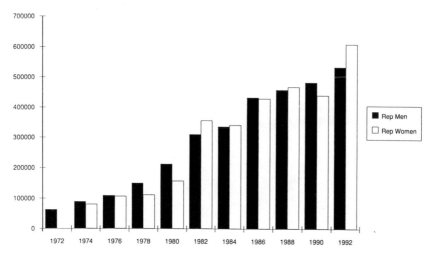

Fig. 6.5. Mean receipts of male and female Republican incumbents, 1972–92

calculation for 1992, female Republicans surpassed their male counterparts, raising an average $365,426 to $322,420 for the men.[6] These data support the contention of chapter 3 that the greater problem for women has been their scarcity as open seat major party contenders not their ability as campaigners.

The Financial Structure of Men's and Women's Campaigns

In addition to the total amount of money candidates accumulate, where and when they obtain their funds are important. Even though male and female major party nominees have raised and spent equivalent amounts of money in their congressional campaigns in the contemporary era, it does not necessarily follow that they have financed their quests in the same manner. The structure of giving may have differed between the sexes. Women may have been more apt to finance their campaigns through many small donations, as the *Christian Science Monitor* contended in 1990, and they may have had less access to political action committee and party money, although if this situation has been the case in recent election cycles, we would have to explain how women in general have been able to raise more funds than men.

6. Districts in which a challenger beats an incumbent in a primary are considered open seats only in the general election. The primary candidates of both parties in these elections are not considered in any of the open seat primary analyses that have been conducted for this study.

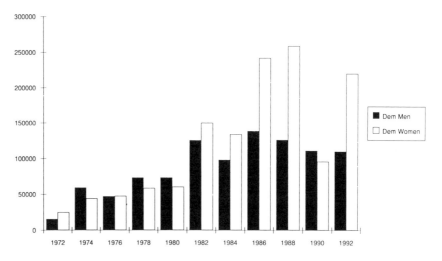

Fig. 6.6. Mean receipts of male and female Democratic challengers, 1972–92

Political Action Committees (PACs)

PACs especially are a significant source of campaign financing, although some candidates have made it a political strategy not to accept PAC contributions. Based on the conventional wisdom described in this chapter's introduction, we would hypothesize that women would have had greater difficulty tapping into the world of PACs, although this disadvantage may have changed over the course of the feminist era. Previous studies of congressional campaigns, however, found only a small gender gap in PAC financing of congressional campaigns in the 1980 and 1982 election cycles (Burrell 1985; Newman et al. 1984).[7] Female nominees had tapped the PAC community almost as effectively as men who had run for national office. Continuing the analysis through the 1992 election shows only a modest "pac" gap in the financial structure of male and female nominees' campaigns for the U.S. House, and in one election, 1988, the gap was in women's favor (table 6.2). These bivariate figures do not control for the fact that PAC money has flowed disproportionately to incumbents in these elections.

Table 6.3 presents the multivariate model showing the relative impact of sex on PAC contributions, controlling for incumbency and party similar to the model developed for campaign receipts. In each of the elections from 1980 through 1992, the disadvantage expressed in the bivariate models disap-

---

7. Data on PAC contributions are not available on FEC data tapes prior to 1980.

TABLE 6.2. Mean PAC Contributions and Total Amounts Raised in Contributions of $500 or More, by Sex, 1980–90

Year	Average PAC Contributions		Average Total Amounts of $500+ Contributions	
	Men	Women	Men	Women
1980	$ 44,703	$ 38,214	$23,104	$14,659
	(708)	(50)	(708)	(50)
1982	71,234	65,186	35,848	35,363
	(703)	(53)	(703)	(53)
1984	91,370	73,833	41,127	26,534
	(661)	(63)	(661)	(63)
1986	106,845	83,636	54,829	45,529
	(660)	(62)	(660)	(62)
1988	120,646	124,625	56,976	67,416
	(649)	(57)	(649)	(57)
1990	128,829	121,059	63,267	58,430
	(631)	(69)	(631)	(69)
1992	139,807	137,776	—	—
	(704)	(105)		

Note: Ns in parentheses. Figures include only candidates with major party opposition.

TABLE 6.3. Relative Effects of Sex, Party, and Incumbency on PAC Contributions

Year	Constant	Sex	Party	Open	Incumbent	R^2
1980	$ 21,703	$ 2,413	$ −4,373	$ 34,105***	$ 46,893***	.21
	(2,670)	(6,273)	(3,183)	(5,265)	(3,388)	
1982	26,305	3,288	7,152*	42,706***	79,203***	.30
	(3,831)	(8,122)	(4,133)	(6,211)	(4,496)	
1984	137,305	10,872	−22,018	248,894***	214,873***	.23
	(12,671)	(26,154)	(14,776)	(29,889)	(15,399)	
1986	14,432	5,418	27,788***	94,043***	146,504***	.45
	(5,317)	(10,588)	(5,913)	(9,732)	(6,326)	
1988	7,910	22,212*	39,764***	131,915***	166,519***	.48
	(5,831)	(12,205)	(6,500)	(13,430)	(6,775)	
1990	41,561	22,458	26,008**	104,656***	130,775***	.24
	(7,566)	(15,109)	(8,721)	(17,018)	(9,156)	
1992	15,323	11,760	52,172***	65,008***	213,561***	.44
	(7,475)	(12,735)	(8,523)	(11,345)	(9,695)	

Note: Figures in parentheses are standard deviations.
*p > .10. **p > .05; ***p > .000.

tive. In nine of the twenty-five cases (five elections by five types of groups) the coefficient for sex was statistically significant. In all of these instances it was positive for female candidates. "The strongest PAC signal for female candidates was from the nonaligned ideological PACs. All five election years had positive coefficients, and in four of those years they were significantly positive. Overall, the PACs of this category contributed between $2,000 and $6,000 more to female nonincumbents than to their male counterparts" (1991:106–7).

Large Contributions

One might still wonder whether the structure of individual contributions has differed for male and female candidates with women having financed their campaigns with many small donations, while men relied more on a smaller number of large donations. The general equality between the sexes in overall PAC contributions and total receipts provides some indirect evidence that this difference has not been the case. Direct evidence is available through a comparison of large contributions to the campaigns of men and women. Large donations are defined as donations of $500 or more from individual contributors. The Federal Elections Commission has compiled data on the total amount of contributions of $500 or more, and the number of donors who have given such amounts from 1980 through 1990. (Data for 1992 are not yet available.) The gender gap in large contributions varies from election to election (table 6.2). In 1982, high donors financed men's and women's campaigns equally. Male candidates as a group surpassed female candidates in 1980, 1984, and 1986, and 1990, while women did better in 1988. High donors then did not consistently give more to male candidates than female candidates in recent elections, but more often than not male candidates have done better as a group.

Table 6.4 presents the coefficients for the multivariate model of the effect of party, candidate status, and sex on the total amount of money raised from contributions for $500 or more. Female candidates' ability to finance their campaigns with large contributions relative to male candidates is mixed throughout the 1980s, although in no election is the coefficient for sex statistically significant, once party and candidate status has been accounted for. In three of the elections between 1980 and 1990, women did slightly worse than their male counterparts raising from $1,500 to over $9,000 less. But in three of the elections they acquired more in large donations varying from $200 to over $17,000. Female candidates can match their male counterparts in acquiring big donations for their campaigns.

An analysis of the size, structure, and source of money has shown that the idea that female congressional nominees have been disadvantaged in the financing of their campaigns has been a myth, unsupported by empirical

TABLE 6.4. Relative Effects of Sex, Party, and Incumbency on Large Contributions—Unstandardized Regression Coefficients

Year	Constant	Sex	Party	Open	Incumbent	R^2
1980	$17,002	$-6,878	$ -162	$ 18,824**	$ 9,067**	.02
	(2,450)	(5,759)	(2,922)	(4,832)	(3,110)	
1982	24,017	277	-8,869*	37,831**	24,219**	.08
	(3,415)	(7,241)	(3,685)	(5,537)	(4,008)	
1984	28,577	-9,075	-10,116*	49,228**	29,406**	.07
	(3,993)	(8,210)	(4,676)	(9,303)	(7,343)	
1986	33,472	-1,489	-17,695*	25,547**	47,099**	.09
	(6,159)	(12,206)	(6,878)	(3,802)	(7,343)	
1988	28,032	17,638	-14,527*	36,522**	59,518**	.16
	(5,250)	(12,205)	(5,992)	(4,009)	(6,230)	
1990	30,743	1,199	-13,455*	89,257**	68,244**	.15
	(5,482)	(10,856)	(6,626)	(12,194)	(6,926)	

Note: Figures in parentheses are standard deviations.
*$p > .10$. **$p > .000$.

evidence. But the case of financial disadvantage cannot be closed until an analysis of primary election money has been undertaken.

Early Money

As studies began to show that female major party nominees raised as much money as men in similar situations, scholars and activists began to focus on women's supposed limited access to early money as a way to explain the minuscule representation of women in public office. The argument was that once women obtained a major party nomination they might have access to the same sources of money as male nominees. But women candidates have had difficulty raising money in primary elections because they could not rely on party identification and structure to help them acquire funds. As Romney and Harrison have described the situation, "In politics, it's the early money that is hard to get and crucial to have. The early money is important partly because it enables the candidate to hire staff, arrange for a headquarters site and set up telephone service, get expensive initial bench-mark polling to provide a reasonably reliable basis for strategy. . . . So far, the main money hurdle for women politicians is getting some to start out with" (1988:86). Indeed, the belief that women candidates need help raising money in the initial stages of a campaign was the inspiration behind the founding of EMILY's List ("Early Money Is Like Yeast") in 1986, an organization devoted to providing "seed money" to progressive female Democratic Party congressional and gubernatorial office-seekers. But the impact of sex on the raising of early money has not been empirically tested.

As noted in the introduction to this chapter, U.S. House and Senate candidates are required to report their financial activity four times during the course of their campaigns. This reporting requirement allows us to test whether female candidates have been disadvantaged in raising early money by examining amounts raised in the first stages of the campaign season and the percentage of candidates who had even raised enough at these points to have had to file reports. The Federal Election Commission has made available the reports for the four periods for the 1988, 1990, and 1992 elections, which will serve as the basis for this analysis.

Table 6.5 compares the average amounts of money male and female candidates raised in the first and second reporting periods. It suggests that women candidates have not been later starters than their male counterparts and have not been disadvantaged in acquiring early funds to fuel their campaigns. If they were, a smaller percentage of women would have filed reports with the FEC for the first reporting period, and they would have had smaller campaign treasuries than male candidates.

In 1988, female major party nominees raised an average amount of money *greater* than that of their male counterparts in the first reporting period. In 1990, while female candidates lagged behind in fund-raising at the end of the first reporting period, they surged ahead by the second. Interestingly, the women candidates who made it to the general election in 1992 raised smaller amounts than the male candidates in both reporting periods. This difference may be accounted for by aggressive fund-raising on the part of besieged incumbents. Thus, it is important to compare the early financing of different groups of candidates' campaigns.

Incumbents and Early Money

Female incumbents in 1988 and 1990 started the campaign season ahead of their male incumbent counterparts, but not in 1992 (table 6.6). A comparison

TABLE 6.5. Average Amounts Raised by Male and Female Candidates, First and Second Reporting Periods, 1988–92

	First Period		Second Period	
Year	Men	Women	Men	Women
1988	$104,058	$123,104	$160,922	$186,169
	(723)	(58)	(723)	(58)
1990	114,386	91,301	155,123	173,282
	(718)	(69)	(718)	(69)
1992	121,368	85,177	185,004	166,348
	(734)	(106)	(734)	(106)

*Note: N*s in parentheses.

TABLE 6.6. **Average Receipts of Male and Female Incumbents, First Reporting Period, 1988–92**

Year	Men	Women
1988	$161,026	$185,465
	(381)	(22)
1990	193,251	210,065
	(382)	(24)
1992	240,112	228,205
	(313)	(26)

*Note: N*s in parentheses. These figures include all incumbents running in the general election, opposed and unopposed candidates, but they exclude candidates for whom special election monies were mixed with general election reporting figures.

of the amount of money raised through the first reporting period of the campaign season in 1988 and 1990 shows that female incumbents had an average campaign treasury exceeding that of male incumbents. In 1992, they slightly trailed their male counterparts. They had 115 percent of what male incumbents had in the bank in 1988, 109 percent in 1990, and 95 percent in 1992. Female incumbents are not shy about maintaining a campaign treasury to scare potential opponents. For example, at the beginning of the 1992 campaign season Helen Bentley had nearly $650,000, and Nita Lowey reported $615,000 in the bank; in the same period in 1990 she reported a campaign treasury of $708,775.

Challengers and Early Money

Female challengers have raised money as early as their male counterparts. In two of the three election cycles they surpassed male challengers in amassing a treasury in the initial stages of the campaign season, and in all three years female challengers outpaced their male counterparts by the end of the second reporting period (table 6.7).

Based on FEC reports, only 46 percent, 32 percent, and 39 percent of general election challengers in 1988, 1990, and 1992 respectively had raised enough money to have required submitting a statement at the end of the first reporting period, but women were not disproportionately among the nonreporters. Greater percentages of female than male challengers had filed reports indicating they had raised some money before the end of the first period in 1988 and 1990, and equal percentages of male and female challengers had filed reports in 1992. In 1988, over half of the female challengers (56 percent)

TABLE 6.7.   Average Receipts of Male and Female Challengers, First and Second Reporting Periods, 1988–92

	First Period		Second Period	
Year	Men	Women	Men	Women
1988	$33,584	$42,700	$64,283	$80,962
	(296)	(32)	(296)	(32)
1990	16,180	15,396	39,122	40,357
	(286)	(37)	(286)	(37)
1992	15,247	29,572	39,672	66,029
	(273)	(41)	(273)	(41)

Note: *N*s in parentheses.

had filed with the FEC at the end of the first reporting period, compared with only 44 percent of the male challengers. Thirty-five percent of the female challengers in 1990 compared to 32 percent of the male challengers reported having raised funds in the earliest stages of the campaign season, and 39 percent of both male and female challengers had filed in 1992. These figures belie the idea that one disadvantage female candidates have had is that they have tended to start later than male candidates.

Open Seat Candidates and Early Money

In 1988, there were 27 open seat primaries, with 17 female and 164 male candidates. In 1990, there were 29 open seats. Twenty women and 145 men competed for their party's nomination in those districts. Eighty-two women and 418 men contested the 75 open seats in 1992. Early money is especially crucial in these particularly competitive situations.

Once again, contrary to expectations, we find female contenders doing better than their male counterparts. Female open seat primary candidates were competing early on and showing fundraising prowess. First, a larger percentage of these female candidates reported having raised funds at the end of the first reporting period—59 percent compared with 57 percent of the men in 1988, 55 percent to 52 percent in 1990. The gap was even larger in 1992 when 52 percent of the female open seat primary contenders reported raising funds in the first period, contrasted with 40 percent of the men. Second, women had larger average campaign treasuries in the early stages of the election cycle in each of these years (table 6.8). Third, an examination of the source of contributions in these races indicates that on average, 15 percent of the female candidates' money had come from political action committee (PAC) contributions compared with only 6 percent for the male candidates in 1988. In 1990,

TABLE 6.8. Average Receipts of Male and Female Open Primary Contenders, First and Second Reporting Periods, 1988–92

Year	First Period		Second Period	
	Men	Women	Men	Women
1988	$42,475	$45,942	$97,160	$103,864
	(164)	(17)	(164)	(17)
1990	37,607	43,910	79,004	132,552
	(145)	(20)	(145)	(20)
1992	29,228	35,854	78,350	104,396
	(418)	(82)	(418)	(82)

Note: Ns in parentheses. Includes all primary candidates, not just nominees.

both male and female open seat primary contenders reported receiving 10 percent of their funds from PACs in the first reporting period. Among those candidates who reported raising funds in the first reporting period of 1992, women had obtained 9 percent of their funds from PACs compared to 8 percent for male open seat primary contestants.

These data have provided a first empirical examination of the relationship between sex and the acquisition of early money. They provide little evidence for the proposition that women are disadvantaged financially in the early stages of the campaign process; indeed, for the most part women began the elections in a stronger position than their male counterparts. All three of the most recent elections exhibited similar patterns. Women were indeed in a positive position in 1992, the one year in which we might have expected them to do better, but that year was not distinctive from the previous two election cycles. Rather it was characteristic of the period. Unfortunately, data are not available for earlier years to determine whether this advantage has been a most recent phenomenon or descriptive of the entire contemporary era. Women's success in raising funds can be at least in part attributed to the support many have received from women's PACs.

Women's Political Action Committees

In the preceding chapter I described the changing relationship of political parties and women politicians and considered the importance of strong parties to women's representation in national office. Political parties in the contemporary era have been challenged in their control of their candidates' campaigns not only by candidates' direct communication with voters through the media, but also by their ability to raise money from political action committees (PACs). In the past two decades, all types of groups have established PACs, including some devoted to the funding of women candidates. In 1974, 608 PACs registered with the FEC. Their numbers had increased to 4,125 by 1992. PACs now play a major role in financing elections.

Candidates can finance their campaigns through personal funds and through contributions from individuals, political parties, and political action committees. Individuals can contribute $2,000 to a candidate for federal office in an election cycle, but PACs can contribute $10,000,[8] making them a more efficient source of financial support for campaigns. Individual contributions have declined slowly from 65 percent in 1978 to 53 percent of a candidate's treasury in 1990, while PACs have increased their share, from 17 percent in 1978 to 32 percent in 1990 (Sorauf 1992).

Incumbents, especially, have become increasingly dependent on PAC money. Both incumbents and challengers received greater aggregate contributions from PACs in 1988 than in 1980, but the proportion of their total funds consisting of PAC money had become much larger for incumbents. PAC contributions to nonincumbents grew by 60 percent from 1980 to 1988 (from an average $27,000 to $43,000), but PAC contributions to incumbents increased by more than 300 percent over the same period (from $65,000 to $196,000). PAC money accounted for 17 percent of nonincumbents' campaign chests in 1980 and had changed little, to 18 percent, by 1988. PAC contributions to incumbents tripled over the 1980s, so that by the end of the decade PAC donations were nearly half (48.6 percent) of incumbents' total contributions (Theilmann and Wilhite 1991:82–83). In the 1990 campaign, twenty-one different PACs gave a million dollars or more to congressional candidates (Sorauf 1992). One of those PACs was EMILY's List, a woman's PAC mentioned earlier.

Women's PACs have become a meaningful part of the political campaign world. They are political action committees founded by women to contribute primarily or solely to women candidates. Some women's organizations combine monetary contributions with recruitment efforts, training, and technical assistance in a multifaceted approach to the election of women.

These groups are by definition risk-takers, since they are especially likely to support challengers (Salmans 1984). Stephanie Solien, former director of the Women's Campaign Fund, has described her organization as "venture capitalists, we invest in women" (Roberts 1984). Corporate PACs have primarily given to incumbents, but nonconnected PACs—the FEC category most of the women's PACs fall into—have tended to give a larger percentage of their money to challengers. In the 1987–88 election cycle, for exam-

---

8. The cycle includes primary and general elections.

ple, only 59 percent of their contributions went to incumbents, compared with 80 percent for corporation and 64 percent for labor PACS. Many nonconnected PACs have long supported challengers and recruited political risk takers.

The Women's Campaign Fund

The Women's Campaign Fund (WCF) is the oldest political action committee established specifically to fund women candidates. The Women's Campaign Fund was formed in 1974 with a loan from the General Motors heir Stewart Mott. It is a bipartisan political committee devoted to providing cash and technical assistance to progressive women running for all levels of public office. In its first year of operation the WCF provided $22,500 to twenty-eight women candidates for state and federal office in amounts ranging from $100 to $1,750. To earn WCF support, candidates must favor ratification of the ERA and freedom of choice on abortion. In 1976, WCF hired a full-time executive director to oversee more than $60,000, which was allocated to over seventy candidates. By 1978, the fund was not only providing direct financial contributions to candidates, it was giving technical assistance and strategic counselling. Since then it has also organized training schools for candidates and campaign managers.

Among the services it offers is assistance in obtaining money from other PACs. It brings women to Washington and introduces them to other committeesthat can provide more money. "The professionals at the fund make appointments, hold hands and give advice to the candidates when they come to town" (Roberts 1984). It arranges meetings with directors of campaign committees of many organizations and trains them in how to ask for money and how to make a presentation (See, for example, Rosellini 1982.)

The WCF raises money primarily through direct mail campaigns. It also hosts parties, gatherings, and other fund-raising events in cities nationwide. In 1981, the fund began an annual fund-raising gala in Washington, D.C., in which a series of dinner parties are held in homes around the city. In 1985, for example, it raised $100,000 at this event. Board members, staff, and other supporters also directly solicit contributions from individuals.

EMILY's List

In March 1992 EMILY's List was profiled on the CBS *60 Minutes* news show. EMILY's List, which stands for "Early Money Is Like Yeast—it makes the dough rise," is a national political organization for Democratic party female candidates. Host Morley Safer described this organization as "one of the most effective political action committees in the country." EMILY's List has become a media phenomenon. It has earned its reputation. In 1992, it raised six million dollars for Democratic women candidates, the top fund-raiser in that political cycle. EMILY's List ended the year with 24,000 members.

As described in *Ms.* magazine, EMILY's List began informally in 1984 when founder and president Ellen Malcolm and other politically active friends came together and circulated a list of Democratic women senatorial candidates to solicit money for their campaigns. As the need to make the group more formal became apparent, they began hosting across the country what political consultant Jeri Rasmussen has termed "the ultimate Tupperware party, with the grand prize being a U.S. Senate seat." A member might invite thirty to forty other women and tell them to bring their address books, which brought new names into the chain. The women, armed with Rolodexes, wrote letters and made phone calls with the goal of raising money early for viable Democratic women candidates. They hoped to enlist one thousand members who would donate $100 to $1,000 each to a campaign (Southgate 1986).

In May 1986 EMILY's List became a formal political action committee (PAC). But unlike traditional PACs, EMILY's List has worked as a donor network. Usually, a PAC receives funds from members, then its board decides which candidates should receive donations and how much. Under federal election laws, PACs are limited to a $5,000 contribution per candidate in federal races. But as a donor network, EMILY's List has had a much greater impact. In addition to paying the membership fee to join EMILY's List, a member of EMILY's List chooses a candidate (or candidates) to support and makes a donation directly to that woman, using EMILY's list as a conduit. In the parlance of the campaign finance literature, this is called "bundling." By the fall of 1986, EMILY's List had twelve hundred members who had donated between $100 and $1,000 and it had raised $183,000 for its candidates before that year's primary. "This difference between the List and a traditional PAC is everything. There is no limit on how much EMILY's List can funnel to endorsed candidates through this process" (Spake 1988).

Candidates selected for support have to be progressive, pro-choice, pro-ERA women. Viability is also a crucial factor in receiving money from the organization. Its primary strategy has been to raise seed money for the earliest stages of a campaign, when funds are hardest to obtain.

In 1986, EMILY's List supported two candidates for the U.S. Senate: Barbara Mikulski in Maryland, and Harriett Woods in Missouri. EMILY's List members contributed $350,000 to these candidates. Mikulski received $60,000 through EMILY's List, 20 percent of her money, in the first quarter of the campaign season when she was struggling to become a viable candidate in the primary. In 1988, EMILY's List members contributed more than $650,000 to ten House candidates. The List raised $1.5 million for fourteen women candidates in 1990, including $400,000 for Ann Richards's successful campaign for governor of Texas. Both EMILY's List and the Women's Campaign Fund have a board of directors who decide which candidates will be endorsed and receive money and services from the organization.

EMILY's List employs a rigorous endorsement process. Candidates must be interviewed by Malcolm and members of her staff at least once. They must present voluminous background information and any relevant polling data. Those who win the recommendation have convinced EMILY'S List that they have a viable campaign strategy and organization, that they can raise money, and most important, that they have a good chance to win (Friedman 1993). Morley Safer characterized it as putting "candidates through a wringer." Its "seal of approval" is greatly valued among Democratic women. But as it has become institutionalized, it has been criticized for becoming risk adverse, not willing to take a chance on a candidate who has not established herself within a traditional campaign framework. (See, for example, Matlack 1992.)

Republican feminists have also established a number of PACs for Republican women candidates. For example, in 1983 Wilma Goldstein, political consultant and former member of the Republican Congressional Campaign Committee, formed the Campaign Fund for Republican Women. It provided funding to U.S. House and Senate candidates. This PAC was active for two election cycles, in 1984 and 1986. It raised funds through personal solicitation and a small personalized direct mail appeal by Goldstein, who later joined with Maureen Reagan, daughter of the president, to expand the project. Its major fund-raising event was a January 1984, $250-a-person affair in Washington with President and Mrs. Reagan. It also hosted events around the country that night, which were hooked to the Washington celebration through a satellite system provided by the chamber of commerce. Goldstein attempted to keep administration costs down and give the vast majority of money raised directly to candidates. However, because no one was able to undertake the task of raising money and maintaining the organization on a full time basis, it dissolved after the 1986 election.[9] The Campaign Fund for Republican Women had no litmus test for endorsement such as support for choice on abortion. The only criteria for assistance was that candidates be Republican women. Maureen Reagan also organized her own PAC for Republican women candidates at this time, the GOP Women's Political Action League (PALPAC).

In 1992, Republican women once again established a PAC to support female candidates for federal office—the Leader PAC. In that election cycle it raised about $100,000 and contributed to every female Republican nominee

---

9. U.S. Representative Lynn Martin took over from Goldstein after the organization got underway. Information presented here was obtained through an interview with Wilma Goldstein.

for the U.S. House and Senate. Some candidates received the maximum donation of $5,000 allowed under law. This PAC raised money through the traditional method of direct mail combined with large and small donor events including fund-raisers at the Republican National Convention.

WISH List

In December, 1991 EMILY's List was joined on the Republican side by the WISH List. WISH is an acronym for "Women in the Senate and House." The WISH List has adopted EMILY's List's strategy of soliciting members who then bundle checks together for endorsed candidates. Indeed, Ellen Malcolm trained Glenda Greenwald, WISH List's founder, in techniques to organize a counterpart structure within the Republican Party. It began with approximately 25 members and $100,000 and by the end of the 1992 election had raised over $400,000 from about 1,500 members. The WISH List supports pro-choice female candidates. In 1992, it endorsed ten candidates.

These political action committees are joined by the National Women's Political Caucus (NWPC) and the National Organization for Women (NOW). These organizations differ from the other PACs in being membership groups with chapters in many communities around the country. They lobby, demonstrate, and initiate public education campaigns in addition to participating in the electoral process.

The National Women's Political Caucus

The central goal of the NWPC, as stated in chapter 1, has been to elect more women to public office. In its initial statement of purpose, it pledged itself to oppose racism, sexism, institutional violence, and poverty through party reform, the election and appointment of women to public office, and support of women's issues and feminist candidates across party lines. Its first major action was to increase the number of women national convention delegates within the two major parties. The caucus has both a Democratic and a Republican women's task force. In 1976 the NWPC had enough money to establish a political action committee. In 1977 it adopted national endorsement guidelines for candidate support. The guidelines required that a candidate be a feminist and express support for caucus goals and purposes— specifically for the Equal Rights Amendment, the 1973 Supreme Court decision in Roe v. Wade on abortion, and publicly funded child care. A past record of support for these positions was considered essential, and the candidate had to be willing to make the caucus endorsement known to the public (Feit 1979). The national arm of the NWPC now endorses and funds only women candidates, although some of its state affiliates provide support for male candidates.

The national caucus endorses candidates for federal office primarily on the recommendation of state caucuses.

The National Organization for Women

In her 1967 report as president of NOW, Betty Friedan proposed that NOW extend its activism to electoral politics. Outlining a Bill of Rights for Women for 1968, she advocated its presentation in the political parties and to major candidates with the promise that:

> we . . . cross party lines to work for and support those candidates who will commit themselves to our Bill of Rights and defeat those who are its enemies. We must also, every single member of NOW, become active in the mainstream of our parties and not in the ladies auxiliary. We must insist that for our support we must sit on a major decision-making committee of the party. And everywhere possible we must use the same courage and confidence in running for political office that we have found in fighting for our own equality in employment. We must make it understood that there are many issues facing our nation today of as great or even greater importance to many of us as equality for women, but that it is by the very nature of our commitment to that equality that we wish to speak out and act on those issues in the decision-making mainstream rather than as members of women's ghettos, whether these be Democratic or Republican Women's Divisions, the League of Women Voters, or Women's Strike for Peace.

In its early years, however, NOW devoted itself to lobbying, consciousness raising, and staging public demonstrations. It was a decade later before it began to involve itself in electoral politics. It did not establish a political action committee until 1978 (NOW-PAC). Moving into electoral politics was not a consensual decision. Many members felt such a strategy would diminish the strength of the organization by making it too partisan, a mere arm of the Democratic Party. NOW should continue with its outsider strategy and leave electoral politics to the National Women's Political Caucus opponents of the PAC argued. But NOW's attention was focused on passage of the Equal Rights Amendment at this time, and some leaders felt that only by threatening recalcitrant legislators at the ballot box could they be convinced to vote for the ERA in their state assemblies.

Electoral politics became an even greater focus for NOW after Ronald Reagan won the White House in 1980, and the ERA was defeated in 1982. As Katzenstein has noted, NOW was convinced that "feminism could no longer afford to be casual about electoral politics. Beginning in 1982, NOW redirected much of its political pitch at voting feminists into office" (1984:5). (See also Herbers 1982.) It contributes financially to men's campaigns as well as women's. It is the only organization in this group to do so. Like the NWPC, NOW usually endorses in conjunction with its state chapters.

Table 6.9 shows the amounts of money the women's PAC community has contributed to federal candidates. Their funds rose steadily from 1974 when the Women's Campaign Fund initiated the process of organizing women financially on behalf of women candidates. The women's community PAC funds more than doubled between 1978 and 1980 and nearly doubled again in the 1982 election cycle. They maintained a steady pace until EMILY's List took off in 1988, becoming one of the top ten PACs in 1992. While one cannot at this point put a statistical figure on the impact the contributions of these groups have made to the viability of the women's campaigns they have supported, they certainly give strong evidence that such PACs have made a difference and made women major players in the electoral process.

Conclusion

This chapter has searched for evidence in support of long-standing conventional wisdom that the inability to raise campaign funds has been a major factor in the dearth of women in the national legislature. But on each of the elements of fund-raising—total amounts raised and spent, PAC contributions, large donations, and the acquisition of early money—women candidates have either competed equally with male candidates or, in recent elections, surpassed them. The conventional wisdom does not need to be explained. Whether we look at totals, sources, or timing, women candidates in similar situations as male candidates generally do as well and sometimes even better in financing their campaigns for national office. Further, a significant phenomenon of contemporary elections has been the involvement of women's PACs, which have been able to supplement or compensate for other financial sources in women's campaigns for national office.

Money is still a problem since so few women have been able to run as incumbents. If challengers in general are to mount viable campaigns against incumbents, either the process has to be changed to provide them with access to more money or limits on the fund raising advantage of incumbents must be established. We have to think about the fact that, for example, EMILY's List spent six million dollars in 1992 to increase women's representation in the U.S. Senate from 2 percent to 6 percent, and to raise the proportion of U.S. House members who are women from 6 percent to 11 percent, still a great underrepresentation.

If we do not need to explain the conventional wisdom about the monetary

TABLE 6.9.   Women's PACs Contributions to Candidates, 1974–92

Year	Women's Campaign Fund	National Women's Political Caucus	National Organization for Women	EMILY's List	WISH List	Committee for Republican Women	GOP PALPAC	Leader Fund	Total
1974	$ 22,500								$ 22,500
1976	60,000								60,000
1978	61,333	$ 14,100	$ 3,800						79,233
1980	72,763	12,268	166,900						251,931
1982	53,975	24,940	337,690						416,605
1984	127,300	49,300	217,149			$30,000			423,749
1986	106,056	8,400	19,924	$ 250,000		2,200	$17,207		403,787
1988	121,012	36,350	34,448	650,000			9,750		851,560
1990	125,355	19,350	141,320	1,500,000			1,000		1,787,025
1992	458,317	176,520	257,586	6,100,000	$250,000			$61,500	7,303,923

Source: Most of these figures are from the D-Index of the Federal Election Commission. The D-Index is an itemized list of contributions to federal candidates. The D-Index is not available before 1978. The 1974 and 1976 figures for the Women's Campaign Fund are estimates based on WCF publications. The D-Index does not include "bundled money"; therefore, a reliance on it to estimate the amounts of money EMILY's List and the WISH List have funnelled to candidates would underestimate their contribution. I have relied on those groups' figures in this table.

aspects of women's campaigns for public office—these data strongly refute the notion that women have been handicapped in their quests for national office by an inability to finance their campaigns relative to men—then what has accounted for the persistence of this belief, and the sense that it was only beginning to be changed in 1992?

First, we must not confuse elite participation and conditions with that of the general public. Unfortunately that is what the media have done. The belief of financial inequality persists in part because elite behavior is extracted from or equated with mass positions. In this case, women in general still earn less than men; women still face a "glass ceiling" in achieving top positions in private industry. Women in our society do not have the same resources as men. Thus, how could they possibly compete with men in raising money to finance electoral campaigns? It does not necessarily follow, however, that the same conditions apply to the minuscule percentage of the population who aspire to public office. They are positioned differently. Distinct processes drive their experiences.

For example, women activists viewed the situation regarding the Anita Hill/Clarence Thomas sexual harassment controversy quite distinctly from women in the general population who were divided evenly with men in their belief about who was telling the truth. But the hearings stimulated women activists to seek office because they were mad—mad at the lack of women among the senators judging the judge and Professor Hill, and angry because she was seemingly not taken seriously in the senatorial system. What we tend to see, however, are things from the perspective of the general public, and conclude that sex was not a significant factor in response to those hearings as measured by various public opinion polls conducted at the time of the hearings. The same psychological process has occurred when it has come to the idea of women seeking money to run for office.

Second, money is crucially important to political campaigns for national office. But money is difficult to obtain for all nonincumbents. Women candidates (as do men) see that difficulty for themselves and perceive it in others like them, and thus extrapolate from their own experience to the belief of a group phenomenon. The candidates help to perpetuate the myth. They do not know there is a different story out there, one that is told through the presentation of empirical data that show equality in fund-raising. Of course, until women achieve greater equality in holding office, they will be perceived to be disadvantaged in the electoral process. Until more women run as incumbents they will be financially handicapped, and of course, it takes more money than nonincumbents usually can acquire to achieve that status. Thus, the women's PACs have become crucial elements in the process of electing women to the U.S. Congress.

CHAPTER 7

The Presence and Performance of Women Candidates in General Elections for the U.S. House of Representatives

Columnist Ellen Goodman (1986) has characterized American women's advances in public office holding as progression by the "drip method." That had been a particularly apt description of women's election to the U.S. House of Representatives in the contemporary era—when each election brought either a one- or two-seat gain, or when turnover (the replacement of retiring incumbents) resulted only in the maintenance of the status quo in the number of female representatives—until 1992, when women nearly doubled their membership in the House and increased their percentage of the membership from 6.4 percent to 10.8 percent.

In part, this slow progress resulted from few women entering primary elections for the House and few realistic opportunities to challenge entrenched incumbents, as I have shown in chapter 3. Yet women's campaigns have changed dramatically in the contemporary era. Increasingly, women with lower-level public office experience are running (chapter 4), making them "good candidates." (See Jacobson 1980.) Major party female nominees are just as accomplished at fund-raising as male candidates (chapter 6); and Darcy, Welch, and Clark (1987) have shown that female House candidates are as effective campaigners as male candidates.[1] What impact have these changes had on women's performance at the ballot box? The bottom line in advancing the numbers of women in public office is how well those who run do in obtaining votes in the general election. This chapter examines the presence of women as major party nominees and voter response to women as general election candidates.

General Election Presence

Headlines over the past twenty years have highlighted the numerical presence of female congressional nominees, usually presenting their candidacies in

---

1. Effectiveness was measured by candidate contacts with the voters.

terms of gains and losses, for example, "Women Candidates: Many More Predicted for 1974"; "More Women Seen in U.S. Congress"; "Number of Women in Congress Could Fall from Present"; and "Women Favored to Capture Many U.S. and Local Races—45 Running for Congress."

Numbers tell only part of the story, however. They must be placed in context to understand the relationship between the campaign process and the number of women in the national legislature. For example, we should examine party differences in nomination patterns; community contexts in which women have obtained party nominations; women's strategic presence among general election contenders (for example, whether women are disproportionately nominated in races unwinnable for their party); and women's vote-getting ability compared to that of male candidates in similar situations.

The number of women obtaining major party nominations increased over fivefold from 1968 to 1992, from a low of 19 nominees to a high of 106, and the number of female winners quadrupled from 11 to 47 (figs. 7.1 and 7.2). The rate of increase in the number of nominees has not been steady, however, but quite variable, with spurts and occasional declines. Prior to 1992, the rate of increase of nonincumbent female nominees was most dramatic between 1972 and 1976 where their numbers more than doubled over the earlier cycle of elections (fig. 7.1). After that, female nonincumbent nominees' presence grew incrementally until 1992 when they nearly doubled their numbers again, going from sixty-nine nominees in 1990 to 106 (table 7.1).

Women, however, have been only a small proportion of all nominees and of all nonincumbent nominees in these elections. They comprised 3 percent of all the candidates in the 1968–72 general elections. They doubled their percentage in the next period, and by the 1986–90 cycle had become 8 percent of all candidates. Their presence among nonincumbents was only slightly better, reaching 11 percent in the 1986–90 cycle (table 7.2). Even in 1992, when their numbers climbed dramatically, women were only 16 percent of all nonincumbents. They were, however, 29 percent of the Democratic open seat nominees and 15 percent of the Republican, a substantial increase over earlier elections.

In the 1968 election, Democrats nominated twelve women and Republicans nominated seven for the U.S. House of Representatives. Six Democratic and five Republican women won. But in the elections immediately following, Democrats dominated in both numbers of female nominees and elected representatives. Between 1968 and 1972, Shirley Chisholm, Bella Abzug, Ella Grasso, Louise Day Hicks, Pat Schroeder, Elizabeth Holtzman, Barbara Jordan, and Vyonne Braithwaite Burke were first elected to the House along with only one Republican, Marjorie Holt, who was elected in 1972. The number of female Democratic nominees grew with each election between 1968 and 1976, after which it leveled off and remained virtually static until 1988, when

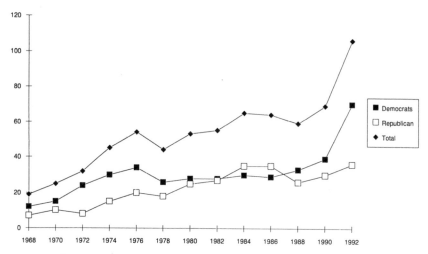

Fig. 7.1. Number of female major party nominees, 1968–92

their numbers began to increase again, and then rose substantially in 1992.

Republicans experienced a different pattern. After a slow start in which almost no new female candidates were nominated and elected, the number of Republican female nominees climbed incrementally through 1984, leveled off, declined, and then began to rise incrementally once again in 1990 and 1992. As the era progressed, the Republicans did make gains in electing women so that by 1986 female House membership was once again nearly evenly split between Democrats and Republicans as it was in 1969; and since the majority of House members were Democrats, these numbers meant that women made up a larger portion of the Republican House membership than the Democratic. The last three elections (1988–92) have been a setback for Republican women, especially 1992.

Republicans in the 1980s were credited with acting more affirmatively to advance their aspiring female politicians (Freeman 1989). For example, U.S. Representative Nancy Johnson (R-Conn.) credited male members of the Republican Congressional Campaign Committee with initiating her successful campaign for an open House seat in 1982 (pers. com., 1988). But the increase in the number of Republican female nominees may have been as much a function of the greater opportunity a minority party has to nominate nonincumbents as it is a reflection of a positive action strategy on the part of the organization. The slow growth in numbers of female Democratic party nominees during those years may have reflected in part a constricted opportunity structure resulting from the large number of Democratic Party incumbents

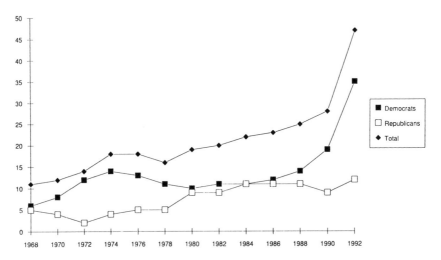

Fig. 7.2.   Number of female major party winners, 1968–92

seeking reelection as much as a hostile organizational environment. A party with little turnover in its incumbency ranks will have little opportunity to nominate women candidates, except in those few situations where the incumbent is a woman.

Once the opportunity structure is taken into account, however, data show that the minority party status of the Republican party in the U.S. House of Representatives has not produced a larger proportion of female nominees than the Democratic party. Democrats surpassed Republicans in the first two subsets of elections in this era; the parties were equal between 1980 and 1984, and the Democrats advanced again between 1986 and 1990, and surged ahead in 1992, when 25 percent of their nominees were women contrasted to only 9 percent of the Republicans (table 7.2).

These data do not necessarily mean, however, that the Democratic party actively recruited more female candidates. A recall of the parties' different cultures, discussed in chapter 3, suggests the nature of the Democratic party has allowed more women to successfully challenge the structure rather than their nominations necessarily being the result of party leadership recruitment. The more important fact, however, is the minuscule proportion of both parties' representatives who were women throughout this period.

State and District Contexts and Women's Nominations

Every state except Montana had a major party female nominee for the U.S. House between 1968 and 1992. Montana, having elected Jeannette Rankin the

TABLE 7.1. Female Major Party Nominees and Winners, 1968–92, by Subgroups of Elections

Election	Female Nominees (N)	Winners %	Winners N	Nonincumbents (N)	Nonincumbent Winners %	Nonincumbent Winners N
1968–72						
Democrats	51	51	26	31	26	8
Republicans	24	46	11	15	7	1
Total	75	49	37	46	20	9
1974–78						
Democrats	90	42	38	56	11	6
Republicans	53	26	14	44	11	5
Total	143	36	52	100	11	11
1980–84						
Democrats	86	37	22	56	4	2
Republicans	87	33	29	65	12	8
Total	173	35	61	121	8	10
1986–90						
Democrats	101	45	45	64	13	8
Republicans	91	34	31	62	3	2
Total	192	40	76	126	8	10
1992						
Democrats	70	50	35	53	40	21
Republicans	36	33	12	27	11	3
Total	106	44	47	80	31	24

Source: Dated compiled from *Congressional Quarterly Weekly Report.*

TABLE 7.2. Women Candidates as a Proportion of all Major Party Nominees and as a Proportion of Nonincumbent Nominees, 1968–92

Year	Proportion of All Nominees (%)	Proportion of Nonincumbents (%)	Democrats[a] (%)	Republicans[a] (%)
1968–72	3.1	3.6	5.1	2.2
1974–78	6.0	7.9	10.5	5.9
1980–84	6.9	9.4	9.7	9.3
1986–90	8.1	10.8	12.8	9.3
1992	12.6	16.0	24.7	9.4

[a]Percentage of nonincumbents.

first woman to Congress in 1916, seems to have rested on its laurels in recent times. In 1968 women were nominated for the U.S. House in fourteen states and won seats in nine of them. In 1990, thirty-one states had female nominees, and women were elected in nineteen states. These numbers increased in 1992 to thirty-six states with female nominees and twenty-seven with female representatives. Those states without a female nominee from either party in 1992 were mainly the smaller population states such as Alaska, Montana, Wyoming, North and South Dakota, Vermont, New Hampshire, Rhode Island, and Delaware. They had less opportunity than those states where redistricting altered district lines creating greater possibilities. Thirty-three states have had a female U.S. representative during this period. Seven states elected their first female representative of this era in 1992.

Rule (1981) found that women elected to the U.S. House in 1974 came from urban, welfare-oriented, high population states. These findings were in keeping with earlier studies of recruitment patterns (Werner 1968; Darcy and Schramm 1977). But by 1983, the association between high population states and states with higher aid to dependent children and the recruitment of women to the U.S. House had disappeared. The most important predictor of election to the House in the 1973–83 period in all fifty states was the percentage of women with professional degrees. State assembly turnover was the second most important predictor. Democratic and Republican congresswomen in 1983 came from urban districts, districts with a sizable minority population, and districts with low rental and housing costs (Rule 1987).

Table 7.3 shows the characteristics of districts electing and reelecting women to the U.S. House at the end of the 1980s. These districts were urban, had a sizable black population, were above average in family incomes, and had voted for Michael Dukakis in the 1988 presidential election. Table 7.3 also compares districts electing and not electing women to the House. On

TABLE 7.3. Characteristics of House Districts, 1986–90

Characteristic	Districts with Women Members	District with No Women Members	Difference of Means	T
Average percentage of population —black	14.5%	11.2%	3.3	−0.97
Average percentage of population in urban areas	84.7%	72.4%	12.8**	−3.80
Median family income	$21,469	$19,915	$1,554*	−1.86
Percent of vote for Dukakis	51.5%	46.0%	5.5*	−1.63

*Significant at the .05 level, one-tailed T-test.
**Significant at the .001 level, one-tailed T-test.

three of the four descriptive characteristics for which we have information, the differences were statistically significant. The cohort of women elected to the House in the 1986–90 period came from more liberal, and wealthier districts in urbanized areas. It remains to be seen to what extent the 1992 election altered these relationships. It certainly expanded southern representation.

Is community context an important factor in the nomination of women for seats in the House? That is, have women been more likely to have obtained major party nominations in certain environments than in others? Environmental contexts affect opportunities by limiting or facilitating the acquisition of criteria deemed appropriate for public office holding and the development of attitudes among the populace and political activists about who should be public officials. The pattern of increase in women's nominations may have been concentrated in a subset of states and districts with particular characteristics, even though all but one state has had a female nominee. Alternatively, a broadening of favorable situations across the country may have characterized the trend in women's nominations, resulting in little relationship between the socioeconomic and political characteristics of districts and the nomination of female candidates.

Congressional districts provide varying opportunity structures for women's nomination and recruitment to the U.S. House. Different political cultures affect the attitudes of the public and activists toward women's involvement in politics. Greater economic development, usually associated with urbanized areas, provides greater educational opportunities for women, allowing more women to acquire the credentials viewed as important for public office holding (Jones and Nelson 1981). In addition, a social welfare oriented community expands opportunities for recruitment to public office to those with concern and/or expertise in such areas as education, aid to dependent children, youth problems, and public assistance. "Those issues appear to be consistent with traditional women's roles as wife, mother and nurturer. Consequently, elites and voters may be more receptive in social welfare contexts to women's candidacy than in non-welfare polities" (Rule 1981).

Contextual factors should similarly affect major party nominations for House seats and election to that body but not necessarily exert the same influence. For example, minority parties may recruit women candidates either as "sacrificial lambs," or in the feminist era, as a means of creating publicity, being different, and making a statement against "politics as usual" in unfavorable contexts for their election. (Note the pattern of growth of Republican female nominees.) But this would not result in more women being elected to the House (unless the political savvy and distinctiveness of such candidates allowed them to disproportionately beat incumbents). The relationship between competitiveness of the party system and party control over nominations has been debated in the past. (See Rule 1981:64.) Studies have found a negative relationship between interparty competition and the election of women to state legislatures (Diamond 1977; Jones and Nelson 1981), but Rule (1981) found no statistically significant relationship between interparty competition within the states and the election of the 1974 cohort of U.S. female representatives. The relationship between interparty competition and the nomination of female candidates remains to be explored. The recent decline in party control over the nomination process alters the opportunity structure for women candidates in a way that has yet to be fully analyzed.

I employ the potentially theoretically significant district characteristics examined in chapter 3 regarding women's candidacies in open seat primaries as independent variables in the nomination process to compare districts having had female nominees with those districts that have not. The analysis is divided into two periods, 1972–80 and 1982–90. Redistricting in 1980 shifted district boundaries and altered their character. Table 7.4 shows the result of a bivariate analysis of the relationship between district characteristics and patterns of female nominations.[2]

In both the 1970s and the 1980s, districts with female Democratic nominees were wealthier, more urbanized areas and had a smaller proportion of blacks living in them than those districts without female nominees. The same relations are found for Republicans, except that the relationship between female nominees and the percentage of blacks in the districts is reversed: the greater the minority population the greater the likelihood of a woman being nominated by the Republicans. However, the relationship between the proportion of blacks in a district and nomination of female candidates does not change within either of the parties if we exclude the southern states and examine presence only outside the South.

Both parties were more likely to nominate women in districts less friendly to their party in presidential elections and less friendly to their party generally as measured by the normal vote. This last relationship could be the result of one of two processes. The first process reflects the "hopeless candidacy" idea in which parties only run women in situations unfavorable to their party. The second explanation for this finding is that districts more favorable to a party already have incumbents who tend to be men, and therefore offer few opportunities to nominate women. Most women are nominated as challengers to incumbents. If, however, the hopeless candidacy thesis explains the negative relationship between percentage of the vote obtained by the party's presidential nominees and districts that have nominated women, then nonincumbent female nominees should have obtained a smaller percentage of the vote than their male counterparts and should have had lower success

---

2. Data are not available for the earlier elections.

TABLE 7.4.   Bivariate Analysis of the Impact of Constituency Factors on the Nomination of Women Candidates, 1972–90

Constituency Factor	Democrats	Republicans
1972–80		
Percentage of population that is black	−.087	.030
Percentage of population in urban areas	.090	.130**
Median family income	.150**	.080*
Region	−.150**	−.100*
Normal vote	−.220**	−.150**
1982–90		
Percentage of population black	−.090*	.120*
Percentage of population urban	.070	.070
Median family income	.230**	.000
Region	−.140	−.090
Normal vote	−.180**	−.160**

*Significant at the .05 level.
**Significant at the .01 level.

rates. The next section addresses the relationship between gender and votes obtained.

Table 7.5 presents the results from a multivariate probit analysis examining the impact of these constituency factors on the nomination of women within both parties. Together these variables explained only a small portion of the variance in the nomination of a woman in either party. In each decade only 7 percent of the variance was explained in the Democratic party and 5 percent in the Republican party. In both decades the only variables that reached statistical significance among the Democrats were the normal vote of the party, which had a negative impact, and region, with women less likely to have been nominated in southern districts. The Republican party experienced the same impact. Only region and the normal vote of the party made a statistically significant difference. The more popular the party the less likely women were to be nominated, and they were less likely to be nominated in the South. In the 1980s, Republican women were also more likely to be nominated in districts with a higher proportion of blacks, not areas traditionally friendly to that party, and Democratic women tended to be nominated in wealthier districts.

To summarize, constituency context seems to have had little impact on the presence of women as candidates and nominees for the U.S. House during the feminist era. Both candidacy and nomination seem to depend on more personal factors than contextual ones. The lack of female candidates and nominees in the South is perhaps the most outstanding, and not surprising,

TABLE 7.5. Probit Analysis of the Impact of Constituency Factors on the Nomination of Women Candidates, 1972–90

Constituency Factor	Democrats		Republicans	
	Probit Coefficient	Standard Error	Probit Coefficient	Standard Error
1972–80				
Percentage of population black	.004	.007	.002	.007
Percentage of population urban	.007	.003	−.001	.003
Median income[a]	.009	.050	.050	.060
Region	−.650**	.240	.400*	.230*
Normal vote	−.040***	.009	.030	.010**
1982–90				
Percentage of population black	.010	.007	.010	.006
Percentage of population urban	−.000	.004	−.003	.004
Median income[a]	.060**	.020	.020	.020
Region	−.420*	.200	.440**	.190
Normal vote	−.020**	.006	.010**	.006

[a]Median income is in thousands of dollars.
*Significant at the .05 level.
**Significant at the .01 level.
***Significant at the .001 level.

finding. But in 1992, nine of the twenty-four newly elected female representatives were from the South, and four of them were black. The South, along with California (which elected five new women to the House and two U.S. senators), had the greatest opportunity to increase its female representation because of redistricting, which created new districts in the region, and the Voting Rights Act, which helped minorities in states such as Florida, North Carolina, and Georgia. Women did especially well in those districts.

Gender and the Vote

Previous analyses of congressional election results from 1970 to 1974 (Darcy and Schramm 1977) and from 1982 to 1984 (Darcy, Welch, and Clark 1987) indicated that "the electorate is indifferent to the sex of congressional candidates," and "there is currently no disadvantage in being a woman candidate." These data have shown that once a woman obtained a major party nomination for a seat in the House, she did as well at the ballot box as male candidates in comparable situations.

In recent elections, female candidates may even have had an advantage in the voters' minds. Recall, for example, Allen Ehrenhalt's comments in 1982, cited in chapter 3, that it helped to be a woman because of the clean image. (Indeed in 1982, two open seat U.S. House races had only female candidates, an unprecedented event, but one that was not repeated until 1992 when four open seat general election contests were all-women races.) As scandals and corruption grew in Washington, the theme of women candidates having an advantage as outsiders became even more pervasive. The outsider theme and the idea of being different, of course, dominated the 1992 election. Thus, in examining women's vote-getting ability in recent elections, our attention is called not just to whether voter bias against women candidates has disappeared, but whether female congressional nominees as a group have surpassed their male counterparts at the ballot box.

Two measures of the relationship between gender and the vote in general election contests for the U.S. House are employed here to evaluate women's candidates' performance over the course of the feminist era. The major questions of concern are does the nomination of a woman candidate depress a party's votes, enhance its position at the polls, or make no difference in outcomes? Has there been a trend in women's favor over the course of these two decades? The effect of gender on the vote is measured first by the average percent of the vote obtained by male and female candidates, accounting for type of candidacy (i.e., incumbent, challenger, open seat contestant) and party affiliation, and secondly, by the win/lose rates of male and female candidates in similar situations.

The data in table 7.6 compare the average percentage of votes male and female general election candidates obtained in the 1968 through the 1992 elections, divided into four subperiods and 1992. The percentages show that female candidates have done less well than male candidates in each of the subperiods within this era and in 1992. However, the eta statistics, which measure the strength of the relationship, indicate a very weak correlation between sex and votes obtained. As a group, women most closely matched male candidates in the earliest period (1968–72), and they actually matched their male counterparts in each of the candidate status subcategories in 1992, but because they disproportionately were among nonincumbents their overall percentage was very slightly less than that for male candidates.

The gender gap in performance has resulted primarily from men's incumbency, and from Democratic party dominance. Once we control for type of race and party affiliation, that is, if we compare vote percentages obtained by each party's candidates separately and within candidate status categories, the gap narrows. The explanatory power of sex then virtually vanishes, accounting for less than 1 percent of the variation in the vote in each of the four sets of elections in this era, and women slightly surpassed men in the percentage of the votes they obtained in 1992.

Female incumbents have been strong vote getters surpassing their male counterparts throughout the era. Female Democratic open seat nominees ran more strongly than their male counterparts in the earlier elections, but fell

TABLE 7.6. Mean Percentage of the Vote, by Sex, Party, and Candidate Status, 1968–92

Candidate status	Democrats		Republicans	
	Men	Women	Men	Women
		1968–72		
Challenged incumbents	65	67	64	63
	(521)	(18)	(459)	(8)
Challengers	36	36	34	28
	(444)	(20)	(516)	(11)
Open seats	50	54	48	40
	(125)	(10)	(132)	(4)
	Unadjusted Mean Score		Adjusted[a] Mean Score	
Men	49.39		49.38	
Women	48.33		48.32	
	Eta = .01		Beta = .01	
		1974–78		
Challenged incumbents	67	73	61	67
	(547)	(27)	(383)	(10)
Challengers	38	36	32	28
	(343)	(50)	(539)	(35)
Open seats	55	57	43	38
	(147)	(8)	(147)	(8)
	Unadjusted Mean Score		Adjusted[a] Mean Score	
Men	49.61		49.56	
Women	44.58		45.25	
	Eta = .07		Beta = .06	
		1980–84		
Challenged incumbents	65	71	65	70
	(551)	(22)	(399)	(19)
Challengers	34	34	34	34
	(379)	(41)	(519)	(54)
Open seats	52	44	47	45
	(111)	(11)	(113)	(8)
	Unadjusted Mean Score		Adjusted[a] Mean Score	
Men	49.83		49.60	
Women	44.81		47.88	
	Eta = .07		Beta = .02	
		1986–90		
Challenged incumbents	68	69	64	67
	(528)	(30)	(379)	(26)
Challengers	34	35	31	30
	(357)	(48)	(505)	(54)

TABLE 7.6—*Continued*

Candidate status	Democrats		Republicans	
	Men	Women	Men	Women
Open seats	50	49	48	45
	(81)	(15)	(90)	(4)
	Unadjusted Mean Score		Adjusted[a] Mean Score	
Men	50.03		49.77	
Women	45.72		48.47	
	Eta = .06		Beta = .02	
		1992		
Challenged incumbents	63	65	62	62
	(175)	(17)	(111)	(8)
Challengers	35	39	36	36
	(94)	(26)	(179)	(14)
Open seats	55	54	44	38
	(62)	(21)	(72)	(9)
	Unadjusted Mean Score		Adjusted[a] Mean Score	
Men	49.23		49.07	
Women	48.48		49.63	
	Eta = .02		Beta = .01	

Note: Ns in parentheses. Incumbents facing no major party challenger have been excluded, as have candidates in races involving two incumbents (redistricted seats), and races involving two female candidates.
[a] Adjusted for party and candidate status.

behind in more recent contests until they once again marginally surpassed the men in 1992. Republican female open seat nominees have consistently lagged behind Republican male open seat candidates. Their small numbers, however, make conclusions about their performance suspect. Open seat nomination patterns are discussed more fully below. A party's fortunes do not improve by nominating a woman to challenge an incumbent, rather within both parties males and females tended to do equally well (or poorly) against incumbents of the opposition party. Overall, female candidates are neither particularly advantaged nor disadvantaged at the polls and that has been the pattern throughout the contemporary era. But do they win as often as male contenders?

Table 7.7 describes the general election success of Democratic and Republican male and female U.S. House candidates from 1968 through 1992. A number of points are clear. Both male and female incumbents are overwhelmingly successful at achieving reelection, and both sexes within both parties are equally unsuccessful in challenging incumbents.

Gender differences emerge when open seat races are examined, however, and the trend is contrary to our expectations. We would have expected female

TABLE 7.7. General Election Success Rate by Party, Race, and Sex, 1968–92

Candidate status	Democrats (# Running/# Winning)		Republicans (# Running/# Winning)	
	Men	Women	Men	Women
1968–72				
Challengers	444/13	20/1	516/14	11/0
	(.03)	(.05)	(.03)	(.00)
Open seats	130/60	11/7	132/72	4/1
	(.46)	(.64)	(.55)	(.25)
Challenged incumbents	521/507	18/17	459/446	8/6
	(.97)	(.94)	(.97)	(.75)
Unopposed incumbents	141	1	19	1
1974–78				
Challengers	343/46	50/2	539/25	35/0
	(.13)	(.04)	(.05)	(.00)
Open seats	156/92	9/5	147/47	8/3
	(.73)	(.56)	(.32)	(.38)
Challenged incumbents	547/524	27/25	383/335	10/0
	(.96)	(.93)	(.87)	(1.00)
Unopposed incumbents	140	5	25	1
1980–84				
Challengers	379/26	41/1	519/36	54/4
	(.08)	(.03)	(.07)	(.07)
Open seats	113/59	12/2	115/62	10/4
	(.52)	(.17)	(.54)	(.40)
Challenged incumbents	551/511	22/22	399/372	19/19
	(.93)	(1.00)	(.93)	(1.00)
Unopposed incumbents	134	5	38	1
1986–90				
Challengers	357/14	48/3	505/9	54/0
	(.04)	(.06)	(.02)	(.00)
Open seats	86/50	15/5	91/47	4/2
	(.58)	(.33)	(.53)	(.50)
Challenged incumbents	528/519	30/30	379/362	26/26
	(.98)	(1.00)	(.96)	(1.00)
Unopposed incumbents	154	3	72	1
1992				
Challengers	94/4	27/2	179/14	14/0
	(.04)	(.07)	(.08)	(.00)
Open seats	64/35	22/15[a]	74/33	9/3[a]
	(.55)	(.68)	(.45)	(.33)
Challenged incumbents	175/164	17/14	111/108	9/9
	(.94)	(.82)	(.97)	(1.00)
Unopposed incumbents	15	0	11	0

[a]These figures exclude the four races in which a Democratic woman and a Republican woman faced each other in the general election. The Democratic candidate won in all of those races. The overall success rate for Democratic women in actually 73 percent, and for Republican women it is only 23 percent.

Note: Success rates are given in parentheses. Races in which an incumbent was defeated in a primary are considered open seat contests in the general election. Incumbent versus incumbent races are excluded. Only incumbents running in the general election are included in incumbent success rates.

candidates in such races to have become increasingly successful given a more favorable national environment for women in politics. But this did not occur for female Democratic candidates until 1992, and Republican female open seat nominees, although quite successful, have been extraordinarily few in number. In the earliest set of elections, Democratic female open seat nominees had a higher success rate than their male counterparts. Sixty-four percent of the Democratic female open seat nominees won compared with 46 percent of the male nominees. Then their advantage disappeared, dropping to a stunningly low 17 percent success rate in the 1980–84 cycle of elections. Only two of the twelve female candidates won. They recovered somewhat in the 1986–90 period, and totally reversed their earlier downward slide in 1992 when they won 68 percent of their contested races against male opponents and had an overall 73 percent success rate, having beaten Republican female candidates in four other races. Conversely Republican women had a particularly bad year in 1992, when only three of thirteen open seat nominees won.

Women won 25 percent of the open seats in 1992. Prior to 1990, they had never won as much as 10 percent of the regularly scheduled open seat elections. (These figures do not include contests in which an incumbent was defeated in a primary.) Women won 3 percent of the contests in 1968 (one out of thirty-one races). They won an average of 7 percent of the open seat contests between 1970 and 1978 and 4 percent of the races between 1980 and 1988. In 1990, they were victors in 11 percent of the elections. The significant jump in the proportion of open seats won by women in 1992 compared with the earlier elections further indicates the positive distinctiveness of that year for women candidates.

Conclusion

Generally, the findings of the analyses presented in this study help to diminish even further the explanatory power of demand side factors for the minuscule representation of women in the U.S. House of Representatives. On all of our measures of campaign experience, women have kept pace with their male counterparts, occasionally falling behind as a group and sometimes surpassing the men. When women have run, women have done as well as men is the description that best captures women's campaign experiences in the contemporary era.

The one factor that has been a bridge between demand side and supply side explanations in accounting for the small numbers of female U.S. representatives has been the opportunity structure of this era. Because of the advantages incumbents have brought to the campaign process and the fact that so many have sought reelection, the demand for new candidates who could realistically expect to run a competitive campaign has been small, and few women have sought these less-than-promising opportunities. Incumbency has been a major drag on movement towards equality.

But the contemporary era has also been characterized on the supply side by women not exhibiting a major presence in the more opportune situations where ultimate election was promising, although the trend has been toward increasing numbers of women seeking open seat party nominations culminating in a significant presence of Democratic women in such elections in 1992. The lack of presence among Republican women, however, especially remains a puzzle to be solved as a result of these analyses, particularly since that party's leadership has been credited with being facilitative toward women's candidacies. One has to assume that the conflict between feminism and the cultural conservatism of the right wing of the Republican party has dampened the enthusiasm of at least some potential female candidates to mount a campaign. One can assume that the Republican party leadership will strive greatly to improve its record in 1994 and beyond. But given their limited ability to control nominations because of the primary election system, their efforts could clash with the agenda of the cultural conservatives, and there is little reason to believe that they will successfully recruit women within a negative environment. The emphasis on the traditional family among the conservatives would conflict with their promotion of women in political leadership positions.

A number of other factors stemming from women's lives help us understand the lack of a greater presence on the part of women during this era, although the surge in Democratic women's candidacies in 1992 hint at the diminishing of some of these barriers. First, although women have steadily increased their presence among public officials at lower levels of office holding, they still represent only a small minority of potential candidates positioned to run strong campaigns for national office when seats become vacant. Fowler and McClure (1989) cite the positioning hypothesis as a limiting factor in increasing the presence of women in open seat House contests. They point out that only 991 women were state legislators in 1988, two per congressional district, leaving few to take advantage of an open congressional seat opportunity. Also, there are four times as many men as women in elective office. In state senates—where many U.S. House nominees come from—women held only 13 percent of the seats in 1989 (Rule and Norris 1992). As Fowler and McClure state,

> Given the small (although increasing) number of women holding and seeking state and local public office across the country, the reservoir of female talent ready to move to Congress will continue to be quite limited. Therefore, the chance that a woman who has the credentials and

desire to win a House seat will also reside in a district with a vulnerable incumbent [or in an open seat district] is exceedingly small. (1989:228)

We must also consider whether if more women were positioned to run for seats in the House more would actually run—not necessarily so, for both personal and political reasons. A move to a seat in the national legislature is qualitatively different from service in the state capitol or the mayor's office. Deciding to run for national office is even more complex for women than men, particularly if women are married and mothers. Wifehood and motherhood, the personal realms of their lives, are significant elements of the decision-making equation with which women must deal. Men do not face these personal factors in the same way. As Sapiro has argued, "Women will not fit into politics if public affairs remains as it is, functionally and normatively detached from private life. A policy of promotion of women into public affairs will not work if the private world is not integrated" (1983:188). The risk of uprooting family is great for women and those who have opted to take that risk continue to face questions on the campaign trail (even in 1992 women candidates with young children had to answer for how they would care for them).

Situational factors are important. So, too, is ambition, for both male and female politicians. The relationship between ambition and quests for seats in the national legislature had become problematic in general in the 1980s. Changes in the attractiveness of a run for the U.S. House for ambitious politicians have implications for both male and female public officials. It is not a problem unique to women. We have traditionally conceived of ambitious politicians following a single-minded path from a state legislature to the national legislature. The desirability of this career path changed for at least some politicians in the 1980s. Satisfying and influential careers could be found in state capitols as opposed to the nation's capitol. (See, for example, Fowler and McClure 1989; and Duncan 1984). Prime candidates have opted not to seek House seats but to continue their careers within their states.

This shift has obvious implications for women state legislators deciding to run for congressional seats rather than to continue their careers in state houses. One activist in the women's campaign community clearly stated the problem:

Frankly who wants it. I look at some of the women who are out there on appropriations committees and speakers of the house [in state legislatures]. . . . Can you really make a difference here being one of 435, being a freshman member, being stuck on some committee you may not even care about just barely bringing home the bacon to your district so that you can get reelected? . . . Policy-making in this country is done by a group of men who meet with Dick Gephardt. Its done by Foley, Gephardt and the boys. They decide whether there is a child care bill. They decide what they are going to give up to the president. It's not done by the Congress really. They're brought in to vote. . . . Frankly if I met somebody who is a real sharp aggressive leader in the state legislature and there was a congressional district being cut there, I don't that I could say to her that she would have more of an impact on public policy coming to Washington. . . . She probably passes more pieces of legislation and probably has more of an impact on the people of her state than she will ever have in 10 years in Congress. (pers. com., 1990)

Term limitation movements in the states may alter this perspective and reverse the trend away from ambitious politicians not seeking congressional seats. The excitement of women's wins in 1992 may have a ripple effect of more women in positions to run seeing the value of undertaking such a task. Congress may once again become an exciting place to formulate national policy.

But translating ambition into pursuit of higher office seems more complex for women than men, too. Bledsoe and Herring (1990) have found that among local officeholders the circumstances under which men and women seek higher office differ. The strength of their current political position and their perception of their political vulnerability had little effect on men's decisions to pursue higher office. They were self-motivated and guided more single-mindedly by their political ambition. The circumstances in which female local officeholders found themselves had much greater impact on their decisions to seek higher office.

A historical factor of the 1980s also has contributed to the lack of growth in female representatives in that decade. The electoral environment in the 1980s may not have favored women's election to the House. The national environment certainly became more favorable to women in public office, and as the data in this chapter have shown, women candidates have faced little discrimination from voters. But the conservative ideological environment of the 1980s worked against the actual nomination and election of women candidates. The public perceives female politicians to be more liberal (Mericle, Lenart, and Heilig 1989), and female U.S. representatives have voted more liberally than their male colleagues (Welch 1985). As Boles states, "given a political environment that is hostile toward the traditional liberal agenda, this view of women in politics also may have a negative impact on female candidacy" (1993:28). The point is not that voters are prejudiced against female candidates, but that they have not been supportive of what female politicians were perceived to have stood for in the elections of the 1980s. Thus, the number of female open seat candidates and their success declined in the

1980s, but began to revive at the end of the decade, and the 1990s is viewed as the decade of women politicians as issue concerns have shifted to areas deemed compatible with women's interests.

This adverse ideological atmosphere of the 1980s would have served as a disincentive for some female aspirants to mount a congressional campaign. It contributed to the poor record of those female Democrats who did obtain their party's nomination in open seat districts. In 1981, for example, no new Democratic woman took a seat in the Ninety-seventh Congress. The Republican tide of 1980 had totally overwhelmed Democratic female (and male) candidates who were not incumbents. The tide, of course, swung in a different direction in 1992.

The emphasis in this latter discussion has been on the paucity of female candidates in the past and the possibilities for the future. But we must not forget that numbers of women have run, and a number have run and been successful. Some have even been the overwhelming favorite not only to win their party's nomination in an open seat district but to be victorious in the general election. Between 1968 and 1990, five women won their party's nomination either unopposed or by gathering over 60 percent of the vote in a primary and then winning over 55 percent of the vote in November. Three more did so in 1992. For example, in 1990, California state representative Maxine Waters, rated during the primary season by *Congressional Quarterly Weekly Report* (Beneson 1990) as "the heavy favorite in the four candidate primary" for the open Twenty-ninth District seat, won her primary with 89 percent of the vote. She faced only nominal Republican opposition in the general election in this overwhelmingly Democratic district, winning her House seat with 80 percent of the vote.

These success stories have research significance. Given all of the difficulties female candidates purportedly have faced, how did these women attain front-runner status, especially in districts dominated by their party? We can learn from these exceptional situations if we direct our attention to how women win. We should ask questions about fund-raising ability, for example. An exceptional recent case is Rosa DeLauro who in 1990, without ever having held public office, drove all potential primary opponents (and district convention contenders) from the race for the Democratic party nomination in Connecticut's Third District by having an indomitable organization and a large campaign treasury in the preliminary stages of the campaign.[3]

---

3. Prior to her candidacy for the House, DeLauro had been executive director of EMILY's List, an organization formed to raise money for female Democratic House and Senate candidates. She had also been chief of staff for U.S. Senator Christopher Dodd and came from a politically prominent New Haven family.

Other important questions include these winners' relations with their party organizations. Have they tended to come from strong party backgrounds? Were local parties relevant to their campaigns? Did their campaigns emerge from outside or in opposition to local party affairs? Investigating the exceptional female candidates' campaigns should enhance our understanding of winning characteristics and facilitative circumstances for women politicians.

CHAPTER 8

Women Members of Congress and Policy Representation

I think it's important for women in Congress to ensure equity for
women. . . . If we don't who will?
—Rep. Olympia J. Snowe, R-Maine

On October 8, 1991, seven Democratic female House members marched
across the Capitol and tried to enter the Senate Democrats' weekly policy
luncheon. Why? Because they believed the Senate was about to proceed with
the confirmation hearings of Clarence Thomas for U.S. Supreme Court justice
without allowing Oklahoma University law professor Anita Hill to testify
about the sexual harassment charges she had made against the judge. After the
extraordinary committee hearings were held in which both Professor Hill and
Judge Thomas testified before television cameras, the National Women's Political Caucus placed an ad in the *New York Times* posing the question "What
if?" "What if 14 women, instead of 14 men, had sat on the Senate Judiciary
Committee during the confirmation hearings of Clarence Thomas?" The ad
was accompanied by a picture of seven women sitting on the panel before
Judge Thomas.

What if more women were elected to national office? In what ways
would it matter? Women in public office stand as symbols for other women,
both enhancing their identification with the system and their ability to have
influence within it. This subjective sense of being involved and heard for
women in general alone makes the election of women to public office important because for so many years they were excluded from power. Because of
their distinctive attitudes, women lawmakers have also impacted on policy
outcomes, bringing substantive as well as descriptive importance to their
presence in public office.

Of greatest effect on the political system, however, is the representation
of women by women. The purposive activity of women within a legislative
body on behalf of women's interests in the polity through the initiation of

legislation to achieve equality is the single most significant aspect of women's presence as political leaders. After reviewing theoretical notions about representation in general and its specific application to women, and exploring attitudinal differences between the sexes as manifested in Congressional voting behavior, this chapter focuses on congresswomen's "acting for" women.

Making government more responsive to the needs and problems of women through the election of more women to public office has been a major goal of the contemporary women's rights movement. Feminists assume that by electing more women to public office, "women [will] represent other women, speak for women's interests, and change the content and direction of public policy" (Kelly, Saint-Germain, and Horn 1991). This study of women's campaigns and election to the national legislature concludes with an analysis of how women in Congress have perceived and performed the charge to act for women.

Theories of Representation and the Election of Women

The importance of electing more women to public office grows out of a belief that representative democracy demands that all citizens regardless of gender have an equal opportunity to participate in politics. Increased representation for women in elective and appointive positions of power is a matter of justice and equity, women's rights activists claim. Furthermore, "as role models for other women and children, women politicians can encourage the erosion of traditional and rigid sex roles" (Leader 1977). Thus, the numerical presence of women in the corridors of power is important for symbolic reasons, and this study of women and their experiences as candidates for Congress is significant for what it tells us about women gaining equity in the political system.

Demands for more women in public office go beyond the symbolic nature of representation, however, to include substantive concerns as well. The policies officeholders enact are a crucial aspect of the representative process (Pitkin 1967). Activists argue that women in public office will make a difference in the policies that are made and the way they are formulated. The 1992 election, for example, was about the substantive as well as the symbolic difference women in policy roles would make. Women candidates campaigned on the theme that their presence in the legislature would make a difference in the policies and processes of that institution.

Why should we expect women to have a differential impact on the workings of the legislature? Some have argued that differences in the voting records of male and female members of Congress are an extension of policy differences that exist between the sexes within the general public (as discussed in chapter 2). Further, many women elected to office are likely to have been motivated by the feminist movement and thus espouse egalitarian policies.

More theoretically, some feminists think natural differences in aptitude or moral outlook between the sexes will predict distinctive behaviors as officeholders. Ecofeminists, for example, believe that only women's values can save the planet from ecological disaster. To them, women and men embody respectively the values of peace and war, nurturing and destruction. Others view differences that exist between men and women as a result of different experiences. Gilligan has claimed that it is the social experiences of boys and girls that lead them to develop different moral outlooks. Ruddick has suggested that distinctive ways of thinking have arisen out of the work that mothers do. (See Bryson 1992, for a discussion of these theories.) Gender role socialization may predispose women to certain styles of leadership according to these latter theories. Distinctive natures or distinctive experiences contribute to distinct behavior in power situations for men and women these theories tell us.

Potentially, women legislators can impact policy making in a number of ways. These ways include affecting the operational process of the system, influencing policy outcomes, and reshaping the agenda to include women's concerns. Studies have empirically tested these ideas.

Women may change the way government works through distinct operating styles and different ways of conceptualizing problems. Women tend to practice a different type of politics, to use Lyn Kathlene's term (1992). She reports that female legislators in Colorado's House of Representatives conceptualized problems differently from their male colleagues. For example, they took more comprehensive and innovative approaches to public policy concerns, especially in the areas of education and family/children's issues. They more often targeted spending directly to help people rather than to fund indirect commissions and regulatory bodies and proposed more accountable policy solutions (1992). She found a "gendered approach to politics." (See also Kathlene, Clarke, and Fox 1991.)

In addition, the Center for the American Woman and Politics (CAWP) 1991 survey of male and female state legislators showed that "when compared with their male colleagues, women are more likely to bring citizens into the process, . . . to opt for government in public view rather than government behind closed doors and are more responsive to groups previously denied full access to the policy making process" (Dodson and Carroll 1991). Women in their study were not only affecting policies. They were transforming the way the system worked.

As more women become successful as legislators and executives and as sex role socialization diminishes, women's ways of making policy should influence the whole policy-making process. Men may learn from women. We can envision women's ways becoming more a part of men's operating styles. Women's ways of politicking may lead to new norms of lawmaking in legislatures, leading to a less distinctively gendered nature to the policy-making process, a process that will have become transformed.

Gender and Liberalism

Beyond affecting the practice of politics, women also may have distinctive political attitudes that are reflected in their voting behavior in the legislative body. The behavioral consequences of distinctive attitudes have received scholarly attention through studies of legislative voting behavior. Primarily, researchers have sought to determine whether female legislators vote in a more liberal direction than male representatives. The potential for greater liberalism on the part of female politicians follows from studies of differences between the sexes in the general public, and from the politics of women's rights activists who believe that government action can create greater equality for women in society. Poole and Ziegler (1985) concluded from their analyses of voting behavior in the U.S. House and Senate that "all things being equal, the more women there are in the House and Senate, the more liberal those institutions will become."

A number of other studies have found congresswomen acting from a more liberal political ideology than congressmen. In an analysis of the Eighty-eighth and Eighty-ninth Congresses, Gehlen found that female representatives supported liberal initiatives such as the Civil Rights Act of 1964 more than did their male colleagues, and that more female than male members cosponsored the Equal Rights Amendment (1977). Examining the voting records of female members of the U.S. House from 1961 to 1975, Frankovic reported congresswomen becoming more cohesive over time in their voting records, and at least in one year (1974) their voting behavior was significantly different from their male counterparts. She concluded that a feminist coalition—if not truly "feminist" in orientation, at least a coalition of feminine members of the House—had come into existence in the early years of the second feminist movement (1977:529). Leader, in her study of liberalism and feminism among members of Congress in this time period, also concluded that women representatives were more liberal and more feminist than male representatives on the whole, but party rather than sex was a stronger predictor of voting behavior (1977).

Welch (1985) has provided us with the most extensive longitudinal analysis of the voting patterns of men and women in Congress. Examining the voting records of male and female members of the House from 1972 through 1980 on issues in which the conservative coalition was present, as defined by *Congressional Quarterly,*[1] she found that women voted in a more liberal direction, even after taking party affiliation into account; but differences decreased over time and were negligible among northern Democrats. The decrease resulted primarily from women members becoming less liberal over time relative to men. The different constituency bases of men and women representatives accounted for a good deal of the "gender gap" in the members' voting patterns rather than sex per se. Women tended to be elected from particular types of districts that were more supportive of liberal policies.

More women were elected to the House in the 1980s; the gender gap prompted attention to policies of special concern to women (Thompson 1988), and women members of Congress formed their own organization to lobby for women's issues. To what extent have they maintained a distinctive liberal ideology in their overall voting behavior? Welch's analysis is replicated here for the 100th, 101st, and 102d Congresses (1987 through 1992). In these Congresses, conservative coalition scores were compiled separately for each session of each Congress. Thus, six individual rankings are used for analysis. Since greater female liberalism may be a result of different party or constituency bases, I control for party and constituency factors through regression analyses to determine the independent effect of sex. Constituency variables are those that were employed in chapters 3 and 7: percentage of the district's population that is black, median family income of the district, percentage of the district that is urban, and region (South and non-South). Do sex differences in voting behavior remain after taking into account the fact that women may disproportionately represent particular types of districts?

Table 8.1 presents male-female differences in conservative coalition support scores under a variety of conditions. Women representatives were not substantially less conservative than men in the latter part of the 1980s and early 1990s. On a scale from 0 to 100, men voted about 9 points more conservatively than women. Both groups fell on the conservative end of the scale, although female representatives, with an average score of 51.36, barely exceeded the midpoint. The average score for the male members was 60.27. Democratic women were the most liberal group, as has been found in previous studies, with an average score of 35.82, followed by Democratic male representatives who had an average score of 41.94. Republican women were much more conservative, with an average score of 73.73, although significantly less so than their male colleagues who averaged 88.03 on the conservative coalition support scale. The lesser conservatism of Republican women compared

---

1. The conservative coalition is measured as a vote in which a majority of southern Democrats sided with a majority of Republicans against a majority of northern Democrats.

TABLE 8.1.   Effect of Sex on Conservative Coalition
Support Scores, 1987–92

	Difference (Male-Female)	r
House Members		
All	8.91	.06**
Democrats	6.12	.04
Southern Democrats	−10.62	.08
Northern Democrats	4.56	.04
Republicans	14.30	.28***
Year		
1987	3.88	.02
1988	2.18	.01
1989	5.66	.04
1990	9.00	.07
1991	16.93	.12*
1992	14.27	.11*

*Significant at the .05 level.
**Significant at the .01 level.
***Significant at the .000 level.

with their male colleagues drove the gender difference that was present during this period. They were both substantially and statistically less conservative than their male counterparts. While northern Democratic women, who made up the bulk of the female Democratic members of Congress in this period, were approximately 5 points more liberal than northern Democratic men, southern Democratic women were somewhat more conservative than their male colleagues, and even more conservative than Republican female representatives as a group.[2]

While Welch found the gap in the liberalism of male and female members of the House lessening over time, it widened between the 100th and the 102d Congress, surpassing in 1991 the smallest gap of the earlier period. The gap began to widen because Democratic women exhibited greater liberalism over these years while the their male counterparts remained static in their level of conservatism. Democratic women scored an average fifty-six points in support of the conservative coalition in 1987, but their score declined each year to a low of thirty-one points in 1991. Republican women did not decrease their support for the conservative coalition, but their presence in the Congress declined in 1991, while Democratic women increased their numbers, helping

2. One would expect to see a sharp decline in the conservatism of southern Democratic congresswomen as a result of the 1992 election. Six Democratic women were newly elected from that region all of whom ran on fairly liberal platforms.

to account for the growth in the gender gap in liberalism in the first session of that Congress.

Party and Constituency Factors

Chapter 7 showed that districts electing women to the U.S. House at the end of the 1980s were more urban, had a larger percentage of blacks, were more liberal, and were above average in family incomes. The female members' slightly greater liberalism during this period may be an artifact of constituency bases rather than sex: that is, women tended to be elected from districts with a more liberal political outlook, fostering a liberal voting record in accord with the ideology of their constituencies rather than an ideology emanating for their gender.

Table 8.2 shows the set of regression coefficients including constituency characteristics for the three Congresses and for the three distinct party/region subcategories. Women have continued to vote in a slightly more liberal direction than men, but constituency characteristics explain a good portion of this difference. Republicans continued to exhibit strong gender differences even controlling for constituency factors. Party, however, was the dominant factor in explaining differences in support for the conservative coalition. Democrats are much more liberal than Republicans.

Before we conclude that the presence of women in Congress in the waning years of the twentieth century made only a minor contribution to the liberalism of that body, it is important to note that the conservative coalition appeared on very few votes and had lost much of its political impact on most legislation. It had become "little more than an academic phenomenon in Congress" (Rubin 1991).

TABLE 8.2. Predictors of Conservative Coalition Support, 1987–92

Predictor[a]	All	Southern Democrats	Northern Democrats	Republicans
Region	.320**			.28**
Party	−.590**			
Percentage of population black	−.090**	−.03	−.150**	−.11*
Percentage of population urban	−.240**	−.60**	−.330**	.04
Median income	.009	.30**	−.001	−.20**
Sex	−.020	.12**	−.002	−.25**
R^2	.590	.29	.180	.18
N	2,164	355	936	870

Republican = 0; Democrat = 1; men = 0; women = 1.
[a]Standardized regression coefficients.
*Significant at the .01 level.
**Significant at the .000 level.

The "endangered species" nature of the conservative coalition by the 102d Congress suggests that it is no longer "the best single measure of congressional conservatism" (Welch 1985:128), although important to this study for longitudinal comparative purposes. The *National Journal*'s annual vote ratings provide a comprehensive alternative measure of political ideology. The *National Journal* compiles overall liberal and conservative vote ratings using a composite index of votes on social, economic, and foreign policy issues. In 1992, fifty key votes were used to construct the index. To supplement the analysis of the gender differences in conservative coalition support, the voting scores of male and female representatives in the second session of the 102d Congress (1992) are compared on the *National Journal*'s liberalism rating.

With 100 being a perfect liberal score across social, economic, and foreign policy issues, female representatives scored an average 62.33 points on the composite measure of liberalism, and male representatives scored 49.21 points, a difference of 13 points. Once again female Democrats were the most liberal with an average score of 75.32, followed by male Democrats with an average score of 66.26. A large gap, then, existed between the parties. Female Republicans scored an average 34.91, while male Republicans scored 22.16. Controlling for party and constituency factors in a multiple regression analysis cut the impact of sex in half, but a statistically significant difference remained. (Data not shown.)[3]

These data show women to be a continuing liberal influence in Congress as theory has suggested. Party is the main divide on political ideology in the U.S. Congress, and women within the parties reflect that divide; but Democratic women enhance the distinctiveness of the parties, making the Democratic party more liberal, while Republican women, being less conservative than their male colleagues, mute the difference and help push the body in a more liberal direction. In terms of general political ideology, female representatives as a group continue to influence the policy preferences of Congress from what they would be if only men served.

Women's Issues

What matters for feminists is that the presence of women in power not only affect public policy generally but initiate policies especially beneficial to women. Women's presence should have the greatest impact when issues of special concern to women are being debated. Conservative coalition support

---

3. The standardized regression coefficient between sex and liberalism was .12, $p > .01$; controlling for party and constituency characteristics decreased the standardized regression coefficient of sex to .05, $p > .05$.

ratings capture the general liberalism of male and female members of Congress. The question of the extent to which women legislators have espoused a distinctive feminist political orientation remains to be considered. Have congresswomen made a difference in voting on women's issues?

Beginning with the Ninety-fifth Congress (1977–78), the National Women's Political Caucus has compiled a voting chart on women's issues. Issues included in the chart for the Ninety-fifth Congress were equal representation of men and women on the National Commission on Neighborhoods, tax deductions for use of a home for day-care services, flextime for federal employees, the Humphrey-Hawkins Full Employment Bill, family planning, extension of the food stamp program, federal funding for abortion, raising the minimum wage, and gay rights. In the 101st Congress (1989–90), the last Congress for which NWPC voting scores are available, women's issues included federal funding for child care programs, an increased minimum wage, family and medical leave, the Civil Rights Act of 1990, and abortion. In the following analysis, the voting records of male and female members of the House on women's issues are compared in the 100th and the 101st Congresses, as compiled by the National Women's Political Caucus.

On a scale from 0 to 100 with 100 being a perfect score in support for women, female members of the House were about twelve points more supportive of women's issues than male members, scoring an average sixty-five points compared with fifty-three for the men, a substantial and statistically significant difference (table 8.3). This difference occurred because female Republicans were so much less conservative than their male Republican colleagues, whereas male Democrats were slightly more supportive of women's rights legislation than their female counterparts. Female Republicans scored an average fifty-five points on the National Women's Political Caucus voting record contrasted with only eighteen points for Republican males. Northern

TABLE 8.3.   Effect of Sex on Women's Rights
Support Scores, 1987–90

Members	Difference (Male-Female)	*r*
All	12.19	.07*
Democrats	−2.88	.03
Southern Democrats	−11.39	.08
Northern Democrats	−1.66	.02
Republicans	37.02	.37**
100th Congress	8.36	.06
101st Congress	15.50	.10

*Significant at the .05 level.
**Significant at the .000 level.

TABLE 8.4. Predictors of Women's Rights Support, 1987–90

Predictor[a]	All	Southern Democrats	Northern Democrats	Republicans
Region	−.16***			−.29***
Party	.72***			
Percentage of population black	−.08**	.10	.13*	.19**
Percentage of population urban	−.12***	.27**	.29***	−.04
Median income	.03	−.05	.13*	.10
Sex	.08***	−.12	−.05	.35***
R^2	.61	.09	.15	.20
N	866	139	373	353

[a]Standardized regression coefficients.
*Significant at the .05 level.
**Significant at the .01 level.
***Significant at the .000 level.

Democratic male and female representatives were equally supportive and the most favorable group on women's issues, scoring an average eighty points on the NWPC voting record. (Southern Democratic males were actually more supportive of women's rights as measured by the NWPC voting record than southern Democratic females, scoring an average sixty-six points on the scale compared with fifty-two points for the women.)

Table 8.4 presents the standardized regression coefficients for the more complete model of factors affecting support for women's rights issues. Even after controlling for party, region, and constituency characteristics, sex remains a statistically significant predictor of support for women's rights issues in Congress. Being a woman increased support for the women's rights issues eleven points after controlling for the other independent variables. Party and region are the major factors accounting for variation in voting records on women's issues, with sex and the urbanness of the district playing a slightly smaller role. Only the wealth of the district plays a minor role in predicting votes on women's issues.

The National Women's Political Caucus ratings on women's issues are supplemented in the second session of the 102nd Congress (1992) with an analysis of votes on issues included in the *Women's Voting Guide,* a publication issued by the Women's Political Action Group for the 1992 election. Members of the House were scored on votes on five "representative bills" affecting women.[4]

Women members of the House had an average support score of 90 percent on these issues compared with 66 percent for male members. Female Demo-

---

4. The bills were the Family and Medical Leave Act, Labor-HHS Conference Report, the veto override attempt for Labor-HHS, civil rights, and the NIH Revitalization Act.

crats scored an average 95 percent; male Democrats scored 86 percent. The chasm was great among Republicans. The nine female Republicans had an average score of 80 percent compared with 35 percent for male Republicans. In these three Congresses, the presence of women made an even greater difference for feminism than their presence did for overall liberalism, although constituencies mediated those effects in both domains. The difference came primarily from the greater support of Republican women on women's rights' issues contrasted with the opposition of Republican male members. However, they did not equal the pro-feminist stances of nonsouthern Democratic men and women, just as earlier studies have found. In order to have a distinctive voice on roll call votes, issues affecting women's roles in society must be placed on the agenda and nurtured through the legislative process. We now turn to the role of women in that crucial process.

Affecting the Agenda for Women

Influencing the Congressional agenda on issues regarding women's place in society is perhaps the most far-reaching of all the ways in which women legislators can affect the policy-making process. Making government more responsive to women's needs by electing more women to office has been a major goal of the contemporary women's rights movement. Having women members in Congress to reshape the agenda for women is central to feminist interests.

Voting on legislation of particular importance to women is one way of influencing policy making on behalf of women. The legislative process, however, is about far more than votes on final passage of a bill. The floor stage is the culmination of a very complex process that favors the nonpassage of legislation. Before feminist issues are voted on, they must be drafted, promoted, and shepherded through the committee system. Members of the legislature must define their legislative agenda and the issues they will emphasize. It is the purposive activity of representatives involving sponsorship and direction of legislation that is crucial to policy representation. Bringing issues to the agenda that have previously been suppressed or overlooked is one element of power (Cobb and Elder 1972).

Studies have shown female state legislators as having acted purposively on behalf of women. They have had distinct issue priorities and have been more active on women's rights legislation than male legislators. The Center for the American Woman and Politics' recent survey of male and female state legislators, reported in *Reshaping the Agenda* (Dodson and Carroll 1991), confirmed this idea. Women officeholders were more feminist and more liberal than men in their policy attitudes. Women were more likely to give top priority to women's rights policies and to public policies related to their

priorities of the caucus in order to capture women members of Congress conceptualization of women's issues and to assess legislative progress on them. An examination of the legislative priorities and bills endorsed by the Congressional Caucus for Women's Issues provides a basis for understanding the substantive nature of the difference women members of Congress have made for women. We want to know not only the extent to which women representatives have acted for women, but of what those actions have consisted.

Individual female (and male) legislators have championed specific pieces of legislation aimed at addressing gender inequality. For example, Martha Griffiths (D-Mich.) forced Congress to include "sex" in the Civil Rights Act of 1964. Other major pieces of legislation passed in those early years, such as the Equal Pay Act, the Equal Credit Act, and the Educational Equity Act. But accomplishments have expanded since the formation in 1977 of the Women's Congressional Caucus. In 1981, the organization changed its name to the Congressional Caucus for Women's Issues (CCWI) and admitted congressmen as members.[5] However, men cannot hold caucus office, serve on the executive committee, vote on policy matters, or elect officers. Thus, it is the women members who set the agenda. Initially, the caucus focused on sponsoring executive briefings, introducing minor pieces of legislation, writing letters to the administration urging more female appointees, and building camaraderie among the female members. Its greatest success in these early years was the passage of a bill in 1978 to extend the time in which the Equal Rights Amendment could be considered for ratification by the states. Caucus members launched an intensive drive to build support for extension. As described by Irwin Gertzog:

> The Caucus had not met and determined that it would consciously devote its attention to passing the Resolution. No such formal decision had to be made. The ERA was one of a handful of measures on which all Caucus members shared enthusiastic, even passionate, agreement. Some were prolife, others prochoice on the abortion issue. And they might disagree on how much federal money to spend to aid wives who are victims of spousal abuse. But the ERA was the litmus test of whether you were for women or against them, and only four congresswomen expressed reservations about unrestricted extension of the time limit, three of whom were not Caucus members. Only one of the four, Marilyn Lloyd, did not vote for final passage. She was "paired against" the Resolution. (1984:204)

---

5. See Gertzog 1984 for an extended discussion of the development and transformation of the caucus.

Expanding into the Congressional Caucus for Women's Issues allowed the caucus to "transform itself into a large and effective body dedicated to legislative achievements" (Thompson 1984:16). The CCWI has aspired to enact major legislation. It has sought to "perform legislative leadership functions, linking members to outside groups, forming legislative proposals, planning strategy, and mobilizing like-minded members for floor debates, amendments, or votes" (Thompson 1985a). According to Thompson, "the Congresswomen's Caucus filled a gap in the representative structures of Congress by dealing with an issue which was of public concern but for which no formal congressional structure could formulate a response" (1984:2).

Each Congress, the CCWI adopts a set of legislative priorities. It also has a formal process for endorsing legislation introduced by its members. A description of the major agenda items of the caucus tells us how the presence of women has substantively transformed lawmaking regarding women. Opportunities for women in our society would be significantly altered if all of the priorities and endorsed bills of the caucus were enacted into law and implemented. (This presupposes that legal remedies that are liberal feminist goals will create greater equality for women across race and class lines.)

The CCWI has been constrained by the need to achieve consensus among its members, the effort to maintain itself as a bipartisan organization, the limited attention members of the House can pay to any one issue, and the many hurdles a piece of legislation must pass before being enacted into law. As explained by Rep. Olympia Snowe (R-Maine) "We try to select issues that generally will not divide our members. For instance, we don't force abortion as an issue for the caucus.[6] We sit down and develop strategies and priorities to get as many of the statutes through Congress as possible" (Gamerakian 1985).

Types of issues addressed and the way in which they are presented have also varied over this period with the ideological makeup of the female membership in the various Congresses and the political realities of the times. Although the 1980s was an era of downsizing national initiatives, the gender gap in women's and men's attitudes and votes that received so much attention in 1983 and 1984 made the Congress of those years a particularly promising one for promoting women's issues. However, while that Congress was the "gender gap" Congress, the next Congress (the Ninety-nineth) became "the

---

6. In 1993, the caucus finally made abortion rights an agenda item. As a result of the 1992 election, nearly all members of the caucus's executive committee were pro-choice. But even though some members were not pro-choice in earlier Congresses, the caucus had made overturning of the gag rule, an administration policy which restricted family planning providers at federally funded clinics from providing information and referrals about abortion, a priority item. A consensus existed among caucus members as to the importance of family planning issues regardless of personal feelings about abortion.

family" Congress after Ronald Reagan's landslide reelection in 1984. As Thompson has explained it, "If women's economic issues were to make any progress in the 99th Congress, a new strategy would have to be found to replace the gender gap approach. Instead of describing legislation as for women, liberals could describe it as 'pro-family' seizing that politically popular label from conservatives and the religious right" (1993).

The Congressional Caucus
for Women's Issues' Priorities

> As the Caucus' second decade begins, we are giving major emphasis to the intertwined issues of work and family. By focusing on a range of issues, such as dependent care, pay equity, and equal credit, we hope to make possible an improved economic, social and personal balance for American women and their families.
> —Representative Olympia Snowe, (R-Maine), cochair of CCWI

The Economic Equity Act

Achieving economic equity for women by helping them "to balance their work and family roles" has been the caucus's focus in the 1980s. In 1981, the caucus teamed up with key senators to introduce the Economic Equity Act (EEA), a package of tax, retirement, and child care/support bills designed to secure women's economic rights. That act, which grew to be a twenty-four-point package of bills, came to "constitute the heart of the caucus's legislative agenda" (Rix 1991). Although originally introduced with some thought to its being a means of implementing the proposed Equal Rights Amendment, the EEA took on a prominence of its own when the requisite number of states did not ratify the ERA to become part of the Constitution. The "feminization of poverty," as highlighted by the U.S. Civil Rights Commission 1982 report— "A Growing Crisis: Disadvantaged Women and their Children," which showed that women were a disproportionate number of America's poor in the early 1980s—served as an incentive for pushing the Economic Equity Act.

Appendix A presents the titles and individual bills that have become part of the EEA. The first measures passed under this omnibus bill in the 1991–92 sessions increased the spousal Individual Retirement Account (IRA), established a sliding scale for the dependent care tax credit, prohibited states from treating military pensions as communal property in divorce cases, and lifted estate tax penalties on rural women inheriting farms.

By the 102d Congress (1991–92), economic equity meant expanded nontraditional job training for women, the provision of educational and professional opportunities in science and mathematics, increased procurement opportunities for women business owners, establishment of a commission to investigate ways to break the "glass ceiling and allow women to advance through management ranks," and changes in the Social Security system so that women would not be penalized for taking time off from the work force. Overall, the EEA consisted of 114 pieces of legislation between 1981 and 1992; some were bills that were introduced more than once. In all, 89 different measures have been initiated as part of the Economic Equity Act.

As the EEA has developed over recent Congresses, the focus of the bills that constitute it has expanded from being primarily equalitarian in character to being affirmative in nature. Equalitarian measures:

> [seek] to elevate women to positions of equality with men in the marketplace, government, and the academy as well as in the public consciousness. . . . Affirmative measures facilitate women's claims to the resources and recognition normally offered men as a matter of course and tend to free them from the social, economic, and cultural constraints under which they have customarily labored. Affirmative measures are those which asservate the importance of women's role in history and society, which support and reinforce women's claims to economic independence, and which assist them in overcoming the social and cultural constraints imposed up them by a male-dominated society. (Gertzog 1984:143)

Early legislation stressed pensions (both for employees and homemakers), benefits in divorce, child support, and inheritance taxes, all measures seeking equality in resources. In later Congresses, resources were being given to women to establish and maintain their own businesses, gain skills in nontraditional employment, overcome the "glass ceiling," and achieve pay equity, all of which would advance women's position in the public realm of society.

When first introduced, the EEA was seen as "a package of bills which would cost the federal government little while improving economic prospects of millions of women" (Thompson 1988:22). But as it has expanded, so have the remedies sought to achieve equity and status change. The policy methods employed in the various bills introduced as part of the EEA to overcome inequities involving women can be categorized into eight types: positive regulations, negative regulations, taxing policy, studies, funding, programs in the federal government, commissions/councils, and symbolic acts. Positive regulations involve federal laws that establish opportunities for women which had been either explicitly closed to them or implicitly limited because of their life situation. Pension reforms are a prime example of these types of policies. Negative regulations eliminate discrimination based on sex. Taxing policy has primarily sought to provide equity based on women's marital and work status within the family. A few bills have called for the undertaking of a study to determine the affect of federal policy on a particular aspect of women's lives and the extent to which a problem exists. Funding has involved grants to states, communities, and groups, and the establishment of demonstration projects in a variety of areas. Programs and commissions are activities set up within federal agencies to work on a particular problem, and symbolic acts have been congressional resolutions. Table 8.5 presents the breakdown in the number of bills that fall into each category. A plurality of the remedies have been positive regulations, followed, interestingly given budget constraints of this era, by funding actions. Overall, a broad range of types of policies has been initiated; thirty of these policies—mainly funding items and positive regulations—have been enacted (the starred items in app. A).

A new piece of legislation in the realm of economic equity, the Unre-numerated Work Act, was first introduced by Rep. Barbara-Rose Collins, a single mother, at the end of the 102d Congress. She reintroduced it in the 103d Congress. It would require the Commissioner of the Bureau of Labor Statistics to conduct nationwide, time-use surveys of all unpaid work per-formed in the United States. The surveys would include, according to the bill, "household work, work related to child care and other care services, agri-cultural work, work related to food production, work related to family busi-ness, and volunteer work." It would require the Commerce Department to include all unpaid work performed in the United States in its calculations of the nation's gross domestic product. This bill is part of an international move-ment to add housework to the gross national products of countries as a way of elevating the status of such work and of those who perform it (Odum 1992). This bill has a traditional element to it in that rather than changing women's roles, it makes their homemaking roles more valuable (although it is aimed at the value of housework no matter who does it). Nonetheless, it is a revolution-ary way of evaluating the economy.

TABLE 8.5.   Federal Remedies Mandated
by Economic Equity Act Bills

Remedy	Number	Enacted
Positive Regulations	37	13
Funding	16	10
Taxing Policy	14	4
Negative Regulations	7	—
Studies	6	2
Programs	3	—
Commissions/Councils	4	—
Symbols	2	1

The Equal Rights Amendment

In addition to economic equity, the Equal Rights Amendment was an early priority of the caucus, as discussed above, and remained so through 1985. Indeed, in the Ninety-seventh and Ninety-eighth Congresses, the ERA was assigned the status of bill number 1. However, it ceased to be a priority after its defeat in 1985 on the floor of the House under a special rule. The ERA continues to be introduced in every Congress, but it no longer receives much attention. None of the congresswomen reporting for *The American Woman 1990–1991* mentioned the Equal Rights Amendment as a priority activity in the 101st Congress.

New Priorities

In addition to economic issues, issues concerning health and violence against women became major priorities of the caucus in the latter part of the 1980s. For example, Rep. Cardiss Collins (D-Ill.) reported that "because of my concern about a significant increase in the number of women afflicted with uterine cancer, on the first day of the 101st Congress I introduced legislation to require Medicare Part B coverage for routine Pap smear tests. The catastrophic health care insurance bill that was signed into law in 1988 included my amendment requiring Medicare to cover mammography/breast cancer screenings for women over age 65."

The Women's Health Equity Act (WHEA) was first introduced late in the 101st Congress and several of its measures were quickly enacted into law. WHEA was a legislative response to a 1990 General Accounting Office report that found that the National Institutes of Health (NIH) had failed to enforce its own policy calling for the inclusion of women in clinical trials, and to an internal NIH report documenting the need to increase funding on women's health research (*Update*, February 5, 1993). The Caucus had actually focused attention on the issue six years earlier when, in 1985, it released a General Accounting Office audit showing that $7 billion a year in federal dollars was being spent on health-care research that largely ignored women.

When first introduced into Congress in 1990, it was a title of the Economic Equity Act. But when reintroduced in the 102d Congress, WHEA was separated from the EEA and made an individual omnibus package of twenty-two bills divided into the areas of research, services and prevention. The package sets a broad agenda for addressing a number of important women's health issues including breast and ovarian cancer, osteoporosis, women and AIDS, contraception and infertility, health and social services for parenting and pregnant teens, prevention of infertility through improved screening and treatment of sexually transmitted diseases, and Medicaid coverage for mammography and pap smear screening.

The Violence Against Women Act also was first introduced in 1990. This act would increase funding for police activities designed to reduce rape and domestic violence, establish services for victims of rape and domestic violence, and provide training for police, prosecutors, and judges in dealing with crimes against women. The bill would also make gender-based violence a federal civil rights violation. Several provisions were incorporated into other bills that became law during the 102d Congress. They included reauthorization of the Family Violence Prevention and Services Act, the only federal program designed to specifically aid victims of domestic violence; requirements that universities and colleges develop campus sexual assault programs; programs to train judges in cases involving domestic violence; and development of a model antistalking law that individual states could adopt. An expanded Violence Against Women Act is a priority of the Congressional Caucus for Women's Issues in the 103d Congress.

In the 103d Congress, the caucus has introduced a fourth package of issues, the Gender Equity in Education Act, consisting of nine bills. In contrast to the other omnibus measures, the Caucus is attempting to enact all of the titles that comprise the Act as one piece of legislation. This measure is aimed primarily at elementary and secondary education curricula. It would create an Office of Women's Equity in the Department of Education which would be charged with promoting and coordinating women's equity policies, programs, activities, and initiatives in all federal education programs and offices. The nine bills of the Gender Equity in Education Act would mandate research, and establish grants and demonstration programs in the areas of sexual harassment in the schools, math and science education, equitable treatment of boys and girls in the classroom, dropout prevention for pregnant and parenting teens, and child abuse education support services for at-risk youth. These bills would also require equity in data collection and disclosure of participation rates and program support expenditures in college athletic programs.

Family and Medical Leave

Job leaves for family members is the issue priority of the caucus that perhaps has produced the most publicity and conflict in recent Congresses. In the words of Rep. Nancy Johnson (R-Conn.), "Today's parents need to know that they can take time off, not only in family emergencies, but also for the school play, the parent-teacher conference, or the chicken pox—the important events in a child's life." Rep. Pat Schroeder (D-Colo.) first introduced a federally mandated family and medical leave policy in Congress in 1985. Eight years later it became law when, as one of the first bills passed by the legislature in the 103d Congress, it was signed by President Bill Clinton.[7] The Family and

---

7. President Bush had vetoed an earlier bill that had passed the House and Senate.

Medical Leave Act provides workers in companies with more than fifty employees up to twelve weeks of unpaid leave each year to care for a newborn or newly adopted child, to care for a seriously ill family member, or to recover from their own serious illness. When first initiated by Representative Schroeder as the Parental and Disability Leave Act in 1985, the legislation would have required employers to provide at least four months of job-protected leave for parents to stay home with a newborn, newly adopted, or seriously ill child and six months of job-protected leave for pregnancy-related and other temporary disabilities. It also would have established a commission to study and make recommendations within two years for a national paid parental and disability leave policy. This bill would have covered all businesses, with no small employer exemption. The history of this legislation demonstrates the possibilities as well as the limits of the legislative process as an arena for change in women's lives. The exclusion of employers with less than fifty workers in the final bill exempts the vast majority of businesses, and because only unpaid leave was mandated it may do little to help low-income individuals. But given the cultural bias in the United States against interference by the government in matters between employers and employees, the passage of this bill was significant.

Civil Rights

The caucus also has had to push civil rights legislation in response to Supreme Court decisions that limited the scope of earlier laws. The Supreme Court's decision in *Grove City* v. *Bell* in 1984 made passage of the Civil Rights Restoration Act a priority of the caucus. In *Grove City,* the Supreme Court had ruled that enforcement of Title IX of the Education Amendments of 1972, which had banned discrimination on the basis of sex in institutions receiving federal aid, was limited to the specific program or activity within the institution that directly received federal financial assistance, not to the entire institution. Congress in 1988 enacted PL 100–259 over President's Reagan's veto, effectively overturning the Supreme Court's decision and restoring the scope of the discrimination ban.

In 1989, the Supreme Court issued six rulings that limited the scope of two major U.S. laws dealing with employment discrimination: Section 1981 of a Reconstruction-era law, and Title VII of the 1964 Civil Rights Act. The Court's rulings had made it harder for women and minorities to prove that they had suffered discrimination. In response, the Civil Rights Act of 1991 made it easier for workers to sue their employers, and for the first time it allowed money damages for victims of harassment and other intentional discrimination based on sex, religion, or disability. However, it capped the amount of damages women could collect in employment discrimination cases, which angered women's rights activists.

In addition to expanding into new areas, the caucus has had to continuously monitor the reauthorization and financing of programs previously enacted. And it coordinated with other groups to produce major legislation. The Family Support Act of 1988, which reformed the welfare system, and the 1991 Child Care Act are major initiatives in which the caucus and its members were principal coalition partners.

This review of the legislative priorities of the caucus shows both the increased prominence of feminist issues, and the constraints on those who would change the system. Constraints have been imposed by the ideology of Congress and a legislative process that not only works to make the implementation of new legislation difficult, but also requires that seemingly settled issues be revisited with new authorizations and new funding, sometimes in an unfavorable climate. But the caucus has not been deterred in its efforts to achieve equity for women, as exemplified by the range of areas it has tackled and the variety of legislative remedies it has proposed. It continues to expand its efforts on behalf of women.

Conclusion

The election of women to Congress has profoundly affected representation in its many facets. It makes a difference whether more women are elected to leadership positions in our society as symbols of what females can achieve. Consider that when asked what the best thing about being a girl is, middle school female students have difficulty articulating an answer. They are apt to draw a blank. When asked what is best about being a boy, boys are likely to reply "not being a girl," according to Professor Cynthia Mee of the University of Wisconsin-Platteville, who has interviewed two thousand middle school students in five states. By the eighth grade, girls and boys both perceived men as having more power.

Mee has written that "The average middle school girl thinks that boys can do more now, will be able to do more as they grow up, have higher-status career expectations and will probably get paid more" (Dorscher 1993). Her study amplified the results of the American Association of University Women's 1991 study "Shortchanging Girls, Shortchanging America," which found that as girls and boys grow older, both experience a significant loss of self-esteem in a variety of areas; however, the loss was more dramatic and had a more long-lasting effect on girls. Sixty percent of elementary school girls said they were "happy the way I am"; over the next eight years, their self-esteem fell 31 percentage points, with only 29 percent of high school girls saying they were happy with themselves; 46 percent of the high school boys retained their high self-esteem (AAUW 1991:4). Girls emerged from adolescence with a poor self-image, constrained views of their future, and much less confidence about themselves and their abilities. Thus, if for no other reason than to provide role models for girls, having women in leadership positions is extraordinarily important. But women in Congress have not just served as symbols. They have acted to help girls gain skills and enhance their self-esteem through the introduction in the legislature of the Educational Equity Act and the nurturing of that bill through the process to enactment as law. The members of the Congressional Caucus for Women's Issues have seen that it has been reauthorized and its funding renewed. In the 103d Congress they have renewed their efforts on behalf of girls with the introduction of the Gender Equity in Education Act.

A clear connection exists between the election of women to office and pro-women public policies, as this chapter has shown. Women in national leadership positions today tend to be articulate feminists. This was especially notable in 1992. Women candidates took clear feminist stands according to a survey conducted by *Ms.* magazine (see Kathlene and Lenart 1993). An overwhelming number of women congressional candidates took feminist positions (87 percent of the survey respondents),[8] and those women who were the most feminist and most liberal were the most likely to win, regardless of party.

Twenty-eight women were newly elected to the U.S. Congress in November, 1992—four in the U.S. Senate and twenty-four in the U.S. House of Representatives. These women have established a legislative agenda to promote issues of special concern to women and families. On December 7, all of the twenty-four new female House members held a press conference calling for full financing of Head Start early-childhood education programs, passage of a family and medical leave bill, codification of legal abortion, and extension of federal laws against sexual harassment to Congress. (All of the first-term women are supporters of abortion rights.) One of the first pieces of legislation passed by the 103d Congress and signed into law by President Clinton was the Family and Medical Leave Act, which, as discussed above, had been a priority of the Congressional Caucus for Women's Issues since 1985.

Women in Congress also have been active on behalf of women in the early stages of the 103d Congress. Thirty-three percent of the bills female Democrats introduced into the House and 30 percent of the bills introduced by female Republicans concerned women and children's issues. Forty-seven percent of the speeches female Democratic Senators made were in this domain as were 30 percent of those made by Democratic congresswomen and 35 percent of those made by Republican congresswomen (Boles 1993). These studies of women candidates and officeholders indicate that women leaders have had a

---

8. Of the 159 U.S. Senate and House candidates surveyed, 129 (81 percent) responded.

clear impact on public policy. They have adopted a strong progressive agenda aimed at achieving greater equality for women in society as far as that is possible through the legal system. The election of more women has affected the representational nature of Congress both descriptively and substantively.

The second half of this chapter described the substantive nature of the issues the Congressional Caucus for Women's Issues has advocated. To explain the role of the caucus in congressional agenda setting and policy making would require an analysis of the genesis of these measures and an investigation of the legislative process surrounding their progress. Comments of members and the studies of others quoted above have suggested both an expediency regarding the introduction of some items considered to be women's issues and an independence on the part of caucus members in the initiation of legislation based on ideological beliefs. Some women members of Congress campaigned as feminists in seeking a seat in the House, others found women's rights to be important to them after entering the legislature, and a few have disavowed the idea of women's issues and often voted against the priorities of the caucus usually because they possess a general conservative philosophy and do not believe in activist government.

Individual members of the caucus have sought out particular issues of concern to women to champion. Thus, Rose Mary Oakar (D-Ohio), for example, was known for her sponsorship of pay equity legislation; Marcy Kaptur (D-Ohio) sought and won federal funding for day-care centers in public housing; Nita Lowey (D-N.Y.) has led the fight for abortion rights; and Marge Roukema (R-N.J.) was instrumental (along with Pat Schroeder) in the passage of the family leave bill. In the addendum to this chapter, these women speak for themselves about their priorities. They see themselves, as the cochairs of the CCWI Pat Schroeder and Olympia Snowe have stated, as bearing "a responsibility beyond their own geographical constituencies to women across America" (Rix 1987:19). In a sense they are fulfilling the suffragist vision of a women's bloc.

APPENDIX A: THE ECONOMIC EQUITY ACT

97th Congress (1981–82)

Title I. Tax and Retirement
  Individual Retirement Accounts for Spouses
  Private Pension Reform
  Heads of Household: Zero Bracket Amount

Public Pension Reform: Civil Service
   Ex-Spouses & Survivors
Public Pension Reform: Military Service
   Ex-Spouses & Survivors*
Displaced Homemakers Tax Credits

Title II. Day Care Program: Tax Credits*

Title III. Armed Forces

Title IV. Agricultural Estate Taxes and Farm Loans*

Title V. Nondiscrimination in Insurance

Title VI. Regulatory Reform and Sex Neutrality

Title VII. Study of Enforcing Alimony and Child Support

98th Congress (1983–84)

Title I. Tax and Retirement Matters
   Private Pension Reform*
   Spousal Individual Retirement Accounts
   Displaced Homemakers Tax Credit
   Civil Service Pension Reform*
   Head-of-Household Tax Reform

Title II. Dependent Care
   Sliding Scale for Tax Credits
   Tax-Exempt Status for Child Care Facilities*
   Refundability
   Information and Referral*

Title III. Nondiscrimination in Insurance

Title IV. Regulatory Reform

Title V. Child Support and Enforcement
   Amendments to Title IV-d, Social Security Act*
   Federal Mandatory Wage Assignment

99th Congress (1985–86)

Title I. Retirement Security
A. Private Pension Reform*
B. Social Security
  1. Earnings Sharing
  2. Full Benefit-Disabled Widow(ers)
  3. Transition Benefit-Displaced Homemakers
  4. Disability Definition
C. Military Pension Reform*

Title II. Dependent Care
A. Title XX of Social Security Act
B. Higher Education Act Amendments*
C. Child Care in Public Housing

Title III. Insurance
A. Nondiscrimination in Insurance
B. Health Insurance Continuation*

Title IV. Employment
A. Pay Equity
  1. Enforcement & Education
  2. Federal Study
  3. Legislative Study
B. Education/Training-AFDC Mothers
C. Women in Business
  1. Commission
  2. Equal Credit

Title V. Tax Reform
A. Head-of-Household ZBA
B. Earned Income Tax Credit*
C. Dependent Care Tax Credit
D. Spousal IRAs
E. Nondiscrimination in Business Expense Deduction

100th Congress (1987–88)

Title I. Work
A. Pay Equity
  1. Federal Study
  2. Legislative Study

B. Women in business
  3. Equal Business Credit Opportunity Act
C. Part-time and Temporary Employees
  4. Part-time and Temporary Employee Benefits Protection Act
D. Economic Security
  5. Earnings Sharing
  6. Disability Definition
  7. Pension Reform Act
  8. Spousal Impoverishment
  9. Nondiscrimination in Insurance
 10. Federal Council on Women

Title II. Family (Dependent Care Package)
A. Improving the Quality of Dependent Care
  11. Training for Family Day Care Providers
  12. Improvement of Child Care Standards
B. Improving Access to Child Care — All Families
  13. Dependent Care Tax Credit
  14. Mortgage Financing for Family Day Care Centers
C. Increasing the Supply of Dependent Care for Lower-Income Families
  15. Title XX Funding*
  16. Latchkey Bill
  17. Child Care in Public Housing*

101st Congress (1989–90)

Title I. Employment
1. Pay Equity Technical Assistance
2. Legislative Pay Equity Study
3. Part-time & Temporary Workers Protection Act
4. Federal Council on Women
5. Vocational Education*
6. Women in Business/Procurement

Title II. Economic Security
1. Earnings Sharing
2. Disability Definition*
3. Pension Reform Act
4. Displaced Homemakers & Single Parents Homeownership Assistance*
5. Housing Assistance for Domestic Violence Victims

Title III. Dependent Care
1. Quality Child Care Demonstration Projects

the Part-Time and Temporary Workers Protection Act that amends the Employees Retirement Income Security Act of 1974 to include part-time employees in pension and health insurance plans on a "pro-rata" basis. Third, I have introduced the Family Building Act which requires that all federal employee health insurance plans cover family building activities, including medical procedures necessary to overcome infertility and necessary expenses related to adoption.

Louise Slaughter: I am currently working on child care legislation that involves a cooperative effort between business and the federal government. . . . I am an original cosponsor of the Family and Medical Leave Act.

Olympia Snowe: I have been a principal sponsor of the Act for Better Child Care Services. . . . As part of a dual strategy to address the crisis in child care, I have also reintroduced Dependent Care Tax Credit legislation to expand the current tax credit for child care expenses and make it refundable to families whose incomes are below current tax liability levels. . . . I have been a leader in caregiver issues, introducing the Alzheimer's Disease Tax Credit Act which would provide a tax credit for family caregivers of victims of Alzheimer's. This is the fourth year that I have introduced the National Osteoporosis Prevention Week legislation, bringing attention to the growing problem of osteoporosis in older women.

Jolene Unsoeld: My top priority in Congress is to help strengthen America's families which are foundations of health communities and a vibrant society. To promote strong families we must ensure that workers are able to find good jobs with decent wages. Parents must be able to buy a home. They should have access to safe affordable child care. Our neighborhoods must be free of drugs and toxic waste.

CHAPTER 9

Conclusion

Lack of national political power inspired activists to organize the second feminist movement. During the contemporary feminist era, the movement resulted in women making extraordinary gains in political influence in the United States. But women continued to have difficulty winning national office, although the role discrimination played in women's lack of success was unclear. Women throughout the era were even trumpeted as the advantaged candidates. Scholars and reporters alike have attempted to explain why women constituted less than 3 percent of Congress in 1968, and were less than 10 percent of Congress as late as 1992.

The 1992 election emerged as a major breakthrough for women candidates seeking national office. It was a watershed year. Negative stereotypes became positive as women's issues once relegated to secondary status became central public policy concerns. As U.S. Representative Pat Schroeder commented, "Our stereotypes are in." Women and women's organizations were formidable fundraisers. They monopolized media attention. They won more than they ever had before.

But even with the striking gains of the 1992 election, the number of nationally elected women in the United States still lags behind many democracies, as shown in chapter 1. Other countries have elected women as heads of state; the United States still has trouble dealing even with the president's wife having a policy-making role, let alone truly coming to grips with a woman as president.

This study has examined women who stepped out of traditional roles and sought national offices during the contemporary era. It has shown that most of our conventional ideas about women's campaigns are myths, which can be laid to rest. Nineteen hundred ninety-two as *the* "year of the woman in American politics" was built on the base of two decades of political learning and the accumulation of political experience. Further, this study has shown that the small number of women in office has not been due to a lack of support by parties, political interest groups, or voters. "When women run, women win," a bumper sticker slogan of the National Women's Political Caucus Democratic Task Force at the Democratic National Convention in 1992, is accurate. When women run for the U.S. House of Representatives they don't always win, but they have won as often as their male counterparts in similar situations, and in 1992, Democratic open seat women candidates were the stars of the congressional elections. Plus, the women who have won have altered the congressional agenda regarding issues of special concern to women.

One of the major reasons that relatively few women have held office is that relatively few women have run. The supply of women candidates has two components—the overall numbers of contenders and the presence of women in the subset of elections where the potential for ultimate victory is greatest. To increase their numbers in the national legislature, women first have to enter primary elections. This study documented that relatively few women have sought party nominations for the U.S. House over the course of the feminist era. Women achieved their highest proportion of nonincumbent primary candidacies in 1992, when more women than ever ran for national office, but that was only 13.2 percent of all the contenders, as a surge occurred in men's candidacies as well. In open seat primaries, we found that only in 1992 did a majority of such contests have a female contender. Women's numbers in 1992 capped a trend toward increasing presence in open seat primaries over the course of the contemporary era. Had Republican women created the same presence as Democratic women, the revolutionary aspects of the 1992 election would have been even more striking.

The women's political community has been divided on strategy with some supporting only the strongest candidates, and others, such as Eleanor Smeal of the Fund for a Feminist Majority, encouraging more widespread candidacies. The issue has been should women candidates be encouraged to run only in potentially viable situations, and should only those candidates who are deemed electable be supported? Or should women, as Smeal has advocated, "flood the ticket" by running in as many situations as possible under the notion that the more women run, the more women will win? One can not always know at the beginning of the campaign season what twists and turns the electoral process will take and when a seemingly hopeless situation may turn into a golden opportunity. U.S. Representative Jill Long (D-Ind.), for example, first ran a sacrificial campaign against U.S. Senator Dan Quayle in 1984, when no other Democrat would challenge him; she went on to run unsuccessfully against his successor as U.S. representative, and when that individual was appointed to the Senate to replace Quayle in 1989, when Quayle became vice-president, Long had the inside track to the Democratic nomination in the special election that followed. She won an upset victory. Carol Moseley Braun's victory over U.S. Senator Alan Dixon in the Illinois primary in 1992, and the incredible fallout for other women candidates of her win surprised many pundits. Sometimes, too, in the past, women have won because the "movers and shakers" did not take them seriously. They have been called "stealth candidates." Further, there is the subjective importance of seeing women take the risk of putting themselves forward, although no one would argue that women should strive to be martyrs to the cause.

Women's PACs, however, have operated from a different strategy. Viability is central to gaining support of women's PACs, which tend not to put their limited resources on long shots. They are tough on potential endorsees. Candidates' political potential is carefully assessed before an endorsement is made (Matlack 1992). Some have criticized this pragmatic strategy, believing it has limited the revolution women might have made in public office. More idealism has been called for.[1]

Women are still greatly underrepresented in the U.S. Congress. What can be done to speed the achievement of numerical equality? Where do we go from here? The advantages of incumbency have been the major barrier for newcomers to be competitive. With little turnover in Congress, the rate of change is slow. After the upheaval of 1992, it is believed that the rate of growth in the number of female representatives will return to a more incremental level. The 124 first-termers will likely run again, the financial benefit that stimulated retirement for some in 1992 is no longer a factor,[2] and we cannot assume another scandal will strike the House or Senate making incumbents vulnerable. Incumbents will also benefit if the economy is seen as improving. So until redistricting after the turn of the century once again shakes up the patterns of districts, opportunities for newcomers will be slim. But we should expect women to continue to run in greater numbers and to continue to win open seats. The perception that they will receive support, as well as the reality of the situation as evidenced by the data in this study, should encourage more women to run, as opposed to the earlier more discouraging environment. Certainly the women's community will continue to recruit candidates and assist their campaigns.

Thus, we should expect women to continue to move forward, increasing their numbers in the national legislature, no matter how incremental the rate of growth. But might we expect a backlash against women's accumulation of political influence? If voters accept conservative rhetoric about family values, which is receiving much attention today,[3] we may see a negative reaction to the increased presence of women contending for political leadership. The pursuit of individual career goals may be viewed as being in conflict with the stress on traditional families and the maintenance of intact two-parent fami-

---

1. Actually one might find a difference in the approaches of the women's rights membership organizations and the national PACs, with the membership PACs following the advice of their local memberships who are less concerned with viability factors.

2. After 1992, House incumbents are barred from keeping excess campaign funds for personal use. Those who retired in 1992 could keep their funds.

3. See, for example, Whitehead 1993.

lies. The combining of motherhood and political responsibility may continue to be a burden for women to explain and to feel comfortable with. It may slow the momentum of women into the political arena. However, strong parties with active women can blunt attempts to blame society's problems on feminism and refute sexist stereotypes. Women in public office will be especially sensitive to any implications in public policies meant to strengthen the family, but which do so at the expense of women playing an equal role in society.

Most major works on women and representation have offered suggestions for more quickly increasing the number of elected women. They have recommended electoral system change, campaign finance reform, and strategies for capitalizing on the limited opportunities afforded within the current system.

Electoral System Change

Evidence from other countries suggests that proportional representation with multimember districts provides the greatest opportunity for women. Rule (1987) has shown that type of electoral system was the most significant predictor of women's parliamentary recruitment in twenty-three countries in 1982. She and Pippa Norris have argued that the single-member district electoral system impedes women's election to the House of Representatives and to state legislatures, which are the recruitment ladders to the House (1992).

The party list/proportional representation system has provided the greatest political opportunity for women. Under this system, the parties in a state draw up either a nationwide or a district list of candidates for parliament for presentation to voters. The proportion of members of parliament elected from each party usually reflects the proportion of votes given each party by the electorate. Accordingly, the list system emphasizes political party representation rather than individual representation, and parliamentary candidates run as a team on a party slate. Women are added to lists as a means of broadening the general appeal of the ticket (Rule 1987:479).

In multimember districts, where more than one candidate of a party can be elected, it would be hard for party organizations to exclude women, especially if feminist groups exist. However, if only one candidate can be nominated, as in our single-member congressional districts, a party committee can do little to achieve balance. Many European political parties require minimum proportions of women on candidate lists. When only one candidate is to be nominated in a district, such quotas are impossible to enforce.

As attractive as a switch to a proportional representation system with multimember districts might be, such a change is unlikely in the United States. A national proportional representation system would require a change in congressional law. In 1842, Congress mandated single-member districts for the House of Representatives. Previously, multimember districts were common (Rule and Norris 1992). No ground swell of public support has emerged to motivate individuals to undertake such a lobbying effort to change the system. Some states, however, still have multimember districts, and Matland and Brown (1992) have shown that district magnitude (i.e., the number of seats per district) has a positive effect on the women's election to state legislatures. Multimember districts at this level increase the number of women with prior political experience, thus, potentially expanding the pool of qualified women candidates for higher office.

Campaign Finance Reform

Campaign finance reform is a major item in the constellation of changes in the electoral process that could benefit women's candidacies. Two rationales drive the belief that reforming the campaign finance system would enhance women's opportunities to gain elective office. First, the current system favors incumbents, and since women are disproportionately among nonincumbents, any changes that would help newcomers would consequently help women. Secondly, since the perception has been that women have greater difficulty raising money from traditional sources (although this study has empirically disproven this notion) efforts to open up the system would facilitate women's candidacies.

The campaign finance reform movement, however, has not been without its problems for the women's community. (See Carroll 1985; Rule and Norris 1992.) Changing the system has consisted of a number of diverse efforts involving different aspects of financing such as spending limits and public financing, and other forms of public support as lowering rates for advertising, banning or restricting PACs, and using "soft" money.

Efforts to introduce public monies have been supported by the women's rights community. They would make money more readily available to challengers and thus to women. Support for public financing, however, has not received a great deal of support in Congress, rather, more attention has been paid to reducing the influence of PACs or eliminating them entirely. That has created a problem for women's rights groups. The women's campaign organizations have used the current system well (as described in chapter 6) and, thus, have been ambivalent about changes regarding PACs. They think that, among other things, the newly elected female members of the House (the class of 1992) will need a hefty campaign treasury to get reelected, although some were elected from strong one-party districts. Elizabeth Drew (1993) describes first-term House Democrats as reluctant to reform the financing system in which they succeeded. First-term women, Hispanics and blacks, and in particular members from poor districts, she notes, have argued that they have difficulty raising individual contributions and are very dependent upon PACs. The women's community has become a formidable source of financial support for women candidates through their PACs, and limiting their ability to underwrite the campaigns of women challengers and the large number of recently elected female members of the House would hurt women's candidacies. The women's community might lose its newly won status in the political community if PAC influence were to be substantially reduced.

Bundling, the creative method of financing that made EMILY's List a dominant player in recent elections, has been sharply criticized (editorial, *New York Times,* April 10, 1993). But it is hard to see thousands of women bundling their checks together as an evil source of political influence. EMILY's List, in the battle over campaign finance reform, has argued that since it does not lobby legislators, its method of financing should be an exception to any PAC limitations.

Ceilings on spending and methods of raising money hurt challengers and advantage incumbents. Putting more money into the hands of challengers is necessary within a system that promotes citizen involvement, tries to control overall costs, and makes elections more competitive. A system of public financing that would match private donations up to a certain amount, rather than one that limits the sources women have, should help women candidates.

Parties

Strong parties would enhance women's opportunities to increase their numbers in Congress. Given the weakness of the American party system and the lack of respect with which parties are held, it may seem strange to argue that stronger parties would facilitate women's candidacies and election. A comparative parties' perspective, however, tells us that party organizations are needed to increase the number of women in public office. Although U.S. parties may have once blocked women from running, contemporary parties are no longer the smoke-filled back room political affairs of the past. They are organizations in which women have influence.

If women are to maximize their ability to take advantage of existing opportunities for election, the parties should be given the means to control the nomination of their candidates. In the strongest sense, this would mean eliminating primary election systems and allowing party organizations to select their slates with little interference from the state. The United States is the only western democracy that has taken this role away from the parties and made it a public function. Nominations should be returned to the organizations.

The United States lacks strong parties and strong party platforms. Beyond lessening women's opportunities, this feature of the electoral system increases campaign costs, discourages candidate and voter public interaction, excessively emphasizes candidate personalities, and decreases party accountability.

The entrepreneurial system which now exists allows an individual who perhaps has no ties to the party to flood the electorate with his (or her) own funds and beat an individual who may have labored within the party and developed responsible positions, or allows an extremely committed group not necessarily representative of the majority of party adherents to overwhelm the party structure in a primary election in which few people vote. Even if the parties encourage women to seek the nomination in winnable seats there is no guarantee that they (or any one else they encourage) will get the nomination. Thus, the notion that the parties will make greater efforts to recruit women candidates, as they have promised to do in recent years, rings hollow because parties have a disincentive to get involved in primary elections, and cannot guarantee the result even when they do. Parties can, and do in some areas, operate under a system of pre-primary endorsements. But sometimes that endorsement is a negative. Outsiders use it to somehow suggest to the general public that such an endorsement is undemocratic or unfair. The entire nomination process has to be returned to the parties to be successful within a system that encourages people to get involved in the organization.

Change of the nomination system in this country is unlikely as a ground swell of support for altering it is not now present. Individuals are suspicious of any efforts that appear to give parties greater control over the electoral process. Nevertheless, changes may be possible in some states. Among other things, one could argue that it would save the state money if the nomination process were turned back to the parties. If a party were to abuse the system by excluding individuals or groups from involvement in their selection process that action could be turned against them in the general election. What I envision are meetings or conventions of party members in which people who belong to an organization select nominees. Therefore, the threat of an outside group dominating would be minimal. Commitment to the party is important in becoming part of the selectorate.

Women would not have to fear such a system. In fact, women candidates would likely be more successful at getting good nominations at less cost within the party organizations than in primary systems, particularly if the women's community remains organized on their behalf. It could be an indomitable force or resource within the organizations. It would be to the advantage of the parties in the "the gender gap" society to encourage local organizations to support women. The parties could draw up lists of potential candidates as they do in other countries. I have earlier described the "backstage revolution" in which women have become more prominent and skillful within the parties and, therefore, are insiders and organizational members present to promote women candidates.

Experiences in strong party systems in other countries provide examples of ways for parties to increase women's candidacies and election. Because of their strong party systems, other countries have increased women's opportunities through party policies. In 1983, for example, the Norwegian Labor Party endorsed an affirmative action proposal to insure that at least 40 percent of its candidates were female. This rule change, while only a guideline for county nominating conventions, has had a strong, rapid effect on the composition of the Labor party parliamentary delegation. In 1981, women constituted 33 percent of its delegation; by 1989 they were the majority—51 percent of its parliamentary delegation was female (Matland 1993).

In Sweden, candidate selection is also the sole prerogative of the political parties, usually undertaken in the constituency organizations at the local level. Party women and women's auxiliary organizations participating in the nomination process have gotten women into winnable positions on the party list. In the early 1970s, the percentage of women elected to public office at the local, regional, and national levels was about 14–15 percent. By the end of the 1980s, the percentages had more than doubled, with the proportion of women in regional and national elected office near 40 percent. Parallel increases have occurred at all levels of public office. Women's presence did not decline the higher the office (Sainsbury 1991).

Sweden and Norway are examples of party list/proportional representation systems. In attempting to redress gender inequalities, it is easier to balance party lists of candidates in multimember systems than to designate candidacies in single- member districts as reserved for women. Party list/proportional representation systems mesh better with popular notions of equality (Erickson 1991). British and Canadian parties working within single-member district electoral systems similar to the United States, but with nomination systems controlled entirely by the party organizations also have struggled with this problem within their nomination process that allows local constituencies to choose their candidates for district nomination. They have adopted affirmative action programs and support mechanisms for women candidates. For example, in Britain, the Alliance and Labor parties require the inclusion of women on constituency shortlists for prospective parliamentary candidates. (See Erickson 1991, and Norris et al. 1989.) Norris and Lovenduski (1992) report that women are well organized in the Labor Party both through official women's sections, which have constitutional status and nominating rights at the branch level, and through grass-roots feminist organizations within the party at large. Neither country, however, has increased the proportion of their women members of parliament much beyond that achieved in the United States, in part because of the incumbency factor. Canada, however, has moved ahead, and both countries can now boast of having or having had a woman as prime minister. In each case, a party selected the woman as leader who became prime minister when the party controlled the government. Women have been more likely to become the head of state in countries in which parties choose their leaders than in presidential election systems in which the voters directly choose the national leader.

If parties are strengthened in the United States, then women's candidacies for public office should be faciliated and perhaps enhanced. Evidence from other countries and the transformation within our own parties indicate that party organizations are no longer the enemies of women politicians with ambition for public office. They are an organizational base of opportunity for women as opposed to the present, more entrepreneurial, system that characterizes contemporary American elections, even though women did well in such a system in 1992. (But no women won any of the special elections for the U.S. House in the first half of 1993, although Kay Bailey Hutchinson won a Senate seat in Texas.)

If terms of office were limited (i.e., the number of years in which a person can continuously be elected to the same office), as has been adopted in some states and has been proposed for the U.S. Congress, that should at least in the short run increase the number of women legislators as it would remove long term incumbents, disproportionately men, from the electoral equation. Women's rights activists generally have favored this change in the electoral process. Yet its implications for the influence legislators would have on the policy making process are uncertain. There is strong potential for the weakening of the legislature relative to the executive branch and outside interests. How would the second aspect of the women's rights community's goals—that more women are needed in office to affect the policy-making process on behalf of women in general—be affected? What would happen to women's rights policies which are change oriented in such systems? Would the status quo more likely be maintained? We have to remember that professional legislatures came into vogue because of the abuses of the system resulting from amateur legislators being influenced by special interests.

Summary

In summary, most women who run for national office in the United States have not been victimized by discrimination on the campaign trail, and this has been true generally throughout the contemporary feminist era. Notions of prejudice are passé. (This is not to suggest that some individuals have not faced instances of prejudice; plus, women were noticeably absent from contests in the South until 1992.) The eagerness with which so many women ran for national office in 1992 and the extent to which their campaigns were supported by other women suggest that socialization and lack of ambition may be fading as explanatory factors for the lack of female candidates in national elections. Family responsibilities may continue to limit women's political advancement, but we can expect women to continue not only to run but to win, and to influence and alter the political dialogue.

Nineteen hundred ninety-two was indeed a Year of the American Woman in Politics, not only because more women than ever took advantage of the political opportunity structure to seek national office; women did better than ever—they did it with the strong support of the women's rights community, and they did it by emphasizing their own issues. They were more successful than in the past because their campaigns were built on the experience and expertise women had gained over the course of the feminist era in politics. A quarter century of organizing by women has profoundly affected the electoral process in the United States in terms of both personnel and policy.

References

AAUW. *See* American Association of University Women.

Abzug, Bella. 1984. *Gender Gap.* New York: Houghton Mifflin.

Alters, Diane. 1987. "Women, Strong at the Polls, Still Lag in Campaign Leverage." *Boston Globe,* May 26, 1.

American Association of University Women, (AAUW). 1991. "Shortchanging Girls, Shortchanging America." Report commissioned from Greenberg-Lake, The Analysis Group, Washington, D.C.

Andersen, Kristi. 1990. "Women and Citizenship in the 1920s." In *Women, Politics, and Change,* ed. Louise Tilly and Patricia Gurin. New York: Russell Sage Foundation.

Andersen, Kristi, and Stuart Thorson. 1984. "Some Structural Barriers to the Election of Women to Congress: A Simulation." *Western Political Quarterly* 37 (March): 143–56.

Baer, Denise. 1990. "Political Parties: The Missing Variable in Women and Politics Research." Paper presented at the annual meeting of the Midwest Political Science Association, Chicago.

Baer, Denise, and David Bositis. 1987. *Elite Cadres and Party Coalitions.* New York: Greenwood Press.

Barone, Michael, and Grant Ujifusa. 1990. *The Almanac of American Politics,* Chicago: R. R. Donnelly and Sons.

Bauer, Monica, and John Hibbing. 1989. "Which Incumbents Lose in House Elections: A Response to Jacobson's 'The Marginals Never Vanished'." *American Journal of Political Science* 33 (February): 262–71.

Benenson, Bob. 1990. "Republicans Are Drawing a Bead on Veteran Incumbent Brown." *Congressional Quarterly Weekly Report,* 48 (May 26): 1675–79.

———. 1992. "Arduous Ritual of Redistricting Ensures More Racial Diversity." *Congressional Quarterly Weekly Report,* 50 (October 24): 3327–32.

Bernstein, Robert. 1986. "Why Are There So Few Women in the House?" *Western Political Quarterly* 39 (March): 155–63.

Bernstein, Robert, and Jayne Polly. 1975. "Race, Class and Support for Female Candidates." *Western Political Quarterly* 28 (December): 733–36.

Bird, Caroline. 1979. *What Women Want.* New York: Simon and Schuster.

Bledsoe, Timothy, and Mary Herring. 1990. "Victims of Circumstances: Women in Pursuit of Political Office." *American Political Science Review* 84 (March): 213–23.

Boles, Janet. 1993. "The Year of the Woman—Continued (Or, the Return of the

Puritan Ethic?)" Paper presented at the annual meeting of the Midwest Political Science Association, Chicago.

Bonefede, Dom. 1982. "Women's Movement Broadens the Scope of Its Role in American Politics." *National Journal,* December 11, 2108–11.

Briscoe, Jerry, B. 1989. "Perceptions that Discourage Women Attorneys from Seeking Public Office." *Sex Roles* 21:557–67.

Broder, David. 1986. "The Third Wave of Women Candidates." *Washington Post,* September 14.

Brown, Elizabeth. 1991. "Why Most Public Officials Are Still Men." *Christian Science Monitor,* February 15, 11.

Bryson, Valerie. 1992. *Feminist Political Theory.* New York: Paragon House.

Buchanan, Christopher. 1978. "Why Aren't There More Women in Congress?" *Congressional Quarterly Weekly Report* 36 (August 12): 2108.

Bullock, Charles S., and Patricia Heys. 1972. "Recruitment of Women for Congress: A Research Note." *Western Political Quarterly* 25 (September): 416–23.

Burrell, Barbara. 1985. "Women's and Men's Campaigns for the U.S. House of Representatives, 1972–1982: A Finance Gap?" *American Politics Quarterly* 13 (July): 251–72.

———. 1988. "The Political Opportunity of Women Candidates for the U.S. House of Representatives in 1984." *Women and Politics* 8 (Spring): 51–69.

———. 1990. "The Presence of Women Candidates and the Role of Gender in Campaigns for the State Legislature in an Urban Setting." *Women & Politics* 3 (Spring): 85–102.

———. 1992. "The Presence and Performance of Women Candidates in Open Seat Primaries for the U.S. House of Representatives: 1968–1990." *Legislative Studies Quarterly* 17 (November): 493–508.

Butterfield, D. Anthony, and Gary N. Powell. 1987. "Androgyny, Good Managers, and U.S. Presidential Candidates." Paper presented at the national convention of the American Psychological Association, New York, August.

Canon, David. 1989. "Political Amateurism in the U.S. Congress." In *Congress Reconsidered,* 4th ed., ed. Lawrence Dodd and Bruce Oppenheimer. Washington, D.C.: Congressional Quarterly Press.

———. 1990. *Actors, Athletes, and Astronauts: Political Amateurs in the United States Congress.* Chicago: University of Chicago Press.

Cantor, Dorothy, and Toni Bernay. 1992. *Women in Power: The Secrets of Leadership.* Boston: Houghton Mifflin.

Carroll, Susan. 1985. *Women as Candidates in American Politics.* Bloomington: University of Indiana Press.

Carroll, Susan, and Ella Taylor. 1989. "Gender Differences in Policy Priorities of U.S. State Legislators." Paper presented at the annual meeting of the American Political Science Association, Atlanta.

CAWP Fact Sheet. 1990. "Women in Elective Office 1990." New Brunswick, N.J.: Center for the American Woman and Politics.

Clark, Janet, R. Darcy, Susan Welch, and Margery Ambrosius. 1984. "Women as Legislative Candidates in Six States." In *Political Women: Current Roles in State and Local Government,* ed. Janet Flammang. Beverly Hills, Calif.: Sage.

Clift, Eleanor. 1990. "Sex Still Matters." *Newsweek,* October 29, 34–35.

Cobb, Roger W., and Charles Elder. 1972. *Participation in American Politics: The Dynamics of Agenda-Building.* Boston: Allyn and Bacon.

Congressional Districts in the 1970s. 1974. Washington, D.C.: Congressional Quarterly Press.

Congressional Districts in the 1980s. 1983. Washington, D.C.: Congressional Quarterly Press.

Congressional Quarterly Weekly Report: The Class of 1980. (January 3): 6.

———. 1993. *Special Report The New Congress.* Congressional Quarterly 51 (January 16).

Cooper and Secrest Associates. 1985. *Women as Candidates in the 1984 Congressional Elections.* Alexandria, Virginia.

Cott, Nancy. 1987. *The Grounding of Modern Feminism.* New Haven: Yale University Press.

Cotter, Cornelius, and Bernard Hennessy. 1964. *Politics without Power.* New York: Atherton.

Cotter, Cornelius, and John Bibby. 1980. "Institutional Development of Parties and the Thesis of Party Decline." *Political Science Quarterly* 95 (Spring): 1–27.

Cotter, Cornelius, James Gibson, John Bibby, and Robert Huskshorn. 1984. *Party Organization in American Politics.* New York: Praeger.

Crotty, William. 1980. *The Party Symbol.* San Francisco: W. H. Freeman.

———. 1983. *Party Reform.* New York: Longman.

Crotty, William, and Gary C. Jacobson. 1984. *American Parties in Decline,* 2d ed. Boston: Little, Brown.

Darcy, Robert. 1982. "Why So Few Women in Public Office? A Look at Oklahoma Politics." In *Southwest Cultural Festival: 1982,* ed. Gordon Weaver. Stillwater: Oklahoma University Press.

Darcy, Robert, and Sarah Slavin Schramm. 1977. "When Women Run against Men." *Public Opinion Quarterly* 41:1–12.

Darcy, R., Susan Welch, and Janet Clark. 1987. *Women, Elections, and Representation.* New York: Longman.

Davidson, Roger. 1992. "The Emergence of the Postreform Congress." In *The Postreform Congress,* ed. Roger Davidson. New York: St. Martin's.

Deber, Raisa. 1982. "'The Fault Dear Brutus': Women as Congressional Candidates in Pennsylvania." *Journal of Politics* 44 (May): 463–79.

Diamond, Irene. 1977. *Sex Roles in the State House.* New Haven: Yale University Press.

DiCamillo, Mark. 1993. "How 1992 Truly Became 'The Year of the Woman' in California Politics." Paper presented at the annual conference of the American Association for Public Opinion Research Conference, Chicago.

Dionne, E. J. 1986. "Primaries Show Women Emerging as Seasoned Political Contenders." *New York Times,* September 11, 1.

Dodson, Debra, and Susan Carroll. 1991. *Reshaping the Agenda: Women in State Legislatures.* New Brunswick, N.J.: Center for the American Woman and Politics.

Donovan, Beth. 1992. "Women's Campaigns Fueled Mostly by Women's Checks." *Congressional Quarterly Weekly Report* 50 (October 17): 3269–73.

Dorscher, Mike. 1993. "Study: Middle School Girls Feel Inferior, Left Out." *Wisconsin State Journal,* April 18, 1.

Drew, Elizabeth. 1993. "Watch 'Em Squirm." *New York Times Magazine,* March 14, 32.

Duncan, Phil. 1984. "House Campaigns Quiet as Few Seek to Run." *Congressional Quarterly Weekly Report* 42 (March 24): 657–60.

Ehrenhalt, Alan. 1982. "The Advantages of the Woman Candidate." *Congressional Quarterly Weekly Report* 40 (March 6): 551.

Eisenstein, Zillah. 1981. *The Radical Future of Liberal Feminism.* New York: Longman.

Ekstrand, Laurie E., and William A. Eckert. 1981. "The Impact of Candidate's Sex on Voter Choice." *Western Political Quarterly* 34 (March): 78–87.

Eldersveld, Samuel. 1982. *Political Parties in American Politics.* New York: Basic Books.

Elshtain, Jean. 1981. *Public Man, Private Woman.* Princeton, N.J.: Princeton University Press.

Erickson, Lynda. 1991. "Making the Ballot: Women and Party Selection in Canada." Paper presented at the ECPR Workshop on Party Responses to Women's Demands, Essex University, Colchester, England.

Farah, Barbara, and Virginia Sapiro. 1980. "New Pride, Old Prejudice." *Women & Politics* 1 (Spring): 13–36.

Farah, Barbara, and Ethel Klein. 1989. "Public Opinion Trends." In *The Election of 1988: Reports and Interpretations,* ed. Gerald Pomper. Chatham, N.J.: Chatham House.

Feit, Rona. 1979. "Organizing for Political Power: The National Women's Political Caucus." In *Women Organizing,* ed. Bernice Cummings and Victoria Schuck. Metuchen, N.J.: Scarecrow.

Fenno, Richard. 1978. *Home Style.* Boston: Little, Brown.

Feree, Myra Marx. 1974. "A Woman for President? Changing Response: 1958–1972." *Public Opinion Quarterly* 38:390–99.

Fishel, Jeff. 1973. *Party and Opposition: Congressional Challengers in American Politics.* New York: David McKay.

Fisher, Marguerite, and Betty Whitehead. 1944. "American Government and Politics." *American Political Science Review* 38:895–903.

Flammang, Janet A. 1985. "Female Officials in the Feminist Capital: The Case of Santa Clara County." *Western Political Quarterly* 38 (March): 94–118.

Flammang, Janet, Dennis Gordon, Timothy Lukes, and Kenneth Smorsten. 1990. *American Politics in a Changing World.* Pacific Grove, Calif.: Brooks/Cole.

Fowler, Linda, and Robert McClure. 1989. *Political Ambition.* New Haven: Yale University Press.

Fowler, Linda, and L. Sandy Maisel. 1990. "The Changing Supply of Competitive Candidates in House Elections: 1982–1988." In *Changing Perspectives on Congress,* ed. Glenn Parker. Knoxville: University of Tennessee Press.

Fowlkes, Diane. 1984. "Ambitious Political Woman: Countersocialization and Political Party Context." *Women and Politics* 4 (Winter): 5–32.

Frankovic, Kathleen. 1977. "Sex and Voting in the U.S. House of Representatives: 1961–1975." *American Politics Quarterly* 5 (July): 515–30.

———. 1982. "Sex and Politics: New Alignments, Old Issues." *P.S: Political Science and Politics* 15:439–48.

Freeman, Jo. 1975. *The Politics of Women's Liberation.* New York: McKay.

———. 1986. "The Political Culture of the Democratic and Republican Parties." *Political Science Quarterly* 101 (Fall): 327–56.

———. 1987. "Whom You Know versus Whom You Represent: Feminist Influence in the Democratic and Republican Parties." In *The Women's Movements of the United States and Western Europe,* ed. Mary Katzenstein and Carol Mueller. Philadelphia: Temple University Press.

———. 1989. "Feminist Activities at the 1988 Republican Convention." *PS: Political Science and Politics* 22:39–46.

Friedan, Betty. 1976. *It Changed My Life.* New York: Random House.

Friedman, Jon. 1993. "The Founding Mother." *New York Times Magazine,* May 2, 50.

Gallup, George. 1976. "Women in America." *The Gallup Poll Index* Report no. 128 (March): 7.

Gallup, George. 1984. "Women in Politics." *The Gallup Poll Index* Report nos. 228/229 (August/September): 2–14.

Gamerakian, Barbara. 1985. "Women's Caucus: Eight Years of Progress." *New York Times,* May 27.

Gehlen, Freda. 1977. "Women Members of Congress: A Distinctive Role." In *A Portrait of Marginality,* ed. Marianne Githens and Jewel Prestage. New York: David McKay.

Gelb, Joyce, and Marian L. Palley. 1982. *Women and Public Policies.* Princeton, N.J.: Princeton University Press.

Gertzog, Irwin. 1984. *Congressional Women: Their Recruitment, Treatment, and Behavior.* New York: Praeger.

Gertzog, Irwin, and M. Michele Simard. 1981. "Women and 'Hopeless' Congressional Candidacies: Nomination Frequency, 1916–1978." *American Politics Quarterly* 9 (October): 449–66.

Gilligan, Carol. 1982. *In a Different Voice: Psychological Theory and Women's Development.* Cambridge: Harvard University Press.

Githens, Marianne. 1983. "The Elusive Paradigm: Gender, Politicals and Political Behavior." In *Political Science: The State of the Discipline,* ed. Ada Finifter. Washington, D.C.: American Political Science Association.

Glenney, Daryl. 1982. "Women in Politics: On the Rise." *Campaigns and Elections* 3 (Winter): 18–24.

Goldenberg, Edie, and Michael Traugott. 1984. *Campaigning for Congress.* Washington, D.C.: Congressional Quarterly Press.

Goodman, Ellen. 1986. "It's Slow Progress for Women in Politics." *Boston Globe,* November 11.

———. 1988. "Arrival of the New Insiders." *Boston Globe,* July 19.

Greenberg-Lake. 1992. *Winning with Women.* A survey commissioned by EMILY's

List, the National Women's Political Caucus, and the Women's Campaign Fund. Washington, D.C.: Greenberg-Lake Analysis Group.

Harris, Louis, and Associates. 1972. *The 1972 Virginia Slims American Women's Opinion Poll.*

Hartmann, Susan. 1989. *From Margin to Mainstream.* Philadelphia: Temple University Press.

Harvey, Anna. 1992. "Uncertain Victory: The Electoral Incorporation of Women into the Republican Party, 1920–1928." Paper presented at the annual meeting of the American Political Science Association, Chicago.

Hedlund, Ronald, Patricia Freeman, Keith Hamm, and Robert Stein. 1979. "The Electability of Women Candidates: The Effects of Sex Role Stereotypes." *Journal of Politics* 41 (May): 513–24.

Heiderpriem, Nikki, and Celinda Lake, 1987. "The Winning Edge." *Polling Report,* April 6.

Herbers, John. 1982. "Women Turn View to Public Office." *New York Times,* June 28.

Herrnson, Paul. 1988. *Party Campaigning in the 1980s.* Cambridge: Harvard University Press.

———. 1992. "National Party Organizations and the Postreform Congress." In *The Postreform Congress,* ed. Roger Davidson. New York: St. Martin's.

Hickman-Maslin Research. 1987. "The New Political Woman Survey."

Hill, David. 1981. "Political Culture and Female Political Representation." *Journal of Politics* 43 (March): 159–68.

Holtzman, Elizabeth, and Shirley Williams. 1987. "Women in the Political World: Observations." *Daedalus* 116 (Fall): 25–34.

Hornblower, Margot. 1992. "Despite Gains, Still a Long Way to Go." *Washington Post,* October 22.

Jacobs, Sally. 1988. "Smeal Urges More Women to Run for Political Office." *Boston Globe,* March 29.

Jacobson, Gary. 1980. *Money in Congressional Elections.* New Haven: Yale University Press.

———. 1987a. "The Marginals Never Vanished: Incumbency and Competition in Elections to the U.S. House of Representatives." *American Journal of Political Science* 31 (February): 125–41.

———. 1987b. *The Politics of Congressional Elections.* Glenview, Ill.: Scott, Foresman.

———. 1990. *The Electoral Origins of Divided Government.* Boulder, Colo.: Westview.

Jacobson, Gary, and Samuel Kernell. 1983. *Strategy and Choice in Congressional Elections.* New Haven: Yale University Press.

Jennings, M. Kent. 1990. "Women in Party Politics." In *Women, Politics and Change,* ed. Louise Tilly and Patricia Gurin. New York: Russell Sage Foundation.

Johnson, Marilyn, and Kathy Stanwick. 1976. *Profile of Women Holding Office.* New Brunswick, N.J.: Center for the American Woman and Politics.

Jones, Woodrow, and Albert Nelson. 1981. "Correlates of Women's Representation in Lower State Legislative Chambers." *Social Behavior and Personality* 1:9–15.

Jordan, Mary. 1984. "Celebrating Women's Right to Vote." *Washington Post,* August 25.

Kaid, Lynda Lee, Sandra Myers, Val Pipps, and Jan Hunter. 1984. "Sex Role Perceptions and Televised Political Advertising: Comparing Male and Female Candidates." *Women and Politics* 4 Winter: 41–54.

Kaminer, Wendy. 1992. "Crashing the Locker Room." *Atlantic Monthly* 270 (July): 59–70.

Kathlene, Lyn. 1992. "Studying the New Voice of Women in Politics." *Chronicle of Higher Education,* November 18, B1–B2.

Kathlene, Lyn, Susan E. Clarke, and Barbara A. Fox. 1991. "Ways Women Politicians Are Making a Difference." In *Gender and Policymaking: Studies of Women in Office,* ed. Debra Dodson. New Brunswick, N.J.: Center for the American Woman and Politics.

Kathlene, Lyn, and Silvo Lenart. 1993. "Who Are the Women Candidates? A Typology of Women Candidates in the 1992 Congressional and State Level Races." Paper presented at the annual meeting of the Midwest Political Science Association, Chicago.

Katzenstein. Mary, 1984. "Feminism and the Meaning of the Vote." *Signs* 10:4–26.

Keeter, Scott. 1985. "Public Opinion in 1984." In *The Election of 1984,* ed. Gerald Pomper. Chatham, N.J.: Chatham House.

Kelly, Rita Mae, Michelle A. Saint-Germain, and Jody D. Horn. 1991. "Female Public Officials: A Different Voice?" *The Annuals of the American Academy of Political and Social Science* 515 (May): 77–87.

Kendrigan, Mary Lou, 1984. *Political Equality in a Democratic Society: Women in the United States.* Westport, Conn.: Greenwood.

Kenski, Henry. 1988. "The Gender Factor in a Changing Electorate." In *The Politics of the Gender Gap,* ed. Carol Mueller. Beverly Hills, Calif.: Sage.

Kiernan, Laura. 1988. "Humphrey: Motherhood Remarks 'Just Plain Stupid.'" *Boston Globe,* September 9.

Kirschten, Dick. 1984. "The Reagan Reelection Campaign Hopes 1984 Will Be the Year of the Women." *National Journal,* June 2, 1082–85.

Klemesrud, Judy. 1983. "Women Study Art of Politics." *New York Times,* November 28.

Ladd, Everett Carll. 1992. "Gender and Party ID." *Public Perspective* 3 (July/August): 27–28.

Ladd, Everett Carll, and Charles D. Hadley. 1975. *Transformation of the American Party System.* New York: W. W. Norton.

Lamson, Peggy, 1968. *Few Are Chosen.* Boston: Houghton Mifflin.

Lapidus, Gail. 1978. *Women in Soviet Society.* Berkeley: University of California Press.

Leader, Shelah. 1977. "The Policy Impact of Elected Women Officials." In *The Impact of the Electoral Process,* ed. Joseph Cooper and Louis Maisel. Beverly Hills, Calif.: Sage.

Leeper, Mark. 1991. "The Impact of Prejudice on Female Candidates: An Experimental Look at Voter Inference." *American Politics Quarterly* 19 (April): 248–61.

Lemons, J. Stanley. 1973. *The Woman Citizen: Social Feminism in the 1920s.* Urbana: University of Illinois Press.

Lewis, Kathryn, and Margaret Bierly. 1990. "Toward a Profile of the Female Voter: Sex Differences in Perceived Physical Attractiveness and Competence of Political Candidates." *Sex Roles* 22:1–11.

Loomis, Burdett. 1990. "Political Careers and American State Legislatures." Paper presented at the annual meeting of the Midwest Political Science Association, Chicago.

Lovenduski, Joni, and Pippa Norris. 1989. "Selecting Women Candidates: Obstacles to the Feminisation of the House of Commons." *European Journal of Political Research* 17:533–62.

Lugar, Richard. 1983. "A Plan to Elect More GOP Women." *Washington Post,* August 21, sec. C.

Maisel, L. Sandy. 1981. *From Obscurity to Oblivion.* Knoxville: University of Tennessee Press.

Makinson, Larry. 1989. *The Price of Admission,* Washington, D.C.: Center for Responsive Politics.

Mandel, Ruth. 1981. *In the Running: The New Woman Candidate.* New York: Ticknor and Fields.

Mann, Judy. 1986. "Ferraro's Legacy," *Washington Post,* September 19, sec. B3.

Mann, Thomas. 1978. *Unsafe at Any Margin.* Washington, D.C.: American Enterprise Institute.

Matlack, Carol. 1987. "Women at the Polls." *National Journal,* December 19, 3208–15.

———. 1992. "Too Little, too Late?" *National Journal,* March 28, 761–62.

Matland, Richard. 1993. "Institutional Variables Affecting Female Representation in National Legislatures: The Case of Norway," *Journal of Politics* 55 (August): 737–55.

Matland, Richard, and Deborah Dwight Brown. 1992. "District Magnitudes Effect on Female Representation in U.S. State Legislatures." *Legislative Studies Quarterly* 17 (November): 469–92.

Matthews, Donald. 1984. "Legislative Recruitment and Legislative Careers." *Legislative Studies Quarterly* 9 (November): 547–85.

Mayhew, David. 1974. "Congressional Elections." *Polity* 6: 295–317.

Mericle, Margaret, S. Lenart, and K. Heilig. 1989. "Women Candidates: Even If All Things Are Equal, Will They Get Elected?" Paper presented at the annual meeting of the Midwest Political Science Association, Chicago.

Mill, John Stuart. 1971. *On the Subjection of Women.* Greenwich, Conn.: Fawcett.

Miller, Arthur. 1988. "Gender and the Vote: 1984." In *The Politics of the Gender Gap,* ed. Carol Mueller. Beverly Hills, Calif.: Sage.

———. 1990. "Public Judgments of Senate and House Candidates." *Legislative Studies Quarterly* 15 (November): 525–42.

Mueller, Carol. 1988. "The Empowerment of Women: Polling and the Women's Voting Bloc." In *The Politics of the Gender Gap,* ed. Carol Mueller. Beverly Hills, Calif.: Sage.

Muscatine, Alison. 1984. "Women in Uphill Struggles for Senate Seats." *Washington Post,* June 25.

Nauman, Eric L., and Tobi Walker. 1992. "Women in the 1992 Presidential Race." *CAWP News & Notes* 8 (Fall): 20.

Nechemias, Carol. 1987. "Changes in the Election of Women to U.S. State Legislative Seats." *Legislative Studies Quarterly* 12 (February): 125–42.

Newman, Jody, Carrie Constantin, Julie Goetz, and Amy Glossr. 1984. *Perception and Reality: A Study of Women Candidates and Fundraising.* Washington, D.C.: Women's Campaign Research Fund.

New York Times. 1986. "$100,000 to be given to Women Candidates." June 8.

Norris, Pippa, Ken Carty, Linda Erickson, Joni Lovenduski, and Marian Simms. 1989. "Party Selectorates in Australia, Britain and Canada: Legal Context, Party Procedures and Outcome." Paper presented at the IPSA/ISA First Annual Workshop on Elections and Parties, Fondation Nationale des Sciences Politiques, Paris, April.

Norris, Pippa, and Joni Lovenduski. 1992. "'If Only More Candidates Came Forward . . .': Supply-side Explanations of Political Representation in Britain." Paper presented at the annual meeting of the American Political Science Association, Chicago.

Odum, Maria. 1992. "If the G.N.P. Counted Housework, Would Women Count for More?" *New York Times,* April 5.

Okin, Susan Moller. 1979. *Women in Western Political Thought.* Princeton, N.J.: Princeton University Press.

Ornstein, Norman, Thomas Mann, and Michael Malbin. 1987. *Vital Statistics on Congress.* Washington, D.C.: Congressional Quarterly Press.

Peterson, Bill. 1986. "Women Vie for Breakthrough in 9 State Primaries Today." *Washington Post,* September 9, sec. A.

Pitkin, Hanna. 1967. *The Concept of Representation.* Berkeley, Calif.: University of California Press.

Polsby Nelson. 1983. "The Reform of Presidential Selection and Democratic Theory." *PS: Political Science and Politics,* 16: 695–98.

Poole, Keith, and L. Harmon Zeigler. 1985. *Women, Public Opinion, and Politics.* New York: Longman.

Public Perspective. 1992. "Do Women Vote for Women?" *Public Perspective* 3 (July/August): 98–99.

Public Perspective. 1993. "The Gender Gap at the State Level." *Public Perspective* 4 (January/February): 100–101.

Quindlen, Anna. 1992. "Gender Contender." *New York Times,* April 26.

Raines, Howell. 1983. "Poll Shows Support for Political Gains by Women in U.S." *New York Times,* November 27, sec. A.

Randall, Vicky. 1987. *Woman and Politics: An International Perspective,* 2d ed. Chicago: University of Chicago Press.

Ranney, Austin. 1976. *Curing the Mischiefs of Faction.* Berkeley: University of California Press.

Ries, Paula, and Anne J. Stone. eds. 1992. *The American Woman, 1992–93: A Status Report.* New York: W. W. Norton.

Ripley, Randall. 1988. *Congress Policy and Process.* New York: W. W. Norton.

Rix, Sara. 1987. *The American Woman 1987–88: A Report in Depth.* New York: W. W. Norton.

————. 1991. *The American Woman 1990–91: A Status Report*. New York: W. W. Norton.

Roberts, Steven. 1984. "They're Capitalists, and Their Venture Is Women." *New York Times,* May 17.

Romney, Ronna, and Beppie Harrison. 1988. *Momentum: Women in American Politics Now*. New York: Crown.

Rosellini, Lynn. 1982. "For Women Only: Campaign Primer." *New York Times,* August 20.

Rosenwasser, Shirley, Robyn Rogers, Sheila Fling, Kayla Silvers-Pickens, and John Butemeyer. 1987. "Attitudes toward Women and Men in Politics: Perceived Male and Female Candidate Competencies and Participant Personality Characteristics." *Political Psychology* 8:191–200.

Rosenwasser, Shirley, and Jana Scale. 1988. "Attitudes Toward a Hypothetical Male or Female Presidential Candidates—A Research Note." *Political Psychology* 9:591–98.

Rosenwasser, Shirley, and Norma Dean. 1989. "Gender Role and Political Office." *Psychology of Women Quarterly* 13:77–85.

Rubin, Alissa. 1991. "Influence of Traditional Bloc Clearly on the Decrease." *Congressional Quarterly Weekly Report* 49 (December 28): 3759–61.

Rule, Wilma. 1981. "Why Women Don't Run: The Critical Contextual Factors in Women's Legislative Recruitment." *Western Political Quarterly* 34 (March): 60–77.

————. 1987. "How and Why Do Women and Men's Congressional Recruitment Patterns Differ and What Is the Significance of This Difference, If Any?" Paper presented at the annual meeting of the Western Political Science Association, Anaheim, California, March.

Rule, Wilma, and Pippa Norris. 1992. "Anglo and Minority Women's Underrepresentation in the Congress: Is the Electoral System the Culprit?" In *The Impact of U.S. Electoral Systems on Minorities and Women,* ed. Joseph Zimmerman and Wilma Rule. New Haven, Conn.: Greenwood.

Rupp, Leila J., and Verta Taylor. 1987. *Survival in the Doldrums: The American Women's Rights Movement, 1945 to the 1960s*. New York: Oxford University Press.

Sabato, Larry. 1985. *PAC Power*. New York: W. W. Norton.

Sainsbury, Diane. 1991. "Bringing Women into Elected Office in Sweden and the U.S.: Political Opportunity Structures and Women's Strategies." Paper presented at the annual meeting of the American Political Science Association, Washington, D.C.

Salmans, Sandra. 1984. "The Rising Force of Women's PACs." *New York Times,* June 28.

Sapiro, Virginia. 1981–82. "If Senator Baker Were a Woman: An Experimental Study of Candidate Images." *Political Psychology* 3:61–83.

————. 1983. *The Political Integration of Women*. Urbana: University of Illinois Press.

Schattschneider, E. E. 1942. *Party Government*. New York: Farrar and Rinehart.

Schiegel, Sharon. 1992. "Ruth Mandel: Fighting for Women in Public Life." *Trenton Times,* November 22.

Schlesinger, Joseph. 1965. *Ambition and Politics.* Chicago: Rand McNally.

———. 1991. *Political Parties and the Winning of Office.* Ann Arbor: University of Michigan Press.

Schreiber, E. M. 1978. "Education and Change in American Opinions on a Woman for President." *Public Opinion Quarterly* 42 (Summer): 171–82.

Scott, Austin 1974. "Democratic Women See Gains in 1974." *Washington Post,* March 31.

Shafer, Byron. 1983. *Quiet Revolution.* New York: Russell Sage Foundation.

Shreve, Anita and John Clemans. 1980. "The New Wave of Women Politicians." *New York Times Magazine,* October 19.

Simon, Rita J., and Gloria Danziger. 1991. *Women's Movements in America.* New York: Praeger.

Smith, Tom, and Lance Selfa. 1992. "When Do Women Vote for Women?" *Public Perspective* 3 (September/October): 30–31.

Sorauf, Frank J. 1984. *Party Politics in America,* 5th ed. Boston: Little, Brown.

———. 1992. *Inside Campaign Finance.* New Haven: Yale University Press.

Southgate, Martha. 1986. "EMILY's List: Political Money Where It Counts." *Ms.* 15 (September): 27.

Spake, Amanda. 1988. "Women Can Be Power Brokers, Too." *Washington Post Magazine,* June 5, 32.

Stineman, Esther. 1980. *American Political Women.* Littleton, Colo.: Libraries Unlimited.

Studlar, Donley, and Ian McAllister. 1991. "Political Recruitment to the Australian Legislature: Toward an Explanation of Women's Electoral Disadvantages." *Western Political Quarterly* 44 (June): 467–85.

Tamerius, Karin. 1993. "Does Sex Matter? Women Representing Women's Interest in Congress." Paper presented at the annual meeting of the Midwest Political Science Association, Chicago.

Theilman, John, and Al Wilhite. 1991. *Discrimination and Congressional Campaign Contributions.* New York: Praeger.

Thomas, Sue. 1989. "The Impact of Women on State Legislative Policies." Paper presented at the annual meeting of the American Political Science Association, Atlanta.

Thompson, Joan Hulse. 1980. "Role Perceptions of Women in the Ninety-fourth Congress, 1975–76." *Political Science Quarterly* 96 (Summer): 71–81.

———. 1984. "The Congressional Caucus for Women's Issues: One-Hundred and Thirty Feminists in the House." Paper presented at the annual meeting of the Midwest Political Science Association, Chicago.

———. 1985a. "Lobbying in the House: The Congressional Caucus for Women's Issues versus the Insurance Industry." Paper presented at the annual meeting of the Midwest Political Science Association, Chicago.

———. 1985b. "Career Convergence: Election of Women and Men to the House of Representatives 1916–1975." *Women and Politics* 5 (Spring): 69–90.

————. 1988. "The Women's Rights Lobby in the Gender Gap Congress, 1983–1984." *Commonwealth* 2: 19–35.

————. 1993. "The Family and Medical Leave Act: A Policy for Families." In *Women in Politics: Have the Outsiders Become Insiders?*, ed. Lois Duke. New York: Prentice Hall.

Tolchin, Susan, and Martin Tolchin. 1973. *Clout: Womanpower and Politics.* New York: Coward, McCann and Geoghegan.

Toner, Robin. 1986. "Facing Preconceptions of Women as Candidates." *New York Times,* October 3.

————. 1990a. "For Women, Better Climate Is Seen." *New York Times,* April 22.

————. 1990b. "Gains Seen for Women, But Not Without Fights." *New York Times,* October 29.

Uhlaner, Carole and Kay Schlozman. 1986. "Candidate Gender and Congressional Campaign Receipts." *Journal of Politics* 48 (February): 30–50.

Ware, Susan. 1981. *Beyond Suffrage: Women in the New Deal.* Cambridge: Harvard University Press.

Washington Post. 1992. "Female Candidates, 'Murphy Brown' Have Edge in Poll." June 29.

Wattenberg, Martin. 1986. *The Decline of American Political Parties, 1952–1984.* Cambridge: Harvard University Press.

Welch, Susan. 1978. "Recruitment of Women to Public Office." *Western Political Quarterly* 31 (September): 372–80.

————. 1985. "Are Women More Liberal than Men in the U.S. Congress?" *Legislative Studies Quarterly* 10 (February): 125–34.

————. 1989. "Congressional Nomination Procedures and the Representation of Women." *Congress and the Presidency* 16: 121–35.

Welch, Susan, and Lee Sigelman. 1982. "Changes in Public Attitudes toward Women in Politics." *Social Science Quarterly* 63 (June): 312–22.

Welch, Susan, and Sue Thomas. 1991. "Do Women in Public Office Make a Difference?" In *Gender and Policymaking,* ed. Debra Dodson. New Brunswick, N.J.: Center for the American Woman and Politics.

Werner, Emmy E. 1966. "Women in Congress: 1917–1964." *Western Political Quarterly* 19 (March): 16–30.

Whitehead, Barbara. 1993. "Quayle Was Right." *Atlantic Monthly* April.

Williams, Christine. 1990. "Women. Law and Politics: Recruitment Patterns in the Fifty States." *Women and Politics* 10:103–124.

Williams, Juan. 1984. "Republicans Told Women on Slate a Help." *Washington Post,* June 4, sec. A.

Witcover, Jules. 1974. "Women Candidates Capitalizing on Clean Political Image." *Washington Post,* June 16.

Witt, Evans. 1985. "What the Republicans Have Learned about Women." *Public Opinion,* October/November, 49–52.

Women's Agenda Conference. *Women and Politics Election '88.*

Women's Political Action Group. 1992. *The Women's Voting Guide.* Berkeley, Calif.: Earthworks Press.

Women in Congress, 1917–1990. Washington, D.C.: U.S. Government Printing Office.

Zipp, John, and Eric Plutzer. 1985. "Gender Differences in Voting for Female Candidates: Evidence from the 1982 Election." *Public Opinion Quarterly* 49 (Spring): 179–97.

Index

Abzug, Bella, 9, 78, 82, 93, 132
Age, 10, 17, 41, 59–66, 70, 71, 74, 79, 80, 84, 91, 169
Alliance for Opportunity, 95
Alters, Diane, 89
American Association of University Women, 92, 172
Andersen, Kristi, 1, 85

Baer, Denise, 93, 96
Bailey, John, 83, 191
Bauer, Monica, 36
Benenson, Bob, 39
Bernstein, Robert, 40, 42, 52, 53, 55, 63, 65, 80
Bernay, Toni, 59
Bibby, John, 85
Bird, Caroline, 6
Bledsoe, Timothy, 52, 84, 148
Boles, Janet, 173
Bonefede, Dom, 92
Bositis, David, 93
Boxer, Barbara, 27, 32, 179
Braun, Carol Moseley, 27, 32, 184
Briscoe, Jerry, 75
Broder, David, 58, 59
Brown, Deborah Dwight, 187
Bryson, Valerie, 153
Buchanan, Christopher, 52
Bullock, Charles, 61, 75
Burrell, Barbara, 10, 13, 18, 39, 40, 102, 112
Bush, George, 89–92
Butterfield, D. Anthony, 21

campaign finance, 101–23. *See also* Federal Elections Commission; Political Action Committees
campaign finance reform, 186–88
early money, 104, 117–22, 128
and incumbency, 101, 106, 109, 112, 116, 118
large contributions, 113–16
and political parties, 96
Canon, David, 9, 60
Cantor, Dorothy, 59
Carroll, Susan, 7, 10, 11, 57, 59, 62, 68, 76, 102, 103, 153, 161, 187
Clark, Janet, 4, 6, 7, 10, 13, 18, 35, 40, 41, 44, 52, 109, 131, 141
Clarke, Susan, 153
Center for the American Woman and Politics, 58, 90, 153, 161
civil rights, 26, 77, 154, 159, 164, 166, 170, 171
Clemans, John, 58
Clift, Eleanor, 102
Clinton, Bill, 89, 90, 170, 173
Cobb, Roger, 161
Coehlo, Tony, 94, 95
Collins, Barbara-Rose, 169
Collins, Cardiss, 60, 73, 169, 179
community activism, 76
competence, 19–21, 59
Congressional Caucus for Women's Issues, 162–66, 170, 173, 174, 179, 180
congressional election procedures, 48
conservative coalition support scores, 155